Skills Builder

HANDBOOK FOR EDUCATORS

Teaching and assessing essential skills

Apart from any fair dealing for the purposes of research or private study, or criticism or review, as permitted under the Copyright, Designs and Patents Act 1988, this publication may only be reproduced, stored or transmitted, in any form or by any means, with the prior permission in writing of the publishers, or in the case of reprographic reproduction in accordance with the terms and licenses issued by the CLA.

© Tom Ravenscroft 2022

Published by Skills Builder Partnership

Printed in the United Kingdom

The right of Tom Ravenscroft to be identified as the author of this work has been asserted by him in accordance with the Copyright, Designs and Patents Act 1988.

Paperback ISBN: 978-1-7391465-0-4
eBook ISBN: 978-1-7391465-1-1

Cover design and layout by www.spiffingcovers.com

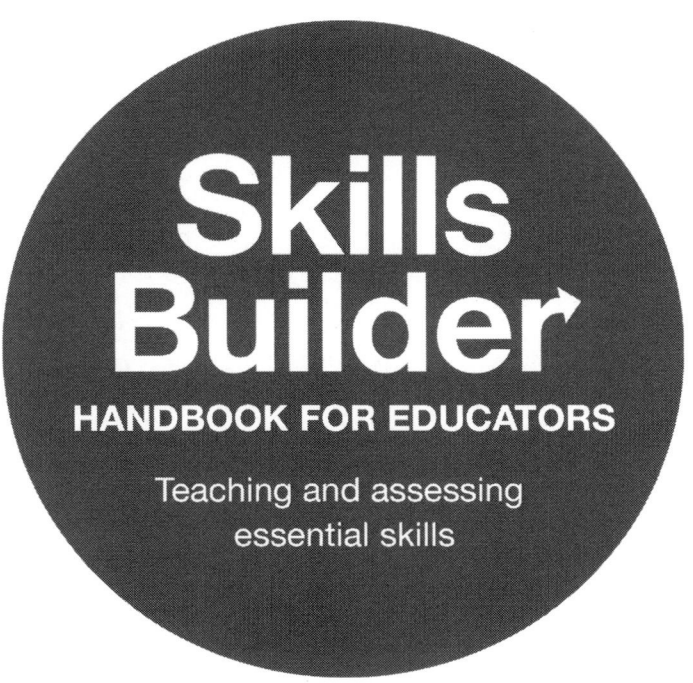

Tom Ravenscroft

Skills Builder Partnership

"Most people agree that young people need essential skills to be successful in the world of work: speaking, listening, problem solving and more. The challenge has always been how you teach and assess these skills with rigour and authenticity. This is where the Skills Builder approach comes in. Through iteration, reflection and focus, Tom and the team have developed a way of working that is helping young people across the country reach their potential by developing these skills for life. I encourage every school to delve into the approach and in so doing prepare children for the future."
- *Oli de Botton, Chief Executive, Careers & Enterprise Company and Co-Founder, School21*

"The Skills Builder approach offers educators worldwide a highly accessible, comprehensive methodology to ensure that the teaching of skills is implemented in a systematic way. It supports pupils to progress and teachers to assess this progress."
- *Susan Douglas, Chief Executive, Eden Academies Trust & Senior Advisor, British Council*

"For more than a decade Tom Ravenscroft has advocated for the importance of essential skills. As a result of his personal leadership Skills Builder was born. This handbook is a powerful tool for any educator who wishes to go beyond the rhetoric of transferable skills and really understand how specific skills can be cultivated in a range of contexts and what these look like as they are developed."
- *Professor Bill Lucas, Professor of Learning, University of Winchester*

"This handbook is a vital tool for educators at a time when it is more important than ever to help the next generation become world ready, not just exam ready."
- *Jo Owen, Founding Chair, STIR & Co-founder, Teach First*

"My passion is the future of working lives and one thing is sure – that there are a number of critical human skills that make a real difference to creating the choices and options people have. Yet these human skills are complex and need to be built across a whole lifetime. That's why I am such a supporter of the work that Skills Builder is doing and why I am so impressed with the model they have built. It has already changed the lives of hundreds of thousands of young people and will continue to do so in the future"
- *Professor Lynda Gratton, London Business School*

Contents

Introduction 11
Essential skills and the Skills Builder Framework 14
    How essential skills fit in 14
    Essential skills in the Skills Builder Framework 15
    Why essential skills matter 16
    Skills Builder Universal Framework 18
    How to navigate the Framework 19
    Inclusion 20
    Tools & Resources to help 21
Skills Builder Principles 22
    Principle 1: Keep it simple 23
    Principle 2: Start early, keep going 25
    Principle 3: Measure it 27
    Principle 4: Focus tightly 29
    Principle 5: Keep practising 31
    Principle 6: Bring it to life 33
Listening 35
    Skills Builder Framework for Listening 36
    Listening Step 0 37
    Listening Step 1 40
    Listening Step 2 43
    Listening Step 3 46
    Listening Step 4 49
    Listening Step 5 52
    Listening Step 6 55
    Listening Step 7 57
    Listening Step 8 59
    Listening Step 9 62
    Listening Step 11 69
    Listening Step 12 72
Speaking 75
    Skills Builder Framework for Speaking 76
    Speaking Step 0 77
    Speaking Step 1 79
    Speaking Step 2 82
    Speaking Step 3 85
    Speaking Step 4 87
    Speaking Step 5 90
    Speaking Step 6 92
    Speaking Step 7 96
    Speaking Step 8 98
    Speaking Step 9 101
    Speaking Step 10 104
    Speaking Step 11 107
    Speaking Step 12 110
Problem Solving 113
    Skills Builder Framework for Problem Solving 114
    Problem Solving Step 0 115
    Problem Solving Step 1 117
    Problem Solving Step 2 120

- Problem Solving Step 3 122
- Problem Solving Step 4 125
- Problem Solving Step 5 128
- Problem Solving Step 6 131
- Problem Solving Step 7 134
- Problem Solving Step 8 136
- Problem Solving Step 9 139
- Problem Solving Step 10 141
- Problem Solving Step 11 144
- Problem Solving Step 12 148

Creativity 151
- Skills Builder Framework for Creativity 152
- Creativity Step 0...153
- Creativity Step 1...155
- Creativity Step 2...158
- Creativity Step 3...160
- Creativity Step 4...162
- Creativity Step 5...165
- Creativity Step 6...168
- Creativity Step 7...170
- Creativity Step 8...172
- Creativity Step 9...175
- Creativity Step 10...177
- Creativity Step 11...180
- Creativity Step 12...184

Staying Positive 187
- Skills Builder Framework for Staying Positive 188
- Staying Positive Step 0..189
- Staying Positive Step 1..192
- Staying Positive Step 2..196
- Staying Positive Step 3..199
- Staying Positive Step 4..202
- Staying Positive Step 5..205
- Staying Positive Step 6..209
- Staying Positive Step 7..212
- Staying Positive Step 8..215
- Staying Positive Step 9..218
- Staying Positive Step 10..221
- Staying Positive Step 11..224
- Staying Positive Step 12..227

Aiming High 230
- Skills Builder Framework for Aiming High 231
- Aiming High Step 0..232
- Aiming High Step 1..234
- Aiming High Step 2..237
- Aiming High Step 3..240
- Aiming High Step 4..243
- Aiming High Step 5..246
- Aiming High Step 6..249
- Aiming High Step 7..252
- Aiming High Step 8..255
- Aiming High Step 9..258
- Aiming High Step 10..261
- Aiming High Step 11..264
- Aiming High Step 12..266

Leadership 269
    Skills Builder Framework for Leadership 270
    Leadership Step 0 271
    Leadership Step 1 274
    Leadership Step 2 277
    Leadership Step 3 280
    Leadership Step 4 283
    Leadership Step 5 286
    Leadership Step 6 289
    Leadership Step 7 292
    Leadership Step 8 295
    Leadership Step 9 298
    Leadership Step 10 301
    Leadership Step 11 304
    Leadership Step 12 307

Teamwork 310
    Skills Builder Framework for Teamwork 311
    Teamwork Step 0 312
    Teamwork Step 1 314
    Teamwork Step 2 316
    Teamwork Step 3 319
    Teamwork Step 4 321
    Teamwork Step 5 324
    Teamwork Step 6 327
    Teamwork Step 7 329
    Teamwork Step 8 332
    Teamwork Step 9 335
    Teamwork Step 10 338
    Teamwork Step 11 341
    Teamwork Step 12 345

Glossary 349
Thanks & acknowledgements 351
About the author 352

Introduction

Back in 2007, I was just starting out my career as a teacher in a state secondary school in central London. I was teaching business and economics to a wide range of learners: from 15- and 16-year-olds who were not expected to get good passes in any of their other qualifications, to 18-year-olds who were studying A-level Economics and who ended up going to highly selective universities.

For most of us, starting out in teaching is daunting. But even as I got to grips with classroom management, goal setting, and assessment, it felt as though something fundamental was still missing. As an education system we had become reductively fixated on the acquisition and demonstration of knowledge as our sole and total focus.

It felt as though we were missing the bigger picture. Yes, we absolutely needed our children and young people to have an understanding of the world, and to be able to easily and intuitively draw on facts and concepts they needed to navigate it. But this was also insufficient. It was quite clear that just doing well academically would not necessarily also equip my learners with the ability to collaborate effectively, or to self-manage, or to structure a problem or use creative tools, or to communicate their ideas.

This broader set of essential skills seems just as fundamental to success as the knowledge which then needs to be plugged in to apply those skills in wider life.

Essential skills

Essential skills are increasingly sought after by employers and called for by educators across the world. That was true back in 2007, and subsequent events and technological shifts - particularly automation - have only made that more so. Highly transferable, highly human skills are increasingly seen as critical for everyone to thrive in education, employment, and their wider lives too.

The challenge is that these skills are often seen as being difficult to pin down. As a teacher, I desperately sought guidance on how to build these skills for my learners but came up short. While we overwhelmingly want our learners to develop these competences, the route to doing so is not clear – nor is how we can actually go about assessing whether they've done so.

The Skills Builder approach

In 2009, while still teaching, I set up Enabling Enterprise which developed and grew into the Skills Builder Partnership. The question I was grappling with then was: "How do we build these essential skills with the same rigour and focus as we would take to any other academic learning?"

We had to learn an enormous amount along the way as we systematically tried out different methods of teaching, practicing, and assessing these skills. Our efforts grew from my secondary school experience to also embracing primary schools, colleges, special schools, and alternative settings too. We realised that in order to apply these skills effectively beyond the classroom, learners had to understand their components fully, and be able to apply them in lots of different settings. That meant a combination of explicit teaching, deliberate practice, and thoughtful application in a range of settings.

The breakthrough really came in 2017, a full decade of testing and experimenting later. We realised that we would never equip everyone to build their essential skills without a common language and model for doing so. By 2020, we had worked with hundreds of educators and employers to create a means of doing just that.

The Skills Builder Framework focuses on building eight essential skills:

The Framework is based on breaking down each of these skills into *steps*: a sequential series of capabilities that build up from being an absolute beginner to mastery in each skill. There are sixteen steps for each essential skill, going from Step 0 to Step 15. These steps can be used both for assessment to measure and quantify an individual's essential skills and as a roadmap of increasingly sophisticated learning outcomes to help structure teaching.

This Framework gives us the *what* of building essential skills. We combine it with six Principles which tell us *how* we can best teach these skills and support progress against the Framework. Together, the Framework and Principles give us the Skills Builder approach.

This Skills Builder approach is now used by millions of learners across the world in countries as diverse as the United Kingdom, Kenya, Czech Republic, Uganda, and Canada - and many more besides. It's also been adopted by employers from multi-national corporations to retailers to start-ups. They use it to support educators, as well as in their own recruitment and staff training, helping to join up the complete journey of essential skill development across lives.

This Handbook

This Handbook gives educators everything the need to be able to teach and assess the essential skills of their learners effectively using the Skills Builder approach. It draws from a strong theoretical and research background but is intentionally practical.

- The next sections of the Handbook covers:
- What we mean by essential skills and why they matter
- The Skills Builder Universal Framework for breaking down essential skills
- The Skills Builder Principles to build essential skills in the classroom effectively
- How school leaders can scale this approach to a whole school or college

After this introduction, the Handbook is divided into chapters for each of the eight essential skills:

- Listening
- Speaking
- Problem Solving
- Creativity
- Staying Positive
- Aiming High
- Leadership
- Teamwork

Within each skill chapter, we break each skill down into the sixteen progressive steps going from Step 0 for an absolute beginner through to Step 15 for mastery of that skill. As you'll see when you explore the Principles, effectively building essential skills requires a combination of direct, explicit teaching ('Focus Tightly') alongside reinforcement and practice ('Keep Practising'), and effective assessment ('Measure It').

This is reflected in the design of each Skill Step in the Handbook, covering:

- **Building blocks:** to structure the step
- **Reflection questions:** to support assessing prior understanding
- **What you need to know:** to cover the core underpinning content of the skill step
- **Teaching it:** to give you ideas of how to teach this step to learners directly
- **Reinforcing it:** to think about how to practice this step across the wider curriculum
- **Assessing it:** to explore how best to assess the skill step

I recommend that you read the introductory parts, and then think about the steps that are the right ones for your learners and dive in with those.

Educators across the world have put the Handbook into practice and seen the impact of it on their learners. As teachers, nothing is as thrilling as seeing our learners make progress – the first time that they are able to express their aspirations, create a new idea, or test a hypothesis of their own.

If you're able, throughout the Handbook you can access more teaching tools and examples by creating a free account on the Skills Builder Hub at www.skillsbuilder.org/hub

We hope you enjoy your journey towards building the essential skills of your learners.

Tom Ravenscroft, July 2022

Essential skills and the Skills Builder Framework

How essential skills fit in

Every teacher has their own philosophy of education and the relative importance of different elements. When we think about a rounded education, there are three key areas that we might consider:

- **Knowledge:** content which can be recalled, understood, and explained
- **Character attributes:** the choices individuals make, manifested as attitudes or behaviours
- **Skills:** the ability to enact a repeatable process successfully

Whilst all three are critical, our focus here is on skills, which we can break down into three broad types:

- **Technical Skills:** those skills which are specific to a sector or role, sometimes drawing off a particular body of knowledge. These skills are not easily transferred beyond the sector or role to which they relate.
- **Essential Skills:** those highly transferable skills that everyone needs to do almost any job, and which support the application of specialist knowledge and technical skills
- **Basic or Foundational Skills:** these are literacy and numeracy, and basic digital skills.

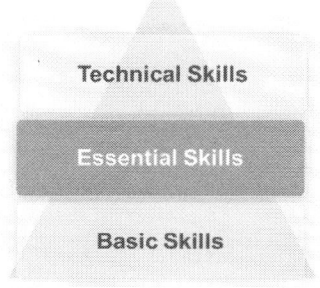

Essential skills in the Skills Builder Framework

The Framework works by turning the broad idea of essential skills into eight specific skills:

Listening: The receiving, retaining, and processing of information or ideas.

Speaking: The oral transmission of information or ideas

Problem Solving: The ability to find a solution to a complex situation or challenge

Creativity: The use of imagination and the generation of new ideas

Leadership: Supporting, encouraging, and motivating others to achieve a shared goal

Teamwork: Working cooperatively with others towards achieving a shared goal

Staying Positive: The ability to use tactics and strategies to overcome setbacks and achieve goals

Aiming High: The ability to set clear, tangible goals and devise a robust route to achieving them

The Framework then goes further by breaking each of these skills into a series of 16 steps, going from the expectations of a complete beginner through to a high level of mastery. In this way, we can support progression in these soft skills in children from as young as 4 years old through their school, college, and well into working life.

Why essential skills matter

The case for building essential skills can seem intuitive, even obvious. How could we object to individuals being better listeners or communicators? Of course we want stronger teamwork and there are no shortage of challenges that need creative problem solvers.

That's undoubtedly why research by the Sutton Trust in 2017 found that 97% of teachers thought that essential skills were at least as important as academic achievements for their learners' future success.

Over the last few years, we've been able to quantify the difference that essential skills make, and the impact is compelling – both within education and beyond it. However, there are real inequalities as to who gets to build their essential skills.

Within education

Essential skills make a real difference to learners. There is strong evidence that during education essential skills are correlated with:

- *Academic achievement:* Cohort analysis using the British Cohort Survey found that higher levels of essential skills were linked with higher academic performance at the age of 10- and 15-years-old. This finding has been reinforced by the *Better Prepared* report which demonstrated that higher essential skill levels were linked to higher qualification levels.
- *Perseverance and self-efficacy:* Building essential skills was linked to higher levels of perseverance shown by individuals when approaching problems or setbacks. Essential skills were also linked to an increased sense that they were in control of their own lives – known as self-efficacy.
- *Wellbeing:* Individuals with higher levels of essential skills also reported higher levels of wellbeing – a finding which was also found with an older cohort too.
- *Higher career aspirations and more successful educational transitions:* There is also evidence that higher essential skill levels are linked to having higher career aspirations, and a reduced likelihood of being not in education, employment or training at the end of compulsory education.

When asked in the *Better Prepared* report, overwhelmingly young people saw the value of essential skills across key aspects of their lives including academic performance (78%), university entrance (66%), successful recruitment (91%), progression in employment (91%), and overcoming wider life challenges (89%).

Beyond education

Beyond education, there is clear evidence that these essential skills are linked to the sorts of positive outcomes that we want for the learners we work with. Most recently, the Essential Skills Tracker looked at essential skill levels and outcomes across the UK working-age population. More than 2,200 adults completed a full self-assessment against the Skills Builder Framework giving each a skill score between 0 and 15, as well as providing other key information about themselves.

This analysis helped to demonstrate the links between skill scores and other outcomes that we care about. The research demonstrated clear links between essential skill levels and:

- *Earnings:* An increase in essential skill scores from the lowest quartile to the third quartile increased average annual earnings by between £3,900 and £5,900, even when controlling for the effect of education.

- *Wellbeing:* The same increase in essential skills score was correlated with an average increase in self-reported wellbeing from 6.0 to 6.5 out of 10. This is consistent with other findings in the space.
- *Reduction in likelihood of being out of work or training:* That increase in essential skills score was also correlated with a reduction in the likelihood of being not in education, employment or training of 42%.

This was reinforced by the views of individuals, 89% of whom felt that essential skills were important for employment, career progression or recruitment success.

Inequality in essential skills

However, while the research demonstrates that essential skills have a real impact on life outcomes, those same skills are not fairly distributed.

The *Better Prepared* report demonstrated that:

- Higher levels of essential skills are correlated with higher social advantage and greater levels of parental engagement, and inversely correlated with attending a specialist setting or having a special educational need.

Similarly, across the adult population, the Essential Skills Tracker showed that individuals in the lowest quartile for their essential skills were:

- 109% more likely to have no formal qualifications
- 8% more likely to have attended a non-selective state school
- 23% less likely to have a parent who attended university
- 22% less likely to have had parents who were engaged in their education

Indeed, in life beyond education, 79% of adults want opportunities to build their essential skills, but only 14% have structured opportunities to do so.

This is a fixable problem

Over the last decade at Skills Builder Partnership we have seen that it is possible for every learner to boost their essential skills and benefit from doing so. Our latest impact report showed that where learners were being taught their essential skills following best practice in their school or college:

- Their rate of progress in essential skills acquisition increased from an average of 0.55 steps of progress per essential skill per year to 1.21 steps of progress where a programme was established.
- This progress could be seen across all age groups, and across all eight of the essential skills.

At Skills Builder Partnership, we think every learner should have the opportunity to build these essential skills as a normal part of a good education. The following pages explore what those best practice approaches look like.

Explore further

You can read all of the reports mentioned in this section and explore the evidence base for building essential skills at www.skillsbuilder.org/insights

Skills Builder Universal Framework

Even with a shared understanding of what the essential skills are, we know that we have to be able to break these skills down into incremental steps. This provides us with a route map of learning objectives to help chart progress, as well as outcomes that we can assess.

The Skills Builder Universal Framework takes each of the eight essential skills and breaks them down into sixteen steps that go from the expectations of an absolute beginner through to what mastery looks like.

It takes the voice of the learners, since ultimately these essential skills belong to them.

To take the example of Listening:

Step 0	I listen to others without interrupting
Step 1	I listen to others and can remember short instructions
Step 2	I listen to others and can ask questions if I don't understand
Step 3	I listen to others and can tell someone else what it was about
Step 4	I listen to others and can tell why they are communicating with me
Step 5	I listen to others and record important information as I do
Step 6	I show I am listening by how I use eye contact and body language
Step 7	I show I am listening by using open questions to deepen my understanding
Step 8	I show I am listening by summarising or rephrasing what I have heard
Step 9	I am aware of how a speaker is influencing me through their tone
Step 10	I am aware of how a speaker is influencing me through their language
Step 11	I listen critically and compare different perspectives
Step 12	I listen critically and think about where differences in perspectives come from
Step 13	I listen critically and identify potential bias in different perspectives
Step 14	I listen critically and use questioning to evaluate different perspectives
Step 15	I listen critically and look beyond the way speakers speak or act to objectively evaluate different perspectives

The Skills Builder Universal Framework was developed and honed over a period of more than four years. During this time, it was shaped through international best practice examples, using employment and jobs data, and drawing on research on skill development. It was also tried and tested with more than 200,000 learners before it was officially launched in May 2020.

How to navigate the Framework

The Framework has been deliberately designed as a flexible tool to support educators to adapt to the learners in front of them. As with all learning, learners progress at different rates. This is particularly true for essential skills where there hasn't been a structured approach in the past to building them.

At the same time, we have tried to calibrate the Framework so that it has clear expectations which are appropriate for mainstream learners in the classroom. An approximate gauge that you can use is:

Step	Age target in mainstream schools (UK)	Age target in mainstream schools (International)
Step 0	Foundation Year	Kindergarten
Step 1	Year 1	Grade 1
Step 2	Year 2	Grade 2
Step 3	Year 3	Grade 3
Step 4	Year 4	Grade 4
Step 5	Year 5	Grade 5
Step 6	Year 6	Grade 6
Step 7	Year 7	Grade 7
Step 8	Year 8	Grade 8
Step 9	Year 9	Grade 9
Step 10	Year 10	Grade 10
Step 11	Year 11	Grade 11
Step 12	Year 12 & Year 13 (Level 3)	Grade 12
Step 13	*College (Level 4+) or university*	*College or university*
Step 14	*College (Level 4+) or university*	*College or university*
Step 15	*College (Level 4+) or university*	*College or university*

In particular, as learners get older, the range of steps that they might be working at expands. As such, it's important to understand the level your learners are working at and where their development needs are in each skill. We find that generally skill steps do move together (i.e. that large step disparities between essential skills are unlikely), but this is not always the case.

While not included here, Steps 13-15 are available online at www.skillsbuilder.org/framework

Principle 3 explores some practical approaches to assessing where learners are.

Inclusion

From the outset, Skills Builder has deliberately worked with learners of all ages and abilities, including children and young people with special educational needs or disabilities. This has included both individuals in a mainstream setting who require extra support, and those who are learning in a specialist setting.

While the previous pages provided some rough guidelines as to how we might choose the right steps to focus on with our learners, when learners have additional needs then age often stops being a useful tool for calibrating expectations. Instead, we would encourage educators to start with the child or young person in front of them and to consider their strengths and development areas against the steps.

Our experience is that sometimes learners with additional needs might have a more 'spiky' profile where they are strong in some skills but struggle in other areas. For example, some learners might be adept at problem solving but find teamwork more challenging.

In other cases, for example if individuals are deaf or non-verbal, then Speaking and Listening are best recast as Communication. The steps can still work well to reflect other non-verbal modes of communication including sign language or written communication.

We have also found that working on a whole step at a time can seem too much for an individual to work on. For these cases, we developed the *building blocks* that you can see at the top of each step page in this Handbook. These *building blocks* help to break down the step into smaller increments that can be built one at a time.

Finally, we have seen schools make great use of Skills Builder to build essential skills into individualised learning plans – sometimes known as Education and Health Care Plans (EHCPs). The specificity of the Framework allows educators to focus on particular steps or even building blocks as a target for the year, and to be able to assess learners' progress accordingly.

We have worked with learners with special educational needs or disabilities in hundreds of settings. We have seen that every learner is able to make progress in these essential skills, and hugely benefits from doing so too.

Explore further

You can find more specialist guidance and tools for building essential skills inclusively at www.skillsbuilder.org/inclusion

You can also find case studies of special schools and alternative provision settings at www.skillsbuilder.org/showcase

Tools & Resources to help

My hope in writing this Handbook is that it gives you everything that you need as an educator to enable your learners to build their essential skills in your classroom.

At Skills Builder Partnership our team of teachers has also created a range of other tools and platforms which can support you too. They all follow the Skills Builder Framework tightly so you can easily bring them in wherever and whenever they are useful:

Skills Builder Hub

www.skillsbuilder.org/hub

Skills Builder Hub enables educators to teach essential skills in line with the Skills Builder Framework. You can set up groups and carry out assessments of your classes' essential skills. You are then directed to appropriate teaching resources, including short lessons which directly teach each skill step, longer projects, and other useful tools and materials like learner worksheets and posters.

Skills Builder Homezone

www.skillsbuilder.org/homezone

Skills Builder Homezone is used by a lot of primary schools to encourage parents and carers to support their children's development at home. The platform combines exploratory material, including videos and reflections, as well as weekly challenges that families can complete together.

Skills Builder Benchmark

www.skillsbuilder.org/benchmark

Skills Builder Benchmark enables individuals to reflect on their own essential skills. It is appropriate to use with young people from the age of about 11- or 12-years-old. The structured reflections allow for individuals to explore their own strengths and development areas and produce useful output reports for learners to use.

Skills Builder Launchpad

www.skillsbuilder.org/launchpad

Skills Builder Launchpad is for individual learners to use to build their own essential skills. It is widely used in colleges and some secondary schools as learners gain greater independence and take more ownership of their own skills development. The platform is designed for mobile use and includes more than 150 short modules to cover each skill step as well as space for reflection and building a portfolio of examples for future use.

Skills Builder Principles

In the last decade, we have had the privilege of working with thousands of educators across primary schools, secondary schools, special schools and colleges. Despite the huge diversity of these organisations, we have found remarkable consistency in what they do well.

In honing these principles over the years, we have gone back and forth between the theoretical backdrop to these skills, and what we have seen and researched ourselves on the ground.

Briefly, educators, schools and colleges who are building essential skills effectively are following six principles to:

Keep it simple: They focus on a simple, consistent set of essential skills, making these as clear and universally understood as possible – among learners, parents, and educators.

Start early and keep going: They see these skills as supporting learning and learners' wider development, and as something to be sustained rather than being built as a quick-fix at the point of entering employment.

Measure it: They take care to understand properly the existing strengths and development needs of their learners in relation to essential skills. They also track progress over time to keep every learner on track for success.

Focus tightly: They use their prior understanding of learners' essential skills to focus on the next steps. This includes explicit and direct instruction on essential skills – not just hoping that they get picked up along the way.

Keep practising: They reinforce these essential skills in other parts of the curriculum and beyond it, including by linking up with other impact organisations whose programmes can support their learners.

Bring it to life: They make the essential skills real by bringing the working world into the classroom and showing learners how these skills are useful across their lives. This boosts their transferability beyond education.

The following pages explore how each of these principles can be brought to life in your classroom, school, or college.

The Bronze, Silver and Gold indicators relate to what we expect to see for a school or college to achieve a Skills Builder Award. We've included them here, because we think they help to illustrate what realising these principles might tangibly look like.

Explore further

You can also find case studies of how other schools and colleges have applied these principles at www.skillsbuilder.org/showcase.

Principle 1: Keep it simple

The principle

Teachers, schools, and colleges that are effective in ensuring progression in essential skills focus consistently on those skills and the steps of progression.

The trap

The reason why this principle is important is because essential skills can easily become confusing; there is so much variation in language and terminology. An individual might use terms like 'teamwork' and 'collaboration' interchangeably, but this can quickly become confusing to a child or young person. It means that they cannot build a clear, consistent mental map of what their skills look like.

We also need to avoid the risk of abstraction – that is, trying to work on or too readily claim progress against, broad learner dispositions like "confidence" or terms that are ill-defined like "charismatic communication".

What we should be aiming for

The most important thing is to try to make the language around the essential skills as simple and consistent as possible. This is vital because we all need to have a shared mental map of what building the essential skills looks like – and that includes teachers, parents, and the learners themselves. The essential skills should be a consistent thread through a learner's learning – but they will not be able to follow that thread if the way it is described keeps changing.

The other part of keeping it simple is to focus on skills at their most tangible. That's why in the Skills Builder Framework we have avoided using intangible concepts like confidence or resilience. From the start, we set ourselves the challenge that if we were not able to assess objectively whether a learner had achieved a particular step, then the step was not defined with enough clarity.

Putting it into practice

Schools and colleges who are putting this into use effectively often do some of the following things:

- *Build awareness of the essential skills:* For example, by having them up on the walls of school hallways and in classrooms and by training staff on how to define and to build them.
- *Ensure learners understand:* They introduce learners to the Skills Builder Framework as a consistent way of thinking about how the skills are built, step by step.
- *Use the language consistently:* Avoid introducing other language and terminology around essential skills.
- *Recognise the value of essential skills:* They demonstrate that achievement in the essential skills is valued alongside academic achievement. For example, by updating parents and carers on their children's progress in reports or update meetings or through other awards.

The Skills Builder Award descriptors

Bronze Award	Silver Award	Gold Award
The language of essential skills is used in some aspects of school or college life and among some members of the community including learners, teachers and leaders. Some events such as assemblies also begin to reference the essential skills.	Development of essential skills forms part of strategic planning and policy development, with the result that the language of essential skills is used across many areas of school or college life and among many members of the community. Assemblies and other events often reference the skills.	The essential skills are embedded within teaching and learning policies and curriculum plans across the school or college with the result that the language of essential skills is used extensively across all areas of school or college life and among all members of its community. Assemblies, staff meetings, parent meetings and other events regularly reference the skills.
Some teachers recognise and reward learner effort and achievement in relation to essential skills.	A majority of teachers recognise and reward learner effort and achievement in relation to essential skills.	The school or college's policy and approach to rewarding and recognising effort and achievement reflects and builds essential skills. All teachers follow this.
Some classrooms and other spaces where the essential skills are taught have visual cues and reminders of the skills (such as posters) on display.	Many classrooms and other spaces have visual cues and reminders of the skills (such as posters) on display.	Most or all classrooms and other spaces have visual cues and reminders of the skills (such as posters) on display.

Reflection questions

- How could you ensure everyone knows which essential skills you focus on in your school or college?
- How could you ensure all staff and learners use a consistent language when referring to the skills?

Principle 2: Start early, keep going

The principle

Teachers, schools, and colleges that are excelling in this area are introducing essential skills to the youngest learners and working with them throughout their education.

The trap

There are three traps that we see teachers, schools, and colleges sometimes fall into when it comes to this principle:

- In some cases, they link essential skills too closely with employability and so think about these skills as being only relevant when learners are close to leaving education. In these cases, they sometimes introduce essential skills teaching too late
- In other cases, essential skills are seen as being foundational; they are perceived as relevant when getting children started in their learning, but after that they can be left
- Or, finally, they are seen as a nice idea, but are seen as a lower priority than examination success, and so are squeezed out as soon as exams come into view

What we should be aiming for

Teachers, schools, and colleges that are effectively building their learners' skills have another thing in common: they see these essential skills as being important all the way through education, and at all ages. They do not fall into the trap of assuming that essential skills are only important for employability and so only teach them at the end of education. Instead they see them as being key enablers of learning throughout childhood too.

This intuitively makes a lot of sense: we know that learners who can listen effectively and articulate their ideas will get more out of class and be able to share more too. Similarly, learners who can set their own goals and plans are better able to take ownership of their own progress and take responsibility for achieving their educational goals. The ability to think critically and to problem solve also helps to explore, process, and join up different concepts.

It's also important to start young because we see differences in learners' essential skills open up early. There is often a real contrast on the first days of school between those learners who can introduce themselves to others, cope with new routines, and form friendships quickly, and those who struggle. Starting early helps to address those imbalances.

At the same time, it is important to keep going. The essential skills are complex. Against the Skills Builder Framework we anticipate that most learners will get to between Steps 8-12 during their time in school – so there is still plenty more to learn to really master those skills.

The Skills Builder Framework supports teachers, schools, and colleges to create an appropriate structured learning programme because the different steps can be adopted as learning outcomes to provide a sequenced programme over many years.

Putting it into practice

Teachers, schools, and colleges who are doing this effectively are doing some of the following things:

- They talk about the long-term picture of where they want their learners to get to in terms of their essential skills, creating a shared sense of aspiration and intention
- They might then break this down into what they want learners to be able to do at each age, using the Skills Builder Framework as a way of having clear statements to work towards. An important part of this is to think about what children and young people in the school need to do at different ages in order to access learning effectively and thrive in their wider lives
- They set the expectation with educators, learners, parents, and carers that the development of these essential skills is a goal of the education system

The Skills Builder Award descriptors

Bronze Award	Silver Award	Gold Award
Some year groups or classes have regular opportunities for the learning and practising of essential skills.	Most year groups or classes have regular and planned opportunities for the learning and practising of essential skills.	All year groups and classes have regular and planned opportunities for the learning and practising of essential skills.

Reflection questions

- How do you think about these skills for all the learners you work with?
- How could you introduce these skills earlier on?
- Where are there opportunities for learners to build the skills further as they grow up?

Principle 3: Measure it

The principle

Leading teachers, schools and colleges bring rigour to the essential skills through consistent measurement and formative assessment of essential skills.

The trap

There are several traps we see teachers, schools, and colleges fall into when it comes to measuring essential skills:

- Sometimes it is assumed that these skills are too difficult to measure, and so their measurement is ignored.
- Other times, schools assume that those learners who are the most amenable, easy to teach, or talkative must be the highest performing in their essential skills. In fact, a closer, more objective assessment of their essential skills might reveal a very different picture.

What we should be aiming for

It is impossible to see progression without a clear understanding of where an individual started from and then where they got to. In this sense, measurement is critical.

There are a range of approaches that can be effective in assessing essential skills and help to provide the insights that we need to ensure progression:

- *Individual assessment by a teacher:* The most intensive option is for a teacher to make an assessment of each learner individually, reviewing the steps they are secure on, and what they need to be able to do next. This gives the most detailed view but is quite time-intensive and needs a good level of understanding of each individual.
- *Group-level assessment by a teacher:* In a classroom setting, it often works well for a teacher to reflect on the skills of their group as a whole and what proportion of the learners have achieved each step. This takes much less time and gives insights into the needs of the class as a whole.
- *Individual self- or peer-assessment:* A further option is that individual learners can self-assess their own skills, or potentially work with a peer or with a parent or mentor to complete the individual assessment themselves. This works best with older learners, although it can work with younger ones if they have a lot of support.

In this way, teachers and learners can gain insight into which steps have already been achieved on the Skills Builder Framework, and what therefore should be the next focus.

Putting it into practice

At a school or college level it can be challenging to introduce a new type of assessment. We find that those who are doing this well take a thoughtful approach to measuring essential skills:

- *Focus on how the data can be used:* The assessment is only worthwhile if it is actually used. This means that teachers have to have some training to understand the Skills Builder Framework and why progress against it matters for their learners.
- *Lowering the stakes:* There is meaningful teacher judgement needed in some of these assessments – they cannot be traditional examinations so it is important to make clear that this is a low-stakes, formative assessment. It should be used to help the teacher plan learning, not to make a judgement of them or their class.
- *Repeating:* As a formative approach, it is important that this assessment is not just completed once. As teachers return to it, they will become more confident, and will be able to see progress.

The Skills Builder Award descriptors

Bronze Award	Silver Award	Gold Award
Some teachers regularly use formative assessment to prioritise and inform their teaching of essential skills.	A majority of teachers regularly use formative assessment to prioritise and inform the teaching of essential skills.	All teachers regularly use formative assessment to prioritise and inform the teaching of essential skills.

Reflection questions

- How can you use the Skills Builder Framework to support consistent assessment?
- How could you assess progress and tracking it over time?
- Where could you check in on progress regularly?

Principle 4: Focus tightly

The principle

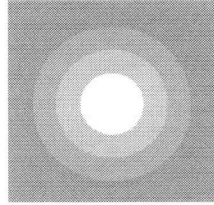

When building essential skills, the best teachers, schools, and colleges are making focused time available to explicitly teach the skills.

The trap

There are a few traps that teachers, schools, and colleges can fall into with this principle:

- Sometimes they focus too much on doing as many activities as possible that use the essential skills, rather than thinking about what learners are getting out of those activities and whether they are pitched at the right level.
- Sometimes essential skills activities are designed without thinking about learning objectives or outcomes.
- In some cases, no links are drawn between different activities to build essential skills, so learners cannot make connections between them.

What we should be aiming for

The insight of what learners can and cannot already do means that we can use this information to focus our efforts on the next critical step. This is a big shift away from the idea of just *using* the skills and hoping that learners pick up what we need them to achieve from the practice.

Instead, with the understanding gained from measuring those skills, we can teach explicitly what is required to make the next step of progress. That might mean teaching about three different styles of leadership, how to take it in turns with other children, how to create goals and a plan to achieve them, or how to use mind maps to generate new ideas. All of these things are better taught directly rather than simply hoping that learners pick them up through good luck.

This direct instruction is often overlooked when it comes to essential skills, but once we have isolated the building blocks of those skills then we can be much more focused about building them.

Putting it into practice

Schools and colleges who are doing this effectively might do a few different things:

- Make dedicated time available to teach essential skills – perhaps only 15 minutes to an hour per week, with just one specific – and measurable - step forward in essential skills as the target.
- Ensure that teachers feel equipped to build skills directly and have the tools and resources available to do so.

The Skills Builder Award descriptors

Bronze Award	Silver Award	Gold Award
Some teachers engage in focused and explicit teaching of essential skills.	A majority of teachers engage in focused and explicit teaching of essential skills.	Most or all teachers engage in focused and explicit teaching of essential skills.
Timetables or planning show that some teachers dedicate time to the teaching of skills, pitching teaching at an appropriate level	Timetables or planning show that a majority of teachers dedicate time to the teaching of skills, pitching teaching at an appropriate level.	Timetables or planning show that most or all teachers dedicate time to the teaching of skills, pitching teaching at an appropriate level

Reflection questions

- How could you create tailored goals for different learners when building their skills?
- Where could you make time just to focus on explicitly developing skills?

Principle 5: Keep practising

The principle

The best teachers, schools and colleges are supplementing focused time on building the essential skills with wider reinforcement and practice across the curriculum, and beyond.

The trap

Some of the traps that teachers, schools and colleges can fall into with this principle include:

- Assuming that the dedicated time available to build essential skills will be sufficient by itself.
- Not making the most of opportunities to apply those skills to other learning, or missing opportunities for deliberate application and reflection on those skills in other contexts.
- Seeing essential skills as being irrelevant to wider learning in the curriculum and the full range of different subject areas.

What we should be aiming for

The importance of direct instruction in the skills that was highlighted in the previous principle does not mean that practising is less important. The big difference is that we are talking about *deliberate* practice.

Deliberate practice is distinguished by focused attention on a particular goal, often with the support of an expert coach.

Schools and colleges build this deliberate practice into their curricula in different ways. Some use a specific project as a basis to apply the essential skills to a real-life challenge: creating a radio show, a school performance, a community event, or a sports competition. These approaches can be highly effective as the sole focus of the learning is on securing progression in the essential skills.

It can also work well, though, to weave opportunities to practice the essential skills through the curriculum without the need to make lots of additional time available. This works best by taking a view across the learning of a particular year group and spotting the natural opportunities to practice applying different steps of the Skills Builder Framework. For example, by giving the opportunity to create a presentation in English, to apply research methods in Geography or to structure problem-solving through Maths.

Of course, the most effective schools and colleges do *both*: offering dedicated time for focused practice which is then backed up by regular reinforcement in other subject areas too.

Putting it into practice

Schools and colleges who are applying this principle effectively do some of the following things:

- Ensure that the language of essential skills is being used the whole curriculum, with common shared standards.
- Include visual cues and reminders to encourage teachers to make reference to those skills in other parts of their teaching. For example, by having the essential skills posted up on the walls in the classrooms or in the front of learner planners or exercise books.
- Some schools and colleges also build in the expectation that essential skills will be reinforced in the design of lesson plans.
- Finally, a extra-curricular offer including sports, arts, drama, or community engagement can provide lots of opportunities to put essential skills into practice.

The Skills Builder Award descriptors

Bronze Award	Silver Award	Gold Award
Some teachers provide opportunities for learners to practise essential skills in the wider curriculum, crossing into different subject areas.	A majority of teachers provide regular opportunities for learners to practise essential skills in the wider curriculum, crossing into different subject areas.	Most or all teachers provide regular opportunities for learners to practise essential skills in the wider curriculum, crossing into different subject areas.
	There are some opportunities for practising essential skills in the written curriculum.	The school's or college's written curriculum makes reference to opportunities for practising essential skills across all subjects.
	Some extra-curricular activities provide opportunities for learners to practise essential skills.	Most or all extra-curricular activities provide opportunities for learners to practise essential skills.

Reflection questions

- How could you ensure regular opportunities for learners to use their essential skills?
- How can you ensure learners are aware that they are using their skills?
- How can you build in regular opportunities to reflect actively on the skills and how they have been developed?

Principle 6: Bring it to life

The principle

Teachers, schools, and colleges which are transforming their learners' essential skills are using links to the working world to increase the depth and transferability of those skills. They give learners opportunities to apply these skills in a wider range of settings.

The trap

Some of the traps that schools and colleges fall into when considering this principle include:

- Lots of schools have only very limited links to employers. In some areas there are a greater range of available employers, and links between schools and employers are better facilitated than others.
- Employer events are separated or isolated from wider learning.
- Teachers struggle to make links between the curriculum as it is taught and how the skills and content could have real-life applications.

What we should be aiming for

The final principle that we have consistently seen make a big impact is linking the essential skills not just to classroom learning, but also to wider life, including the world of work. This is particularly important because we want the skills to be transferable beyond education.

Employers often cite the importance of these essential skills in the workplace too – but then worry that the young people joining them at the end of their education have not built them to the standard that they expect or require. Sometimes this is a challenge of *articulation* – young people have actually built the skills but they struggle to talk about them in a way that is convincing to employers. In this case, it is important that learners have a strong conceptual framework of their own skills which they can communicate with others.

Other times, the skills are not built in such a way that they can effectively use them in a workplace. To build this transferability, it's important that learners have the chance to apply their skills in lots of different settings so that they can see that the building blocks of being able to share an idea are exactly the same whether in a classroom or a workplace or on the football pitch even though the setting looks quite different.

Putting it into practice

There are several approaches that schools and colleges use to put this principle into practice effectively:

- One approach that can be very effective is to use a project-based learning methodology. This is helpful because the project can be focused on a real challenge or problem, either faced by the local community, within the school, or set by an employer. For example, creating a radio show to inform learners about an upcoming festival which allows learners to apply their listening and speaking skills, as well as their creativity in writing an interesting show. This radio show can then be shared with parents and other community members, giving a real life application of the skills.
- Another approach which can be helpful is to work with external partners. This might mean bringing in a volunteer or representative of an employer or the local community to talk about their role and the relevance of essential skills to them and their work.
- Alternatively, depending on the context of the school, it might mean taking learners out of the classroom to visit employers or other community sites. In such instances, a well-facilitated activity and discussion can help learners to connect the essential skills being built in the classroom with their application in the wider world.

The Skills Builder Award descriptors

Bronze Award	Silver Award	Gold Award
The school or college makes some provision of opportunities to apply essential skills. These might include project-based learning, off-timetable days, employer encounters, workplace visits, and enterprise challenges.	The school or college makes provision for the majority of learners to have experiences to apply essential skills. These might include project-based learning, off-timetable days, employer encounters, workplace visits and enterprise challenges.	The school or college makes provision for all learners to have experiences to apply essential skills. These might include project-based learning, off-timetable days, employer encounters, workplace visits and enterprise challenges.
	Some learners use opportunities to apply and develop their skills outside school, for example by volunteering or gaining work experience. *(Secondary and college only)*	Many learners use opportunities to apply and develop their essential skills outside school, for example in by volunteering or gaining work experience. *(Secondary and college only)*

Reflection questions

- How could you frame the skills in terms of their usefulness for education, employment, and wider life?
- Where are there opportunities for learners to use their skills in different settings?
- How could you use links to employers to support building these skills?

Listening

The receiving, retaining and processing of information or ideas

Why it matters

We deliberately put listening as a critical component of communication first when it comes to the essential skills.

Listening sounds deceptively simple as a skill, and we might presume that this should be built in the home environment as a result. This is partly the case, but as teachers we know that listening is not as simple as it sounds – particularly over sustained periods, when taking on more complex information, or when it comes assessing bias.

Without the ability to listen (or receive communication through signing or similar) then we cannot easily receive information. The good news is that it is perfectly possible for all learners to develop their ability to receive and process information.

How listening is built

This skill is all about being able to receive information effectively, whether it comes from a peer, parent, teacher, or someone else entirely.

Initially, the skill steps concentrate on being able to listen effectively to others. This includes remembering short instructions, understanding why others are communicating, and recording important information.

Learners then focus on how they demonstrate that they are listening effectively, thinking about body language, open questioning, and summarising and rephrasing.

Beyond that, the focus is on being aware of how they might be being influenced by a speaker through tone and language.

The final steps are about critical listening – comparing perspectives, identifying biases, evaluating ideas, and being objective.

Skills Builder Framework for Listening

The receiving, retaining, and processing of information or ideas

Step 0	I listen to others without interrupting
Step 1	I listen to others and can remember short instructions
Step 2	I listen to others and can ask questions if I don't understand
Step 3	I listen to others and can tell someone else what it was about
Step 4	I listen to others and can tell why they are communicating with me
Step 5	I listen to others and record important information as I do
Step 6	I show I am listening by how I use eye contact and body language
Step 7	I show I am listening by using open questions to deepen my understanding
Step 8	I show I am listening by summarising or rephrasing what I have heard
Step 9	I am aware of how a speaker is influencing me through their tone
Step 10	I am aware of how a speaker is influencing me through their language
Step 11	I listen critically and compare different perspectives
Step 12	I listen critically and think about where differences in perspectives come from
Step 13	I listen critically and identify potential bias in different perspectives
Step 14	I listen critically and use questioning to evaluate different perspectives
Step 15	I listen critically and look beyond the way speakers speak or act to objectively evaluate different perspectives

Listening Step 0

Step 0: I listen to others without interrupting

To achieve step 0, individuals will have to be able to listen to others without interrupting.

This is the first step in building this skill and provides the foundation for more advanced steps in Listening.

Building blocks

The building blocks of this step are:

- I know what it means to listen
- I know what interrupting is, and why to avoid it
- I know some ways to avoid interrupting

Reflection questions

- What is listening? How do we do it?
- Why do we listen?
- What is interrupting and why do we do it?
- What is wrong with interrupting someone?
- What are some things that we can do to stop interrupting?

What you need to know

What it means to listen

Listening is about being able to receive information through our ears, and then thinking about it so that we understand what is being said.

We cannot listen if we do not try to, if anything is in the way of our ears, or if we are thinking about something else.

It is important to listen because:

- We might learn information that helps to protect us, or to keep us safe
- We might understand how someone else is feeling about something
- We might learn how to do something better
- We might understand something new that we hadn't understood before

What is means to interrupt and why we should avoid it

Interrupting is stopping what someone is saying. You might do this by speaking, or by looking away or doing something that shows that you have stopped listening.

We might interrupt for different reasons – including some positive reasons:

- We might have ideas that we are excited to share
- We might think of something that we want to say right away
- We might agree with the speaker and want to tell them straight away
- We might be running out of time to talk about something

Often though, we interrupt for less positive reasons:

- We might disagree with them and want to put across our point of view
- We might not be finding what they say interesting or relevant
- We might be bored with the conversation

Interrupting others causes several problems:

- It often makes the person you have interrupted feel like you don't care what they are saying, or that they are not interesting.
- It often makes the person you have interrupted feel that you think your opinion is more important than what they have to say
- It means that you have missed out on what is really being said
- If you let someone else talk for longer, you might be surprised about what you learn – and they might say something you did not expect

How to avoid interrupting

We can all get better at not interrupting others. At the start, we may have to take a deliberate approach to thinking actively about how we are behaving and thinking.

Over time, as with all skill development, this will become more of an automatic habit, and not something that requires the same level of thought and attention.

Some strategies to try out are:

- Do try to be quiet, especially if you are normally talkative
- Do try to remember what is being said
- Do apologise if you accidentally interrupt and let the speaker talk again
- Do check if someone has finished before speaking if you're not sure
- Don't presume you know what is going to come next – try to think about whether anything you are hearing is a surprise to you
- Don't use any pause in the conversation to start talking
- Don't feel that you need to say something to show you agree – nodding and maintaining eye contact are much better ways than interrupting someone

If you have to interrupt – for example, because you have run out of time for a conversation, or because there is an emergency – then you can still do this politely and apologetically.

Teaching it

To teach this step:

- Get learners to ask a friend to tell them if they interrupt, or see them interrupting someone else
- Ask learners to get feedback at the end of a conversation to find out whether the other person felt that they had interrupted them at all

If the teacher wants to use an activity to practise this skill step on then you could use a graduated level of challenge:

- Start with one learner delivering a monologue to another – for example, about their weekend, holiday, or what they like doing at home. The other learner has to listen without interrupting for up to 3 minutes. They can then reverse roles.
- Then proceed onto having a conversation where they both have to share ideas and listen to each another. For example, having a conversation about what a great party would look like, or what they would like to do during their school holiday. You can have a third learner to act as an observer to highlight any times that one learner interrupts the other.

Reinforcing it

This is a step that needs regular practice to become a habit. The teacher can:

- Encourage learners to reflect occasionally on whether they have been able to listen to one another without interrupting.
- Model good listening when other learners are speaking or recognise when learners have been showing good listening.
- Keep visual reminders around the learning space about this specific skill step.
- Maintain achieving this step as a target for all learners over a sustained period – for example, by having it as a target for the month.

Assessing it

This step is best assessed through observation:

- During class, the teacher could keep a tally of when learners interrupt the flow of conversation or one another.
- The teacher could observe learners' interactions with their peers, to see how well they can listen to one another without interrupting.
- The teacher could set a target for the class to reduce the number of interruptions over time

Listening Step 1

Step 1: I listen to others and can remember short instructions

To achieve Step 1, individuals will have to demonstrate that they can listen to and recall a short series of 3-5 instructions.

This builds on the previous step of being able to listen without interrupting and starts to focus on the retention of information. It might apply to listening to a manager, instructor, or a peer.

Building blocks

The building blocks of this step are:

- I know why recalling instructions matters
- I concentrate when listening to instructions
- I store and recall simple instructions

Reflection questions

- When do you have to remember instructions?
- Why is it important that you do so accurately?
- When do you struggle to listen to instructions?
- What could you do to better listen to instructions?
- What can you do to help remember three simple instructions?

Why recalling instructions matters

We have to listen to instructions in many different parts of our lives, whether we are being taught something new, being given a job to do, or just completing tasks in our wider lives.

We must listen to instructions carefully to make sure that we do exactly what is being expected and so that we don't make mistakes or place ourselves into situations of danger.

Sometimes people struggle to listen to instructions because:

- They think they already know what to do – perhaps because they think that they have done the same thing, or something very similar in the past
- They are distracted by other things that they are thinking about
- They are distracted by things that are going on around them – for example, background noise, visual distractions or fiddling with things

How to concentrate and focus

To help learners to concentrate we suggest a three-step approach:

- *Stop* anything that might be a distraction. That might include putting down stationery or tools, not writing or reading anything else, and ensuring that there are no distracting background noises.
- *Focus* on the speaker by looking at them and being ready to receive the instructions. Your brain should be actively trying to remember what is being said.
- *Repeat* the instructions in your head several times so that you have processed them and checked that you understand what they mean.

How to store and recall simple instructions

It should be possible to store and recall three simple instructions within our *working memories*. They then need to be considered and processed to pass into our longer-term memory. To help things to stick in our long-term memories we can:

- Think about whether the instructions follow patterns that we already know – for example, there might be links between how we clean different objects, how we write different things down, or how we play different games
- Visualising ourselves completing the task by following the instructions
- Breaking the instructions into three separate packages and imagining them in order

If there are more than three instructions it can be hard to remember them. We might need to put them into smaller sub-sets of instructions. In most cases though, we would write down lengthier sets of instructions. We come on to doing this in *Step 5*.

Teaching it

To teach this step:

- The teacher can give learners a simple set of instructions – for example, to create a model or to rearrange objects in a particular way. As their teacher, model how you would take an instruction, repeat it in your head, and then try to visualise it.
- Working in pairs, one learner is given a simple set of instructions which they then have to share with a partner who then has to remember and enact those instructions to complete the task.

Reinforcing it

This is a step that lends itself to regular practice in the classroom setting, and once mastered will support learning and a positive classroom dynamic. As a teacher you can:

- Remind learners of the three-step process (Stop, Focus, Repeat) to ensure that they are ready to take on instructions before you start
- When giving instructions, model to learners how they can process those instructions, making sure that they have taken them on board
- As learners become more confident in this skill step, provide less scaffolding when giving instructions – perhaps replacing verbal reminders to Stop, Focus, Repeat with visual reminders in the classroom
- Be confident over time in giving sets of instructions without substantial repetition and demonstrate your confidence that learners will be able to follow these instructions

Assessing it

This step is best assessed through a practical exercise:

- By giving learners a simple set of instructions – for example, to fold a piece of paper, draw a particular picture on one side and write something on the inside – and then observe who has been able to recall and follow those instructions
- By asking learners to give each other simple sets of instructions and to observe how learners can cope with that structure

Listening Step 2

Step 2: I listen to others and can ask questions if I don't understand

To achieve Step 2, individuals will show that they can listen and then ask questions to clarify their understanding.

This step builds on the previous two steps of Listening, which focused on being able to listen without interrupting, and then being able to recall basic instructions.

Building blocks

The building blocks of this step are:

- I know why it is important to understand what I have heard
- I think about whether I understand what I have heard
- I ask questions when I have not understood

Reflection questions

- When is it important to check understanding?
- How do you check if you understand something?
- How can you check your understanding of something through questions?
- What are good or bad questions to ask?

What you need to know

How to check your understanding when listening

Even if you are a good listener, what you understand will only be as good as how clear the communication is that you are receiving.

Before you can expand your understanding further, it is often helpful to check that you have understood what you have heard. If you don't, sometimes misunderstandings can grow.

Some ways of checking your understanding are:

- Repeating back what you think you heard
- Rephrasing what you heard to check that you understand the meaning
- Drawing a link to something comparable to check your understanding – for example, 'is that like the time that...' or 'is this similar to...?'

Using questions to check your understanding

When you ask questions to check your understanding, you should first reflect on what you have already understood so that your questions are relevant

Some ways of thinking through whether you understand something, might be to think through the key questioning words:

- Who: who is involved, and how?
- What: what is happening?
- Where: where is this taking place?
- When: when is this happening; at what time and for how long?
- How: how is this going to happen; what are the steps that will be followed?

To make sure you are asking good questions, make sure that they are *relevant* to the situation. Questions that are not relevant will waste time and suggest to the speaker that you have not been listening.

Teaching it

To teach this step:

- The learners could be given some basic information about something – for example, an upcoming event. They should then formulate the questions they need to build up a full understanding of what is going on, e.g. when the event is, what will happen, who will be invited, and what is going to happen to get that event ready.
- They can then try it out with one another. For example, one learner can be given a set of information but can only share it when they have been asked a question that gives them the chance to share that information. This can be extended, where relevant, to sharing of subject knowledge like historical events or scientific ideas.
- Learners could be given a topic to investigate by developing the questions to which they would like to understand the answers, and then inviting in an expert to help address those questions.

Reinforcing it

This step can be regularly practised in the classroom. Some things that the teacher could do include:

- Reminding learners of the key clarifying questions that they might ask – visual reminders of these around the learning environment might be helpful.
- Deliberately encouraging learners to ask questions to expand their understanding of a particular topic or in classroom learning more widely.
- If learners have opportunities to share their work, encourage other learners to find out more by asking clarifying questions to deepen their understanding of what is being shared. The teacher should praise learners who ask effective clarifying questions.

Assessing it

This step can be assessed through observation and structured activity:

- The teacher can encourage learners to ask questions of one another after having presented an idea or a piece of work. Observe and record which learners can ask good questions.
- The teacher can set an activity where learners are only given partial information, which then requires that learners ask questions to complete their understanding.
- Over the longer-term, the teacher can observe learners and their ability to follow instructions and to check understanding when they are listening.

Listening Step 3

Step 3: I listen to others and can tell someone else what it was about

To achieve Step 3, individuals will need to be able to listen, and retain, recall, and share what they have heard.

In Steps 1 and 2 individuals focused on their ability to listen to others and remember simple instructions, and to use questioning to check their understanding. This step builds on this by dealing with the recalling and re-telling of longer pieces of information.

Building blocks

The building blocks of this step are:

- I listen effectively and stay focused
- I retain and process information I have heard
- I recall and explain information to others

Reflection questions

- How do you make sure you are listening?
- How do you help ensure that you stay focused?
- How do you make sure you remember a longer piece of speech, a series of instructions, or a story?
- When do you find this easier or more difficult?
- When are you good at recalling information that you have heard?
- What are the most important things to share?

What you need to know

Listen effectively and stay focused

In the previous steps, some approaches to ensuring focus were discussed, along with the importance of being in the right frame of mind.

One simple model introduced in Step 1 to achieve this is to:

- *Stop* anything that might be a distraction. That might include putting down stationery or tools, not writing or reading anything else, and ensuring that there are no distracting background noises.
- *Focus* on the speaker by looking at them and being ready to receive the instructions. Your brain must be in a place of actively trying to remember what is being said. You cannot be thinking about other things.
- *Repeat* what you are hearing in your head several times so that you have been able to process it, and check that you understand what it means in your head.

Retaining and processing information

Most people find it difficult to recall anything verbatim (that is, exactly in the same way that they were told it). Recalling what is being heard is not like trying to record in real-time what is being said.

Instead, people remember extended things they hear in one of several ways:

- They relate a new piece of knowledge to what they already know and fit it into an existing *conceptual framework*. For example, they might link something geographically, or place it in a historical context. Or they might link a concept in science to something that they have observed themselves.
- Alternatively, people turn the information into a *sequence or story* that they can follow – humans are good at using stories as a way of storing information.
- Finally, thinking about the *implications and feelings* about what is being heard can be a very effective way of processing information.

In any case, it often takes a little time to think and to process what has been heard before we can pass that information on to someone else. *Taking a bit of thinking time* is a good idea.

Recalling and sharing information

It is very difficult to share information that you have not had time to think about first.

When you share information, you are very unlikely to share it exactly as you heard it. The key thing is to focus on keeping the same *key points* – not to get all the words right.

If you have been able to process what you have heard, you might already have turned this into a *story*, or be able to link what you are saying to other *concepts* or *experiences* that will be familiar to the listeners.

The most important information to share will depend on the situation, and it is worth focusing on this key information.

Teaching it

To teach this step:

- The learners should listen to an extended talk of 3-5 minutes, then take time to think about what they have heard and decide what the most important facts are. The teacher can model and scaffold this initially by listening with them and showing them how to think about what the most important pieces of information are.
- Once this has been modelled to learners, they can practice by listening to an extended talk or story for 3-5 minutes. The teacher should give them a chance to think about what they heard, and then try to tell the story back to one another.
- Another good activity, if the group makes it feasible, is to play a version of 'Pass It On' – they each pass a short story along to someone else, try to recall it, and then pass it on to the next person.

Reinforcing it

This is a step that lends itself to regular practice in the classroom setting and, once mastered, will support learning and a positive classroom dynamic. The teacher can:

- Routinely remind learners before they are listening to an explanation that they will need to be able to tell someone else what is going to happen next. The teacher could even only tell half the learners, so that they then need to explain what is happening to the other half.
- Encourage learners to listen to a story or learn something new at home and come to class ready to recall and share what they learnt.

Assessing it

This step lends itself well to being assessed through a simple exercise, although it can also be observed over time:

- The teacher could get learners to listen to a short explanation of something that they are studying, either on video or purely by listening. The learners could then work with a teaching assistant to recall what they can from what they have heard.
- The teacher could observe learners when they are being given some new information, and how well they can pass that information on to someone else.

Listening Step 4

Step 4: I listen to others and can tell why they are communicating with me

To achieve Step 4, individuals will need to understand the main reasons why others may want to communicate with them and to be able to identify each of these reasons.

In the steps so far, the focus has been on the tools of effective listening, but to make progress individuals need to be able to start identifying what the purpose is behind what they are hearing.

Building blocks

The building blocks of this step are:

- I know the key reasons why people communicate
- I know why it is important to know why someone is communicating
- I can identify why someone is communicating with me

Reflection questions

- Why do you communicate with people?
- Why do people communicate with one another?
- Why does it matter why someone is communicating with you?
- What could happen if you misunderstand the purpose of their communication?
- What are the ways of telling why someone is communicating with you?
- Are there any reasons that are more difficult to identify than others?

What you need to know

Why people communicate

Some of the main reasons why people communicate are:

- To share information
- To share an opinion or view
- To express their feelings
- To request something that they need
- To learn about others
- To build relationships
- To give instructions
- To encourage others

Sometimes communication might combine two or more of these purposes:

- To give instructions and encourage someone to follow them
- To share both information and their opinion on that information

Why it matters why someone is communicating with you

Understanding the purpose behind someone's communication with us helps us to be as prepared as possible for processing what is going on and responding appropriately.

If we misunderstand the purpose of the communication, we might be unprepared to take any necessary actions after listening to the other individual. For example, if we think someone is presenting information, we might not be prepared to process instructions. Or if we think someone is trying to be encouraging, we might be unhappy when they express a different opinion to us.

Communication always works better, and is easier to listen and respond to, when we are clear on what the purpose of the communication is.

The signs of why someone is communicating with you

There are some signs you can spot to help understand why someone is communicating with you:

Purpose	How you can tell
To share information	They might start with 'Did you know...' and talk in terms of facts and events
To share an opinion or view	They might use phrases like 'I think that...' or 'In my opinion...' and normally use more adjectives (describing words)
To express their feelings	They might use phrases like 'I feel...' and use emotional language or adjectives (describing words)
To request something that they need	A request will normally be posed as a question, although sometimes it is easier to say No than at other times
To learn about others and build relationships	They might be asking questions or sharing small pieces of personal information followed by related questions about you
To give instructions	They will talk directly and normally with a focus on actions and verbs (doing words)
To encourage others	They will talk in positive terms about what someone is doing and the effect it is having

Teaching it

To teach this step:

- Learners should listen to several short examples of the teacher speaking and match these to the correct purpose of speech.
- This could be extended by a matching exercise, with examples of each type of talk written down and learners having to match the phrase to the correct communication purpose.
- This could be built on further, with learners coming up with examples to illustrate each purpose of communication.

Reinforcing it

This is a step that lends itself to regular practice in the classroom and supports effective learning. The teachers can ask learners to think about the communication they have just heard in the classroom and what the purpose of the communication was. For example, was the teacher encouraging, giving instructions, presenting facts, or sharing an opinion?

This sort of modelling can be undertaken regularly and supported by visual reminders of the different purposes of communication on display in the learning area.

Assessing it

This step lends itself well to being assessed through a simple exercise such as a matching exercise where learners are asked to link what they have heard to what they think was the purpose of the communication, or by creating their own examples of communication with different purposes.

Listening Step 5

Step 5: I listen to others and record important information as I do so

To achieve Step 5, individuals will be able to listen effectively and then be able to identify and record key information.

This builds on previous steps that focused on how to listen effectively to simple instructions, how to recall longer speech, and how to understand the different purposes of communication.

Building blocks

The building blocks of this step are:

- I can sustain concentration when listening over a longer period
- I identify key words and information from extended talks
- I record information in a way that makes it accessible again in the future

Reflection questions

- How do you find listening for 20-30 minutes?
- What causes you to lose focus and concentration?
- Do you have any ways of helping to maintain concentration?
- Can you just write down everything you hear?
- If not, how do you know which information to write down?
- How do you take notes at the moment?
- What tricks can you use to save writing words when you're listening?

What you need to know

Sustain and concentration over a longer time

Many people have cycles of concentration which last for 15-20 minutes so it is not unusual for someone to find it challenging to listen for up to 30 minutes.

Concentration requires effort and after a few minutes we become much more easily distracted than we were at the outset of the activity.

There are some things we can do to support sustained concentration over a longer period:

- We can actively try to avoid anything that might distract us – for example, by putting away stationery, tools, papers, or notes that we don't need.
- We can also avoid looking at other things or people who might distract us, e.g. by not looking out of the window.
- Finally, as our concentration weakens, we become more aware of any discomfort we might feel, e.g. a squeaky or uncomfortable chair. Making sure we're comfortable before listening for a sustained period can set us up for success.

Identifying key pieces of information

It is near impossible for anyone to record exactly what is being said when someone is speaking when the average person says between 125 and 150 words per minute. On the other hand, the average person can only write up to 20 words per minute by hand, or around 40 words per minute when typing. Therefore, it is important to be selective in what is being written down.

Normally, when someone is writing as they listen, they are *note-taking*. This is about selecting the most important facts or pieces of information and ensuring that they are recorded. For example, in history you would want to record key dates, individuals, and places but might not need to record all of the narrative around them.

If the person you are listening to makes the same point more than once, or emphasises it, then it is likely to be an important piece of information that you should record

Record information in an understandable way

Some important techniques to use when taking notes include:

- *Be clear on what the topic is:* If you start with an understanding of the objective and what is being covered when you listen, it is much easier to organise your notes.

- *Bullet points:* Instead of writing in long sentences, use bullet points to write down the key facts in shortened sentences. These are normally arranged under a particular theme, exactly as we've been modelling in this Handbook.

- *Drawing out links between ideas:* Particularly if you're writing notes by hand, you don't need to be constrained by writing all your notes in lines. Instead, you might draw links, or use flow diagrams to highlight how different concepts link together. Arrows are a good way of showing links and flows between things.

- *Find your shorthand:* Over time you might find abbreviations that work for you and stop you from having to write long words over and over again. For example, '=' instead of 'means that', or '→' instead of 'led to', or '~' instead of 'about'. You can also use *acronyms* or *abbreviations*.

- *Separate key facts or vocabulary:* You might want to use a different part of your page to record key facts or vocabulary so you have them all together.

At the end of your notes, it can sometimes be helpful to take time to think about everything that you heard. You can then use this time to create a summary of the main points.

Teaching it

To teach this step:

- Learners could listen to a modelled example of a talk. The teacher can listen with the class to a video or an audio track and show them on the board how to make notes, modelling some of the techniques that have been used above.
- The teacher can build up from this by getting learners to listen to a short video or audio clip and again ask them to make notes and then share what they came up with. If the teacher completes this at the same time, then it can act as a helpful exemplar.
- Finally, learners can build up to listening for a longer time, with the teacher supporting them to maintain concentration and make notes as they go.

Reinforcing it

This is a step that lends itself to regular practice in the classroom setting, and once mastered will support learning. It also lends itself well to assessment. The teacher can:

- Find opportunities to deliver content in a block of time and encourage learners to make notes as they go. These notes can be reviewed or marked as the teacher would another piece of written work
- Regularly remind learners before they listen for a sustained period about how to maintain their concentration
- Create some shared guidelines as a class for what good note-taking looks like in your classroom, possibly including a shared shorthand notation

Assessing it

This step lends itself well to being assessed through a simple exercise:

Give learners the challenge of listening to a sustained presentation on a relevant topic and set them the challenge of making notes as they listen.

Afterwards, the teacher can check whether they have secured the step by reviewing the quality and accuracy of the notes they have made. Alternatively, learners could be given a short test of the key facts, with access to their notes so that if they have recorded the information appropriately then it will be available to them.

Listening Step 6

Step 6: I show I am listening by how I use eye contact and body language

To achieve Step 6, individuals will be able to demonstrate that they are listening by using eye contact and other positive, encouraging body language with whoever is speaking.

In earlier steps, individuals focused on their experience of receiving information and how to take that information on effectively. The next steps, Steps 6 to 8, focus on how individuals can demonstrate effective listening to others.

Building blocks

The building blocks of this step are:

- I actively listen for a sustained period
- I maintain an appropriate level of eye contact with a speaker
- I show that I am listening through my body language

Reflection questions

- Why do you think eye contact is important to show you are listening?
- How do you feel when someone is not making eye contact when you are speaking?
- What does positive body language look like?
- What is the effect of positive body language?
- What do you do already to show you are interested?

Using eye contact

Eye contact is a helpful part of showing that you are listening to someone, and to show that you are not being distracted by other things.

Eye contact is also important because seeing someone's face and their expressions give you extra information about how they feel about what they are saying. It also helps you to understand what they are emphasising, and therefore what they think is important.

However, maintaining eye contact does *not* mean that you should be staring into someone's face. This can be even more off-putting than limited eye contact. Instead, an approximate target of 60-70% eye contact is probably the best balance.

Positive body language

We look at someone else's body language to build our understanding of how they are feeling, and also how interested they are in us and what we have to say. So, to be a good listener you should try to ensure that your body is giving the signal that you are interested in what you are hearing and that you want to hear more. Some of the ways that you can do this are:

- *Face the speaker:* You should turn your body so that you are naturally facing the speaker. This might mean moving your chair – if you are uncomfortable looking at them, it will show, and they might interpret that as your being uninterested or uncomfortable with what they are saying.
- *Not fidgeting:* Fidgeting with your hands, feet, or anything else is distracting both for the speaker and you. It indicates that you want to be somewhere else.
- *Being open with your arms:* Folding your arms can look defensive and suggest that you want to be somewhere else or that you are trying to protect yourself. Instead, try to use open gestures to show that you are open to what you are hearing.
- *Leaning forwards:* When you are engaged, you naturally lean forwards to show that you want to take part in the conversation and also to listen more effectively to what is being said.
- *Engaged face:* Seeing someone smiling helps the speaker to relax and feel that you are enjoying what they are saying. Obviously, depending on the message, smiling is not always appropriate, but you can still look engaged.

Teaching it

To teach this step:

- Learners can be put into pairs. They should take it in turns to talk for 3 minutes on a topic of their choosing, e.g. what they would like to change about school, their favourite television show, or a hobby.
    - For the first go, encourage learners to disregard actively the guidance on how to show that they are engaged by avoiding eye contact, fidgeting, using closed body language, and scowling. Ask the speakers how they felt.
    - Repeat the exercise, encouraging learners to put in effect all of the guidance on how to use eye contact and positive body language. Ask the speakers and listeners how they felt – hopefully, much better.
- Highlight to learners that, whilst eye contact and positive body language are really important when they are speaking and listening in pairs, it is also useful when they are listening as part of a larger group too.
    - When speaking to the class as their teacher, encourage them to demonstrate that they are listening, and highlight good practice

Reinforcing it

This is a good step to reinforce regularly in the course of normal teaching:

- Before paired work, learners can be reminded how to do their best work together – starting by how they show that they are ready to listen and to learn from one another.
- During day-to-day learning, the teacher can remind learners how to be ready for learning, and how they can demonstrate that they are ready through these same techniques.
- The teacher could also include visual reminders of what it looks like when someone is listening, based on the tips and techniques shared above.

Assessing it

This step is best assessed through observation in day-to-day learning, although a particular scenario or role-play could also be created. The teacher could also create a check-list, based on the reminders above, and assess whether individual learners are demonstrating the required behaviour. This could be extended to peer assessment too.

Listening Step 7

Step 7: I show I am listening by using open questions to deepen my understanding

To achieve Step 7, individuals will be able to use appropriate open questions to demonstrate that they are listening and to open up the conversation to learn more.

In earlier steps, the focus has been on how to listen effectively, and then how to use body language and eye contact to show listening.

Building blocks

The building blocks of this step are:

- I follow the thread of a discussion to make appropriate contributions
- I understand the difference between closed and open questions
- I identify how I can expand my understanding of what is said

Reflection questions

- What is the difference between open and closed questions?
- Can you give any examples of the difference?
- How can you use open questions to support being a better listener?
- Can you come up with examples of open questions?

What you need to know

The difference between open and closed questions

An important part of asking good questions is to know the right type of question to ask at the right time. There are two big types of questions:

- *Closed questions* are those which can be answered with a 'yes' or 'no' response, e.g. 'Is that…' or 'Did…' They are useful for confirming or denying facts. However, they are not good at expanding conversations further.
- *Open questions* are those that cannot be answered with a 'yes' or 'no' response. They tend to start with the bigger question words like 'who', 'what', 'why', 'when' and 'how'. Sometimes these questions can still be answered with short factual answers, but they have the potential to be much broader.

Creating open questions to extend conversation

Key points:

The value of open questions is that they can demonstrate to the speaker that you have listened to what they have said so far, as well as permitting the speaker to expand upon the topic they are sharing. This may open up new and interesting lines of enquiry.

It is possible to combine a closed question with an open question to extend the conversation further too, e.g. 'did you consider doing that, and how did you make your decision?' or 'do you like this, and why?'

Teaching it

To teach this step:

- Learners could look at a list of questions and decide whether they are open or closed questions.
- Learners can then listen to a talk from a peer or their teacher and then create closed questions to confirm or deny specific facts. They can then create open questions to broaden out the conversation.
- Learners can interview one another by using open questions to build up their understanding of something

Reinforcing It

This step lends itself to easy reinforcement across learning. For example:

- Before introducing questions to the class, the teacher could ask whether they are open or closed questions
- The teacher could put visual reminders of the difference between open and closed questions on display in the classroom
- If learners present to each other at different times, the teacher could encourage other learners to ask closed or open questions depending on the purpose

Assessing It

This step can be assessed through a simple assignment or observation:

- The teacher could set learners a challenge of creating three open questions and three closed questions in response to a stimulus
- The teacher could give learners a list of questions and challenge them to sort them into a list of open questions and closed questions

Listening Step 8

Step 8: I show I am listening by summarising or rephrasing what I have heard

To achieve Step 8, individuals will show that they can demonstrate their understanding of more complex ideas by repeating or rephrasing what they have heard.

In the earlier Steps 6 and 7, individuals showed they were listening by using eye contact, body language, and open questions. This builds further by showing engagement with the content itself of what they are hearing.

Building blocks

The building blocks of this step are:

- I understand what it means to summarise information
- I understand what it means to rephrase information
- I find appropriate points in conversation to summarise or rephrase

Reflection questions

- What does it mean to summarise what you have heard?
- What is the value of rephrasing what you have heard?
- How would you choose between summarising or rephrasing?
- How can you effectively build this into the flow of conversation?

What you need to know

Summarising or rephrasing what you have heard

Summarising is about capturing the key points of what has been said (the methods of doing this were discussed in *Step 5*, when taking notes).

Summarising works well when what you are listening to is not too complicated, i.e. it is about a process, a set of directions, or instructions. Here the focus is on making sure that you can repeat back the key points without significant change, and to ensure that you have not missed anything important.

Rephrasing is an extension of summarising. Similarly, you take the main points that a speaker has made, but instead of playing that back directly, you change the way that an idea has been expressed.

Rephrasing is most helpful when the speaker is talking about more complex concepts, e.g. explaining a broader principle, or an academic concept. In this case, rephrasing is a helpful test of whether you have understood and been able to process what has been heard. Putting something 'into your own words' requires that you have understood what has been heard already.

Working summarising and rephrasing into conversation

Summarising and rephrasing can be extremely helpful tools to help structure the flow of information. If done well, it can ensure that:

- Anything that wasn't clear or that you misheard when listening can be addressed quickly
- It provides the speaker with greater confidence that you are understanding what they are sharing
- The process of summarising or rephrasing helps you to process and store the information, making it more likely that you will remember it in the future

Timing is critical for making summarising and rephrasing effective tools, though:

- If you interrupt to summarise or rephrase then it can break the flow of conversation or thought of the speaker
- If you leave too little time, the conversation becomes disjointed because there hasn't been time for the speaker to explain the idea or instructions fully
- If you leave too much time, you might miss the opportunity to correct a misconception on your part

Ideally, the speaker would make clear that they had finished a point or idea by asking if that all made sense, or whether you had any questions. However, even if they don't do that, they may well pause as they consider what is coming next. At that point, you can always chip in, starting with something like 'So, what you're saying is...' or 'To check my understanding, am I right that...' or 'So, is it the case that...'

You can tell if you've got your timing right, because:

- If you've timed it right, then your speaker should seem appreciative of what you've checked or encouraged to speak more
- If you summarised or rephrased too soon then they might seem flustered or snappy as they feel that they've interrupted
- If you leave it too long then they might start trailing off or appearing to lose confidence in what they're saying because they're questioning in their head whether you can keep up

Teaching it

To teach this step:

- For *summarising*, the teacher can start by modelling a conversation containing some key information or a set of instructions, perhaps between themselves and a teaching assistant, or one of the learners. At appropriate points, the teacher can model how to summarise what they have heard so far and how this can be built into the flow of a conversation.
    - The teacher might also want to model what it looks like to try to summarise what you have heard too soon, or to leave it too late and show how you might have got lost by that point.
- The learners can then work in pairs, giving a long set of instructions or information (of up to 5 minutes length). This lends itself best to repetition. Encourage the listener to summarise at least twice, and probably three times during that conversation.
- For *rephrasing*, it is worth starting by rephrasing a single idea first. Perhaps this is a subject-related concept, or for a more meta-approach the teacher could rephrase some of the key concepts in this step.
    - Learners can practice this individually by being given a concept or idea, and then telling one another or to writing it down in their own words, rephrasing what they heard.
- Then, in pairs, learners should explain a concept or idea to one another. The listener has to find an appropriate point to check their understanding by rephrasing what they have heard.

Reinforcing it

This is a skill step that lends itself well to being reinforced in class:

- During regular lessons, the teacher could pause at moments to ask the learners to summarise what they have learnt or heard so far, or to rephrase it to demonstrate their understanding.
- The teacher can also continue to model this technique when teaching concepts or ideas that learners find challenging by demonstrating how they rephrase these to help build understanding. This is something that teachers do naturally anyway.

Assessing it

This step can be assessed through observation or a deliberate activity:

- The teacher could check that learners can summarise and rephrase by giving them all something to listen to for 2-3 minutes and then asking them to summarise or rephrase it, either verbally or in writing.
- The teacher will then want to check that learners can build this naturally into the flow of conversation. This could be done through peer assessment of learners as they work in pairs, or through observation of conversations.

Listening Step 9

Step 9: I am aware of how a speaker is influencing me through their tone

To achieve Step 9, individuals will have to understand what is meant by 'tone', how it varies, and the impact of different tones when communicating.

In earlier steps, the focus was on listening effectively and demonstrating listening. This step, and Step 10, focuses on increasing listeners' understanding of how they could be influenced by the speaker.

Building blocks

The building blocks of this step are:

- I understand what tone means and can identify the key elements
- I explain how a speaker's tone can change
- I understand how different tones can influence my understanding of what I hear

Reflection questions

- How do our voices change when we are speaking?
- What do you understand by 'tone' in the context of listening?
- How can tone vary? Can you give examples?
- How do you think each of the elements of tone affect the listener?
- Why is it important as a listener to pay attention to tone, not just the words?

What you need to know

What tone is and how it matters

For now, imagine that someone is saying the same thing, e.g. "Could you get that piece of work to me tomorrow?"

Without changing the words, the way they sound and the meaning they convey can change a lot depending on the way in which someone says them. It is amazing how much meaning comes from the *way* that something is said, rather than just *what* is being said. This simple sentence could sound:

- *Positive*: you are doing them a favour by getting the piece of work done for tomorrow.
- *Exasperated*: the piece of work should have been done today or sooner.
- *Relaxed*: getting the piece of work done for tomorrow would be great, but it could plausibly be at a later date.
- *Like a direct instruction:* it is actually a command, not a question.

We refer to the *way* that something is said as the *tone* of speaking. Five main elements go into creating tone:

- *Pitch:* How high or low someone is speaking
- *Tempo:* How quickly someone is speaking
- *Volume:* How loudly or quietly someone is speaking
- *Intonation:* How the sentence rises and falls
- *Stress*: Where the emphasis is placed on different words

The elements of tone and what they can mean

We can see how changes in tone have different effects on listeners:

Element	The Variation	The Effect on the listener
Pitch: How high or low someone is speaking	Someone speaks with a high pitch	The speaker can seem stressed or anxious, which might be interpreted as lacking confidence or not being honest.
	Someone speaks with a low pitch	The speaker can seem calm and more confident. However, they might seem less energetic or engaged.
Tempo: How quickly someone is speaking	Someone speaks quickly	The speaker can seem energetic and engaged. However, they might also seem stressed or anxious.
	Someone speaks slowly	The speaker can seem more authoritative and calm. However, if they speak too slowly they might seem unengaged.
Volume: How loudly or quietly someone is speaking	Someone speaks quietly	The speaker can appear calm and in control if they speak quietly. However, if they speak too quietly they might seem to be lacking in confidence.
	Someone speaks loudly	The speaker can seem authoritative if they speak loudly as it suggests that they are in control. However, if they are too loud it can seem aggressive or angry.
Intonation: This is about how the sentence rises and falls	Someone uses falling intonation – where the voice falls at the end of a phrase	The speaker sounds confident in what they are saying – perhaps they are giving an instruction.
	Someone uses rising intonation – where the voice rises at the end of a phrase	The speaker sounds like they are asking a question.
	Someone uses falling and rising intonation	The speaker sounds like they are not sure about what they are saying – they are open to discussion. It can also be a way of softening a direct question.
Stress: Putting emphasis on different words in the sentence shifts meaning, mood and intention	Heavy stress on a word draws attention to its importance	Stress identifies which element of the sentence is of most importance to the speaker, and what their intention is behind it (e.g. *Could* you give me that? implies irritation at a delay in being given something, whereas Could *you* give me that? Is about whether the person addressed is capable or willing to do so and so on…

Deciphering tone

Of course, these different elements of tone can all be used in a variety of different ways. The combination that is used can suggest:

Different emotions: As listeners, we might be able to interpret something of how the speaker is feeling depending on their tone.

- Anger could be suggested by a loud voice and falling intonation
- Anxiety could be suggested by speaking quickly and with a high pitch
- Confidence could be suggested by moderate volume and steady speaking pace
- Excitement could be suggested by a louder voice and quick speaking
- Doubt could be suggested by stressing an uncertain element of a statement

The purpose of the communication: As listeners, we can also infer the purpose of the communication from the tone (this was touched on in *Step 4*). For example:

- Instructions tend to have a falling intonation
- Questions tend to have rising intonation
- An invitation for discussion will often have falling and then rising intonation

There are a lot of different combinations of the five elements of tone (pitch, tempo, volume, and intonation, stress). As such, although we have given some examples, this is a skill step that is worth exploring in greater depth through listening carefully and then identifying the elements of tone and what you learnt as a result of paying attention to them.

Teaching it

To teach this step:

- Firstly, learners must have a clear understanding of what is meant by tone and the elements that make it; they should be able to give definitions and examples and talk about how they vary.
- Secondly, learners can then focus on what changes in these different elements might suggest to a listener. The teacher might be able to model how this works by repeating a similar statement in different ways and demonstrating what variations in each of the tonal elements sound like.
- Once learners have a strong understanding of the different elements, the teacher can play them a series of audio clips (try to avoid visual clues) and ask them to reflect on what they learnt from listening to the tone of the speaker.

Reinforcing it

This is a step that can be routinely practised in a classroom setting:

- To reinforce the ideas of tone and the elements that make it up, visual reminders in the classroom can be helpful
- When listening to any audio of another speaker, the teacher can pause learners and get them to reflect on what they have interpreted from the tone of the speaker
- When the teacher is talking in class, they can pause learners and highlight the different elements of tone in how they spoke and ask the class to interpret what that might mean

Assessing it

This step is best assessed through an assessed activity:

- Testing whether learners remember what the five elements of tone are, how they vary and what the effects of that variation can be on the interpretation of the listener
- Playing a series of short audio clips to learners and asking them to interpret how the elements of tone vary in the clips, and what they can infer from that

Listening Step 10

Step 10: I am aware of how a speaker is influencing me through their language

To achieve Step 10, individuals will focus on how differences in the language that the speaker uses influence the meaning of what they are saying. They will identify some common elements and how to interpret them.

In the previous step, individuals explored how a speaker can influence through their tone and how to infer additional meaning from that tone. This step builds on this by focusing on the language that the speaker uses.

Building blocks

The building blocks of this step are:

- I understand how language can influence emotions
- I identify language features that create different emotional responses
- I identify how language tools can influence the listener

Reflective questions

- How can changes in language affect how you feel about something?
- Can you give some examples?
- Why is it important to be aware of how language can influence our emotions?
- What are some of the other ways that a listener can be influenced by what as speaker says?
- What have you experienced as the impact on you?

What you need to know

Language for emotional responses

As listeners, we are influenced by the tone with which someone speaks to us, but we are also emotionally influenced by the language that a speaker uses.

It is important to be aware of how a speaker's language can influence our emotions so that we can consider whether we want our emotions influenced in that way. If we are not aware then we can be easily manipulated by a speaker.

If we are focused on listening to something, then we can often start to mirror the emotions that we are hearing. For example:

- If a speaker starts talking about being excited, then we start to feel excited too
- If a speaker talks about being anxious, nervous, or uncertain then we start to take on that emotion too

There are a wide range of emotions that one might feel at any time, based on what you are hearing:

- Joy
- Fear
- Surprise
- Disappointment
- Trust
- Anger
- Anticipation
- Disgust
- Boredom

What is important is to avoid being overwhelmed by the emotional reaction that you might have to what is being said. While it is helpful to be able to identify the emotional response that a speaker wants you to have, it is also important that this is balanced by being able to think objectively about the *content* of what is being said, to be able to engage critically with what the speaker is saying, and to remain detached so you can make your own mind up as to whether you agree with them or not.

Language tools that can influence a listener

There are other language tools that a speaker can use to influence a listener.

While it is important to listen carefully, it is also important to be able to identify what is influencing you as a listener so that you can be in control of your reaction. In Step 4, we explored some of the purposes that a speaker might have when they are communicating with you as their listener. Each of these has associated language tools that a speaker might use:

Purpose	*Language tools they might use*
To share information	• Facts • Statistics
To share an opinion or view	• Assertions of truth – "It is well known that…" • Selective statistics and facts
To express their feelings	• Emotive language • Hyperbole and exaggeration
To request something that they need	• Emotive language • Compliments
To learn about others and build relationships	• Humour • Self-deprecation • Queries
To give instructions	• Direct instruction
To encourage others	• Flattery • Compliments • Self-deprecation – for example, that they could never have done that.

It is particularly important when a speaker is requesting something, encouraging, or sharing an opinion to be mindful that they are likely to be selective in the language that they use. They might be trying to influence and change your mind about something, or encouraging you to take some action which might not be correct or in your own best interests.

Teaching it

To teach this step:

- Firstly, the teacher should ensure that learners understand why a speaker might want to influence them through their use of language.
- Secondly, learners should understand that language can influence by encouraging a particular emotional response, or through selective provision of information to back up a particular idea.
- They can then look at this by modelling what it looks like to try to influence someone. These modelled examples can come from a teacher in the first instance, but then learners could also create their own.

Reinforcing it

This step can be reinforced in the classroom:

- The teacher can encourage learners to identify emotive language in what they hear or read, and to reflect on how that is being used to influence their emotions.
- Learners can also be encouraged to take a critical view of some of the other language tools they might come across (e.g. hyperbole or exaggeration, selective use of facts and statistics or compliments) and to appreciate how that might influence them as a listener.

Assessing it

This step can be assessed through observation or a carefully designed activity:

- Learners could listen to a couple of speeches or pitches (video is fine for this step) and try to identify where the speaker is looking to influence an emotional response from the listeners.
- They can also look to identify where language tools are being used to influence.

Listening Step 11

Step 11: I listen critically and compare different perspectives

To achieve Step 11, individuals will show that they can listen to two or more different perspectives on an issue and compare them.

In the previous steps, the focus was on how to demonstrate active listening, and then to be aware of how a speaker might try to influence us as listeners. This step thinks about how to listen critically to different perspectives and compare them.

Building blocks

The Building blocks of this step are:

- I explain and can define what perspective means
- I understand the value of different people's perspectives
- I use core points made in a discussion to identify different perspectives

Reflection questions

- What does it mean to have different perspectives?
- What is the value of looking at multiple perspectives?
- How can we identify the core points being made?
- How can we compare perspectives?

What you need to know

Different perspectives

A *perspective* is a view of something. That something might be as small as a specific problem, or as substantial as the global economy.

We have a diversity of opinions on a topic because we have such diversity of information, insights, lived experience, values, cultural norms, and underpinning assumptions about the world. What drives these different perspectives is explored in a lot more depth in *Step 12*.

A perspective might seem obvious or intuitive to the individual who holds it but look utterly incomprehensible to someone else.

The value of different perspectives

Each of us only has an incomplete understanding of anything. Even experts in their field or academics spend a lot of time talking to one another to share different perspectives, and to debate and try to reconcile different ideas about how the world works.

By being open to different perspectives, we are open to:

- Expanding our knowledge and understanding of the world
- Recognising and benefiting from the skills and experiences of others
- Appreciating different values and cultural norms
- Challenging our unconscious biases and assumptions

There is plenty of evidence that groups that work to incorporate diverse perspectives into their thinking make better decisions and get further as a result. This is because the human brain does not tend to worry about the limitations of what it knows – it presumes it knows enough and then keeps going.

It takes an active effort to try to open up to different perspectives, and to wrestle intellectually with the differences that emerge as a result.

Identifying the key points

Comparing perspectives is not an easy thing to do, particularly when listening. A simple mental model to do this is to take each individual in turn, and when listening try to capture some of this crucial information:

- What do they think the answer is, or should happen?
- What reasons do they give for this perspective?
- Do they recognise any of the arguments against their perspective?

This process of capturing information is helpful as a starting point, and to aid us in processing what we are hearing.

Comparing perspectives

To compare perspectives successfully, though, we need to build up our mental models of the options and how to reconcile what we are hearing.

- As we build up our view of the different perspectives, we are looking to:
- Identify the range of available options
- Capture the arguments for and against each of those options
- Assess which of the perspectives we have heard is most *credible* – that is, most likely to be true
- Evaluate which of the options has the most compelling case, balancing the arguments for and against

Teaching it

To teach this step:

The teacher should introduce the idea that there exists a diverse range of perspectives on any question, and that diversity is valuable because each of us only holds a small part of the answer.

- Learners can discuss the value of diverse perspectives. The teacher could illustrate this idea with examples such as highlighting how a decision in the context of school or college, like lengthening the learning day, would be seen quite differently by different members of the community. Learners could discuss what some of these different perspectives might be.
- The teacher can then model how to reconcile these different views. In this simple example, there are two initial options (to extend the learning day, or not to extend the learning day). Additional options might also be introduced, such as reducing the length of holidays.

- The teacher can illustrate how to draw out these three options, add arguments for and against each option in a grid as they are heard, and then use this to help make a choice.
- Ultimately, the teacher should remind learners that lots of decisions are not clear-cut but are about trade-offs between options, and linked with values as much as to outcomes.

Reinforcing it

This step lends itself well to reinforcement in the classroom. For instance, debate can be a way of deepening learners' engagement with a topic, and those listening have to decipher what they are hearing and decide what they think at the end, having reflected on a variety of options and views.

This step is also useful when learners are listening to different perspectives in other areas of learning. This sort of comparison is often an essential part of learning at a more advanced level.

Assessing it

This step is best assessed through a structured activity where learners have to listen to a range of perspectives on a problem or question. They should demonstrate that they can capture critical information, and then organise it in a simple model to compare the options and reach a justified view of their own, based on what they hear.

Listening Step 12

Step 12: I listen critically and think about where differences in perspectives come from

To achieve Step 12, individuals will have to show that they can think about where differences in perspectives might come from.

In the previous step, the focus was on recognising and comparing different standpoints. This step builds on this by encouraging individuals to think more deeply about where diverse views come from, the better to build empathy and understanding.

Building blocks

The building blocks of this step are:

- I am aware of the factors which can influence a person's perspective
- I link information that I have heard to a person's perspective
- I build knowledge of people and events to better understand different perspectives

Reflection questions

- What causes us to have different perspectives?
- Why is it helpful to understand where perspectives come from?
- What are the challenges in being able to do this?
- How can we start to understand those perspectives?

What you need to know

Where different perspectives come from

We all have different perspectives on life. It's easy to forget that our view of the world is uniquely ours. Several layers forge that view:

- Firstly, our *knowledge, experiences*, and *skills*. These can vary according to the education and life experience we have had.
- Secondly, we would also recognise that we have different *interests* – things that we are affected by day-to-day. For instance, a business owner and a worker might have different interests, as the business owner might want to maximise their profits, while a worker wants to get a good salary and work safely.
- Thirdly, we have different *beliefs and values* – which might be religious or not – about how we should act and behave in the world. These are the things that we view as making up good behaviour.
- Finally, we also have an underpinning set of assumptions about the world, which may be entirely unconscious. For example, the relationship between humans and the earth, the nature of time, or what happens beyond death.

With all of these different layers, what we see as the world is simply our view of it and so it is no wonder that we have different perspectives.

The value of understanding where perspectives come from

When we share our views on something, we are only sharing the very surface of this thinking. We are most likely to talk about how our perspective is informed by what we know, what we understand, and our experiences. This is often the most comfortable level to talk at – these things are harder to dispute, and they are also impersonal, so people feel most comfortable sharing them.

Sometimes individuals might talk about how their interests differ from others. This is less comfortable because it highlights individual self-interest and we often want to project that we are taking a perspective for objective reasons, rather than for our advantage.

It is even less likely that the conversation will come to beliefs and values unless these are commonly shared. That is because individuals sometimes find it hard to identify the drivers of their own 'gut reaction' to something. At other times, if their beliefs and values differ from others, they might feel uncomfortable setting themselves apart as different.

When it comes to underpinning assumptions, these are very rarely shared because they are often unconscious to the individual themselves.

For all of these reasons, it is essential to remember that sometimes the perspective and the rationale that we hear for something is only the very tip of the iceberg. There is likely to be a lot more than underpins a particular opinion that we might not see but is still helpful to understand.

Analysing different perspectives

We often struggle to understand fully where our view on something comes from. We simply don't have the brainpower to be able to unpack consciously everything that underpins our view of the world.

It is at least as challenging to analyse this for someone else when we only ever have imperfect information about them. Therefore, we need to move carefully and modestly when we try to understand what is unspoken in someone's perspective.

In *Steps 13 and 14,* we look at how to identify bias when listening, and how to use questioning to better understand different perspectives. For now, a good approach is to think about several layers when we hear individuals giving different perspectives:

- What other reasons might they have to hold this perspective?
- What skills, experience, or knowledge might they have?
- What is their stake in this – how will they personally win or lose depending on this decision?
- How might their beliefs or values be part of their perspective?

Asking these questions will help to widen our understanding of the issue and avoid just taking the views we hear at face value.

Teaching it

To teach this step:

- The teacher should start by asking learners why they think people have different views of things. This can be extended to a structured conversation about the layers from the explicit reasons people give for their opinions to the more implicit.
- Learners could think about a topical issue that they have a strong view on and analyse for themselves where they believe this view came from. Encourage them to peel back the layers of their views one at a time to try to uncover the interests that drive their perspective, and then the underpinning beliefs or values. These could be shared as a group, if appropriate.

- The teacher can lead a discussion of why it is helpful to be able to understand what underpins the different views that individuals present, but also the limitations of being able to gauge these accurately.
- Learners could be challenged to look at a topical issue – for instance, by seeing different politicians' perspectives on a current issue. They could be asked to think about what might be underpinning that particular view.
- After they have shared their analysis, the teacher should remind learners that they will never know for sure why those perspectives come about, and they should avoid assuming too much. However, there is still value in trying to deepen their thinking beyond the view as it is presented.

Reinforcing it

This step can be reinforced effectively by encouraging learners to take a more critical approach to how they take in information and assess different perspectives. When they read differing accounts or opinion pieces, they can be challenged to analyse what they see as causing those differences.

Assessing it

This step is best assessed through a structured analysis task, either based around something that is topical in current affairs or related to their wider subject learning. Learners can be asked either to discuss or write about a comparison of perspectives, and their analysis of where those different perspectives come from. The teacher is looking for evidence of the learner identifying and exploring some of the layers above.

Speaking

The oral transmission of information or ideas

Why it matters

Speaking is the complement to Listening, and together they make the two sides of communication skills.

Whereas Listening is about receiving information, Speaking is about being able to share or transmit information. For some learners with special educational needs, speaking might be replaced by other forms of sharing information including sign language.

Without the ability to communicate like this, learners will struggle to share their ideas, work with others, or to lead.

How Speaking is built

This skill is all about how to communicate effectively with others, being mindful about whether learners are talking to peers, teachers, parents, or others in authority. Initially, this skill focuses on being able to speak clearly. We start with building these skills when talking to individuals who they already know well, then to small groups, and then to strangers.

The next stage is about being an effective speaker by making points logically, by thinking about what listeners already know and using appropriate language, tone, and gesture. The focus is on speaking engagingly through the use of facts and examples, visual aids, and expression and gesture.

Beyond this stage, speakers will be adaptive to the response of their listeners and ready for different scenarios. The final steps focus on speaking influentially by using structure, examples, facts and vision to persuade listeners.

Skills Builder Framework for Speaking

The oral transmission of information or ideas

Step 0	I speak clearly to someone I know
Step 1	I speak clearly to small groups of people I know
Step 2	I speak clearly to individuals and small groups I do not know
Step 3	I speak effectively by making points in a logical order
Step 4	I speak effectively by thinking about what my listeners already know
Step 5	I speak effectively by using appropriate language
Step 6	I speak effectively by using appropriate tone, expression, and gesture
Step 7	I speak engagingly by using facts and examples to support my points
Step 8	I speak engagingly by using visual aids to support my points
Step 9	I speak engagingly by using tone, expression, and gesture to engage listeners
Step 10	I speak adaptively by changing my language, tone and expression depending on the response of listeners
Step 11	I speak adaptively by planning for different possible responses of listeners
Step 12	I speak adaptively by changing my content depending on the response of listeners
Step 13	I speak influentially by changing the structure of my points to best persuade the listeners
Step 14	I speak influentially by changing the examples and facts I use to best persuade the listeners
Step 15	I speak influentially by articulating a compelling vision that persuades the listeners

Speaking Step 0

Step 0: I speak clearly to someone I know

To achieve Step 0, individuals will be able to speak clearly to someone that they know – perhaps to ask a question, to talk about something they are familiar with, or give an answer to a question.

This is the first step of speaking in the Skills Builder Universal Framework, and starts with a focus on speaking clearly so that others can understand the words that are being said. This is the foundation for everything else.

Building blocks

The building blocks of this step are:

- I understand what speaking is
- I respond to simple questions and prompts
- I speak clearly so another person understands me

Reflection questions

- What is speaking?
- Why do we speak to each other?
- What does it mean to speak clearly?
- How do we know if we are speaking clearly?

What you need to know

What is speaking?

Speaking is how we communicate using speech. It is also called talking. We form words using our mouths and add sound to them using our lungs.

There are other forms of communication, including writing, performance, sign language, song, and electronic methods of communicating. Some of the principles of speaking can make sense for other forms of communicating too.

- We speak for several reasons:
- To share information
- To share an opinion or view
- To express our feelings
- To ask for something that we need
- To learn about others
- To build relationships
- To give instructions
- To encourage others

How to speak clearly

When we speak, we want someone else to understand what we are saying

Speaking clearly means that someone else can understand what we are saying. If we don't speak clearly then we might not be understood.

Some ways of making sure we speak clearly are:

- Thinking about what you want to say before you start speaking
- Take a deep breath
- Make sure you have the attention of the person who will be listening
- Look at them and speak loudly enough so that they can hear
- Speak slowly so that they can follow what you are saying
- Do not try to say too much all in one go

Teaching it

To teach this step:

The teacher can continue to model good practice - when talking to the class they could explain how they prepare to talk to an individual. (See key points above)

Learners should be encouraged to talk to one another. This can start as a structured activity where you go through the checklist to help them structure how they are talking.

Over time, this structure can be taken away so that learners can speak clearly to others that they know.

Reinforcing it

This step lends itself to regular reinforcement in the classroom, in particular by asking learners to talk about their ideas or thoughts about something to a friend before talking about it in a bigger group. Some learners will find this much easier than others, and confidence-building and gentle encouragement is needed along the way.

Assessing it

This step is best assessed through observation:

- By asking learners to talk to a friend about what they did at the weekend or at break time or about an interest they have outside of school
- They can then be observed to ensure that they have been able to speak clearly to another learner that they are friendly with.
- However, it is also possible to observe this step easily in the context of normal classroom and playground interactions.

Speaking Step 1

Step 1: I speak clearly to small groups of people I know

To achieve Step 1, individuals will show that they can speak clearly to small groups of people that they know.

This builds on the previous step which focused on being able to speak clearly to one other person that they know.

Building blocks

The building blocks of this step are:

- I understand how to engage more than one person
- I speak in front of others
- I speak clearly so more than one person understands me

Reflection questions

- What is different about speaking to a small group rather than an individual you know?
- Which do you find more difficult?
- Why do you think that is?
- How can you speak clearly in front of a group?

What you need to know

What is different about speaking to a small group

Generally, people find it more challenging to talk in front of a small group than to an individual, for several reasons:

- There are more people to engage, and it can be harder to know whether you are being successful in engaging all of the individuals in the group
- You might also feel that more people are looking at you, and so you might feel more shy or self-conscious
- Other people might also want to speak, so you might worry about whether you will be interrupted
- You might need to talk louder for more people to hear you

This is very normal, and you should not worry if you don't feel comfortable speaking in front of a group to start with, even if they're all people that you know well.

How to speak clearly in a group

Many of the same things that help you speak clearly to an individual that you know will also help you speak to a small group that you know.

It is useful to be reminded about the things that help you speak clearly, whatever the setting:

- Thinking about what you want to say before you start speaking
- Taking a deep breath
- Making sure you have the attention of the people who will be listening
- Looking at them and speaking loudly enough so that they can hear
- Speaking slowly so that they can follow what you are saying
- Not trying to say too much all in one go

The big difference between this step and the previous step is that you will need to think about how to engage more than one person. That means:

- *Making sure that you look at everyone* that you want to be listening to you – not just focusing on one person. That way, everyone will know that you are speaking to them.
- *Speaking more loudly* because in a group you are likely to be stood further apart, and it is harder to hear otherwise.
- *Leaving more space to check that everyone has understood you*. You can check that everyone is following what you're saying by looking around.

Teaching it

To teach this step:

- It is helpful for the teacher to model what it looks like to speak to a group. For example, they can show how they get the attention of a group before they start speaking, how they look around to make sure everyone can understand and make sure that they are speaking loudly enough.
- Learners can be encouraged to talk about something to a pair of other learners they know, and then to gradually increasing numbers to build up their confidence in ever-larger groups.
- Learners can also be reminded of the key things they need to be aware of if they are going to communicate effectively with small groups of others they know.

Reinforcing it

This step can be reinforced effectively in a classroom setting:

- Whenever a teacher is speaking in front of the class, they can model how they are getting ready to speak and ensuring that the learners in the group are ready to listen to them.
- Many primary schools use 'Show and Tell' and similar opportunities to get learners used to speaking in front of their peers for short periods. Learners could also be encouraged to share other pieces of work they produce in front of the class.
- Group work also provides ample opportunities for reinforcing this step. Here, it is important to ensure that the teacher intervenes as necessary to ensure that learners' confidence is being built through positive experiences of speaking clearly to a group and that every learner is having that opportunity.

Assessing it

This step is best assessed through structured observation:

- Asking learners to prepare a short talk about something they are interested in, or a piece of work that they have completed. They can then be observed to see whether they can speak clearly to a group they know for up to 3 minutes.

Speaking Step 2

Step 2: I speak clearly to individuals and small groups I do not know

To achieve Step 2, individuals will be able to speak clearly to others that they don't know.

This moves beyond the previous steps where the focus was on speaking clearly to individuals and then to groups who they already know. The shift, therefore, is mainly in having the confidence to apply the same approach to speaking clearly but in a context where they are less familiar with the individuals.

Building blocks

The building blocks of this step are:

- I understand what is different about talking to people I don't know
- I speak clearly to individuals I do not know
- I speak clearly to small groups I do not know

Reflection Questions

- What is different about talking to people you don't know?
- Which do you find easier – talking to people you know or don't know?
- Why do you think that is?
- How do you speak clearly in front of people you don't know?
- What is different to speaking in front of people you do know?

What you need to know

The difference when you don't know people

Most people find it more difficult to speak to people that they don't know well than to people they do already know.

There are several reasons for this:

- When you know someone, it is easier to predict what their reactions will be to something that you say
- You are likely to feel less shy when speaking to someone who you already know
- When you know someone, you have a better idea of how much they already know about what you are talking about

However, many of the same things that help you speak clearly in front of individuals and groups who you already know will also help you to speak clearly in front of those you don't know as well.

How to speak clearly to people you don't know

Many of the same principles that help you to speak clearly to people you already know – whether as individuals or in a group – will also help you with those you don't already know.

As a reminder, these are:

- Thinking about what you want to say before you start speaking
- Taking a deep breath
- Making sure you have the attention of the people who will be listening
- Looking at them and speaking loudly enough so that they can hear
- Speaking slowly so that they can follow what you are saying
- Not trying to say too much all in one go

The significant differences when you don't know the people you are speaking to are:

- *Spending a bit more time thinking* about how to be as clear as possible – you don't know what the people you are speaking to know already or don't know
- *Making sure you are looking at them* as this will help you to see whether they understand what you are saying or not
- *Trying to make what you are saying as simple as possible* as this will help to ensure that individuals can understand you

With practice, it is possible to build the confidence to speak clearly in front of individuals and groups who you do not already know.

Teaching it

To teach this step:

- The teacher can model the difference in how they would approach talking to a group that they know (e.g. the group of learners in front of them) compared to another group of learners that they did not know. For instance, exploring how they would prepare to talk more simply and as clearly as possible.
- Learners could talk about something to another teacher, or in front of learners from a different class. Before the exercise, be explicit about what they should be doing to ensure that they are speaking clearly. Depending on the maturity of the learners, they could give one another feedback afterwards about how clearly they spoke.
- Learners might speak in front of a broader group such as parents or in a school assembly if those are options. Beforehand, they could prepare and practice to ensure they speak as clearly as possible.

Reinforcing it

This step is slightly more challenging to practice in the context of a classroom, because often learners and teachers become very familiar with one another. However, other opportunities include:

- Occasionally sharing work with other classes and groups of learners, so that learners build confidence in speaking clearly in front of others that they do not know as well.
- Giving all learners the chance to lead assemblies, to speak in front of parents, or to present their work to teachers they are less familiar with.

Assessing it

This step is best assessed through observation:

- In existing activities, learners could be evaluated when they are delivering an assembly or other activity.
- An activity could be designed expressly for assessment – for example, creating a piece of work to present.

Speaking Step 3

Step 3: I speak effectively by making points in a logical order

To achieve Step 3, individuals will be able to make points in a logical order when speaking so that a listener can follow and understand the meaning of what is said.

In earlier steps, individuals focused on how to speak clearly, so that the words they were saying could be understood. The shift now is to focus on the meaning of their communication – particularly ensuring that the points they are making are in a logical order.

Building blocks

The building blocks of this step are:

- I understand what it means to say things in a logical order
- I understand why putting things in a logical order is important when speaking
- I use different approaches to putting things in a logical order

Reflection Questions

- What do we mean by putting ideas in a logical order?
- Why does it matter?
- How do you think you can put things in a logical order?
- Do you do this at the moment? Could you try it?

What you need to know

Logical ordering and why it matters

A logical order is putting ideas in an order that means they make sense when they follow on from each other.

The contrast is putting lots of ideas into a random order.

- For example: "British history has spanned the Romans, Saxons, Vikings, Medieval period…" puts historical periods into a logical order. In contrast "British history has spanned Victorians, Tudors, Romans, Saxons, Georgians…" is much harder to follow because there is no sequence.
- As another example: "The chicken lays the egg, which hatches into a chick, and then grows up to become a chicken" puts a cycle into a natural pattern. In contrast: "An egg makes a chick which was made first by a chicken, and then the chick becomes a chicken too" is somewhat harder to follow.
- As another example: "First take the screw and place it in the hole. Then take the screwdriver and place it on the top of the screw. Then screw clockwise to tighten." The alternative being: "You screw clockwise with the screwdriver once it's in the top. You want to put the screw in the hole first."
- When speaking for longer, the importance of putting ideas into a logical order is even greater. If ideas are not in a logical order, it is difficult for a listener to understand what is said and to be able to process and remember what they are hearing. The meaning that the speaker was trying to communicate gets lost.

How to put things in a logical order

There are three main ways of arranging ideas logically:

- *Talking about causes and effects*: Making a clear connection between how one thing led to another
- *Putting things in the order in which they happen:* Putting events in the order that they occurred, also known as chronological order, makes it easier for them to remember and retell the story
- *Starting from the most straightforward idea:* Thinking about what someone needs to understand to understand the meaning of what is being said, then beginning with the most straightforward idea and building up from there

Teaching it

To teach this step:

- The teacher can model to learners what it looks like to speak without any logical order. For example, the teacher could retell a historical event in a random order or introduce a new topic without reference to anything learners have heard before. The teacher can use this to elicit from the learners what the effect is on them when there is no logical order in what they are hearing, how it made them feel and what they can recall.
- Then, the teacher can model to learners what it looks like to introduce a logical order and how that can support recall and linking new knowledge to existing knowledge.
- Learners can then be encouraged to explicitly think about how to put ideas into a logical order. For example, by giving instructions, talking about an event that happened to them, or explaining a sequence or cycle that they have learnt. Depending on the maturity of learners, they might be given feedback from a peer about whether they put things in a logical order when they were speaking.

Reinforcing it

This step is good to practice in the classroom. Although the focus in this step is on speaking, logical ordering of ideas is useful in written work too.

- When asking for explanations from an individual, the teacher can remind learners of what it means to give a logical response and how a logical answer looks
- The teacher can also explicitly model how they are putting ideas in a logical sequence when they are teaching themselves
- Learners can also reinforce their learning by practising giving explanations to one another

Assessing it

This step can be assessed through observation of speaking or a structured activity. For example:

- Asking learners to talk about an event, create instructions for completing a task, or explain a concept.
- Testing whether learners can put things into a logical order such as: cause and effect; the order in which things happened; building up ideas from the most straightforward to the most complex.

Speaking Step 4

Step 4: I speak effectively by thinking about what my listeners already know

To achieve Step 4, individuals will show that they have considered what their listeners already know when they are speaking.

In Step 3, individuals focused on how to speak effectively by making points in a logical order. Step 4 builds on this by considering what listeners already know, so what they say is pitched at the right level.

Building blocks

The building blocks of this step are:

- I understand why it is important to know what my listeners already know
- I know how to build on what my listeners already know
- I explain new concepts in a way that listeners are able to follow

Reflection questions

- Why is it helpful to know what your listeners already know before you speak?
- What would happen if your listeners understood less than you expect?
- What if they know more than you expect?
- How can you find out what listeners already know?
- How can you use this understanding?

What you need to know

Why what your listeners already know matters

Being an effective speaker is about being able to share ideas and build understanding in your listeners. Therefore, good speaking means thinking about how best to help your listeners to understand you.

When we speak, we all have a view on what our listeners already know. We might call this an *expectation* or an *assumption*. For example:

- When we talk about other people, we change how we talk about them depending on whether our listeners know them or not. We explain who the people are if they don't know – or just use their names if they do know them.
- When we use technical language or acronyms, we are assuming that listeners understand what they are. If we do this without thinking, it is possible for listeners to become confused quickly.
- When we talk about events, we might give our opinion or perspective but this is of no use if the listener does not know anything about the event.

If the listeners understand less than we assume:

- They might quickly become lost and unable to follow the meaning of what you are saying and if technical language will make no sense to someone who has not be taught it or used it
- Or they might misunderstand what you are saying without realising that they have not understood

On the other hand, if listeners understand more than we assume:

- They might quickly become bored and disinterested because lots of the explanation they are hearing is evident to them
- When they become uninterested, they stop listening to what else is said

As a result, it is crucial to think about what listeners already understand so that what you are saying is targeted at just the right level – not too simple and not too complicated.

How to build on what listeners already know

If you are not sure about what listeners already know, you can ask some simple questions to help work it out:

- These might be simple, closed questions, e.g. "Do you know David?" or "Have you been following the election?" to help work out what people already know.
- For more complicated concepts, you might ask more open questions which encourage a fuller response, e.g. "What do you already know about the Tudors?" or "What have you seen about the events in France?"

Once you know how much they know, you can change how you talk, to make sure you don't repeat information they already have. For example, you might choose to introduce individuals that you are talking about, or you might put events in the context of when or where they happened.

If you cannot tell whether you are managing to target what you are saying at the right level, then you can always ask little checking questions as you go:

- Am I making sense?
- Am I giving too much detail?
- Would it be helpful if I explained a bit more about that?

Teaching it

To teach this step:

- The teacher can model what it looks like to talk at the wrong level. For example, the teacher might start by talking about a complex scientific idea and then ask the learners what they learnt. Then the teacher could go to the other extreme and talk about something very introductory at great length, e.g. how to put their coats on.
- The learners can then practice this themselves using different ideas, e.g. talking about someone or somewhere that their audience doesn't know as if they did, before explaining something straightforward or that they already know.
- This exercise can be extended to give learners topics to talk about, having first taken the time to think about what their listeners already know. They can also try using some of the questioning to build that understanding.
- The learners can practice delivering these talks and getting feedback about whether it is pitched at the right level.
- In reflection, they can think about what they should have done differently to make their examples appropriate for the listeners, based on what the listeners already knew.

Reinforcing it

This is a step that can be easily reinforced in the classroom setting:

- When learners speak in class, they can be reminded by the teacher to think about what the listeners already know.
- Similarly, the teacher can model how when they teach something, they think about what the learners already know to make sure that what they are saying is not too easy and not too complex.

Assessing it

This step is best assessed through observation of interaction in the classroom:

- The teacher can observe the learners over some time to see whether their explanations are pitched at the right level.
- This could also happen in a designed exercise where learners are given suggestions of speaking topics. They can be encouraged to use the questioning to work out the right level to pitch what they are talking about too.

Speaking Step 5

Step 5: I speak effectively by using appropriate language

To achieve Step 5, individuals will understand that they need to consider the language that they are using when speaking and choose appropriate language to the setting.

Previously, in Steps 3 and 4, the focus was on speaking effectively by making points in a logical order and thinking about what listeners already knew. This Step builds on this but focuses on the *way* that someone is speaking. This theme continues in Step 6, which introduces tone, expression, and gesture too.

Building blocks

The building blocks of this step are:

- I understand why language changes in different settings
- I explain the difference between formal, informal, and technical language
- I judge what language is appropriate in different settings

Reflection questions

- How does the language we use change in different settings?
- What are some examples of different language that give us a clue as to how formal or informal it is?
- Thinking about the three broad types of language (formal, informal, and technical), which do you think is appropriate in what setting?
- Why do you think it is vital to get this right?

What you need to know

Language and how it varies

There are lots of ways to communicate the same meaning. *Register* is the term used to describe the kinds of words we choose to communicate something. There are three broad *Registers* or types of language that we need to consider:

- *Informal:* This is relaxed language, where we might be speaking to friends outside of school or in the playground. We might use slang or speak in a jokey way. We can use this because there is a shared understanding of what we mean that might be particular to those relationships.
- *Formal:* This is 'speaking properly'. We would avoid using slang or speaking in a jokey way. Instead, we use full sentences, conjunctions, and more sophisticated vocabulary. This way of speaking can be understood much more widely, and so we can use it in lots of different settings.
- *Technical:* This is advanced language that we might use when working closely with someone where we have shared expertise. For example, two plumbers or lawyers or teachers might be able to use language, abbreviations, or acronyms with each other that would not make any sense in the wider world. This way of speaking works well for people who share that technical understanding, but it is impossible to understand if you don't.

Choosing the right language for the setting

It is crucial to select the right register for the setting so that those people who are listening to you have the best chance of understanding what you are telling them:

- It would feel strange to use formal language with your friends. Although they would understand you, they might not continue to follow you if you start using unfamiliar technical language.
- Similarly, many people would feel uncomfortable being spoken to informally by someone who they did not know well. They might be confused about what their relationship is with you or think that you were disrespectful towards them.
- Finally, anyone who does not have the same sort of technical expertise as you would find it very hard to follow technical language and might feel that they were looking foolish if they couldn't understand what you were saying.

In summary:

- Informal language: For friends and people you know well
- Formal language: For most people and settings, and people you don't know
- Technical language: For speaking to others with shared technical expertise

Teaching it

To teach this step:

- The teacher could give examples of different types of language and ask the learners to identify which they are using
- They could then ask the learners to practice how they would talk about the same subject using those three different types of language – informal, formal, and technical
- This idea can be reinforced by asking learners to give a talk targeted at different audiences, giving them the chance to practice various types of language

Reinforcing it

This step can be practised within the classroom setting:

- For example, the teacher can model how to explain a concept using informal, formal, and technical language. Learners could then be encouraged to explain a concept using different language which both reinforces this step and their subject knowledge.
- Teachers can also identify when learners are using different types of language when they speak in class to raise awareness of how language changes depending on whether they are talking to their friends, sharing an idea, or providing a technical answer.

Assessing it

This step is best assessed through a simple testing activity or through observation:

- Learners could listen to different clips of speech and encouraged to identify which type of language is used
- A teacher can observe learners over a period to see whether they can appropriately modify the language they are using according to the setting

Speaking Step 6

Step 6: I speak effectively by using appropriate tone, expression, and gesture

To achieve Step 6, individuals will have to show that they can use the appropriate tone, expression, and gesture in different settings.

In the previous step, the focus was on how to speak effectively by using appropriate language – that is, the right *words*. This step is about the other elements that give meaning to what is said – the tone, expression, and gesture.

Building blocks

The building blocks of this step are:

- I know what tone is and what is appropriate in different settings
- I know what expression is and what is appropriate in different settings
- I know what gesture is and what is appropriate in different settings

Reflection questions

- What is tone, and how can it vary?
- Why is tone an important part of speaking?
- What is meant by your expression?
- How does expression affect the meaning of what someone is saying?
- What is meant by gesture?
- What do we learn from the gestures someone makes?

What you need to know

Tone: What it is

Simply put, tone is *how* we say the words that we are speaking.

We can explore this with a simple example: "You could do that better." Without changing the words, the way that sounds and the meaning it conveys can vary a lot depending on how someone says those words.

- That simple sentence could sound positive – that you can do that better than someone else
- Or it could sound exasperated – that you should have done something better, or that you doing it is a low expectation, and someone else should have done better
- It might sound like a question – an invitation to answer whether you think you could do it better?
- Or it might seem like a direct instruction – that the expectation is that you could, and now will do something better

It is incredible how much meaning comes from the *way* that something is said, rather than the words themselves.

We can refer to this *way* that something is said as the *tone* of speaking. This tone varies by several dimensions:

- *Pitch:* This about how high or low someone is speaking
- *Tempo:* How quickly someone is speaking
- *Volume:* This is how loudly or quietly someone is speaking
- *Intonation:* This is about how the sentence rises and falls
- *Stress:* This is about the speaker highlighting what is important to their meaning by emphasising certain words

Tone: How it varies

Element	The Variation	The Effect on the listener
Pitch: How high or low someone is speaking	Someone speaks with a high pitch	The speaker can seem stressed or anxious, which might be interpreted as lacking confidence or not being honest
	Someone speaks with a low pitch	The speaker can seem calm and more confident. However, they might seem less energetic or engaged
Tempo: How quickly someone is speaking	Someone speaks quickly	The speaker can seem energetic and engaged. However, they might also seem stressed or anxious.
	Someone speaks slowly	The speaker can seem more authoritative and calm. However, if they speak too slowly, they might seem unengaged.
Volume: How loudly or quietly someone is speaking	Someone speaks quietly	The speaker can appear calm and in control if they speak quietly. However, if they speak too quietly, they might seem to be lacking in confidence.
	Someone speaks loudly	The speaker can seem authoritative if they speak loudly – it suggests that they are in control. However, if they are too loud, it can seem aggressive or angry.
Intonation: This is about how the sentence rises and falls	Someone uses falling intonation – where the voice falls at the end of a phrase	The speaker sounds confident in what they are saying – perhaps they are giving an instruction.
	Someone uses rising intonation – where the voice rises at the end of a phrase	The speaker sounds like they are asking a question.
	Someone uses falling and rising intonation	The speaker sounds like they are not sure about what they are saying – they are open to discussion. It can also be a way of softening a direct question.
Stress: This is about where the emphasis is placed on different words	Stressing one word above others	The speaker highlights which element of their sentence is most important to them by stressing a word within it

In different settings, different tone will be seen as appropriate.

- For example, in a workplace, your volume will be expected to be lower than, perhaps, when playing sport
- Different tone can come across as rude or aggressive if used wrongly

Expression: What it is and how it varies

Expression is how your face communicates information as you are speaking. By moving our faces in different ways, we convey a range of emotions:

- Joy
- Fear
- Surprise
- Disappointment
- Trust
- Anger
- Anticipation
- Disgust
- Boredom

As you read through these, you might be able to picture the facial expression which might accompany that emotion.

Our faces convey a lot of emotional information like this without using any words at all. There is some evidence that when listening to a speaker, people take more meaning from facial expressions than from the words.

Because of the amount of information that our expressions give, we should pay attention to how we look, mainly because we might not want to convey that information at that time. For instance, disgust, boredom, anger or fear might not be appropriate emotions to express in a particular situation.

Gesture: What it is and how it varies

A gesture is a movement of the body which means something:

- An outstretched arm inviting someone in
- Crossed arms which suggest defensiveness
- Leaning forwards when speaking to show engagement
- Leaning backwards suggesting that you want to leave
- One finger raised is often used when making a point, but one finger pointing at someone suggests aggression or strong disagreement

Gestures might mean different things in different cultures.

Alongside facial expressions, gestures help to convey meaning in support of what you are saying. The listener will take meaning from the combination of the words you say, the tone in which you say them, and the expression and gestures that you use while you are saying them.

While we can control our gestures when we think about them, sometimes we automatically make certain gestures without thinking about it. As with facial expressions, sometimes these will not be appropriate for the listener, or for the message that we are trying to convey.

For example, it is hard to convey that you are getting excited if your facial expression and gestures suggest that you are bored and want to leave. Similarly, you will not appear confident and knowledgeable if your tone, face, and body all suggest you are nervous.

Teaching it

To teach this step:

- The teacher can lead learners in modelling different elements of tone by repeating the same sentence (such as: "That was a big surprise!") in different tones to give it a different meaning, e.g. excited, disappointed, angry, bemused.
- The teacher can then lead learners in modelling how they might gesture and use facial expression when they are feeling a range of other emotions – joyful, embarrassed, nervous and others.
- This can be extended into looking at other examples, and learners trying to work out how the speaker is feeling about something based on their tone, gesture, or expression.
- This activity could be extended to working in pairs, where one learner has to convey a meaning in a simple phrase (such as: "I've got a lot going on at the moment") through their tone, gesture, or expression, while their partner has to guess what they are conveying.

Reinforcing it

This step can be reinforced in several ways in the classroom:

Before learners speak in class, they can be reminded to think about how they will use their tone, expression, and gesture.

When learners are modelling good or bad practice, they can be reminded of how they come across.

When learners come back in to learn from break time or at the start of the school day, they can be told to think about how their tone, gesture and expressions might need to be different now to how they were before.

Assessing it

This step is best assessed through observation:

- By observing over a sustained period whether learners can use their tone, expression, and gestures appropriately.
- This could also be assessed through learners speaking on a particular topic and conveying their feelings about it.

Speaking Step 7

Step 7: I speak engagingly by using facts and examples to support my points

To achieve Step 7, individuals will show that they can reinforce their arguments and ideas by using facts and examples effectively.

Up to now, the focus on Speaking has been about how to speak effectively by thinking about the logical order of content, what their listeners already know, and using appropriate language, tone, expression, and gesture. This next stage of mastering speaking focuses on how to speak engagingly.

Building blocks

The building blocks of this step are learning:

- I understand the value of using facts and statistics when speaking
- I support the ideas I share with appropriate facts and examples
- I know how to structure an opinion or argument

Reflection questions

- What are facts, and what are statistics?
- Why can they help structure an argument?
- How can you build facts and statistics into speaking?
- When have you seen this done well?
- When have you seen it done poorly?

What you need to know

The value of facts and statistics

Facts are things that are known or proven to be true.

Statistics are pieces of numerical data, e.g. the size of a country, the proportion of people who like pizza, the number of fish in the average lake.

Facts and statistics are important when speaking because they provide *evidence* that adds truth to the argument that you are making. Proper use of facts and statistics make it more difficult for other people to disagree with you and will be more effective in convincing people that you are correct.

When used well, facts and statistics are also interesting – they might help someone to learn something new, and humans respond positively to learning new things.

However, any facts or statistics must be relevant to the argument that you are making or what you are saying otherwise they become distractions. They should also be accurate, or you can quickly lose the trust of your listeners, and they stop listening to what you are saying.

Building facts and statistics into your speaking

Using facts and statistics effectively is all about using them at the right moment when you are speaking - and not using them too much!

One simple structure that is widely used for sharing an argument is:

- Opinion
- Rationale
- Facts or Statistics
- How those justify your opinion

An even simpler model is to use [Opinion] because [Facts or Statistics].

This sort of approach is the basis of debating, where individuals talk about different topics and present different ideas or arguments about them – the team who speaks most convincingly about a topic wins.

Teaching it

To teach this step:

- The teacher can start by modelling how they can use facts and statistics to back up opinions or assertions.
- Learners can then model a simple example of how they can use a fact or statistic to back up an opinion. This works particularly well if linked to learners' recent subject learning.
- This can be built on by introducing the idea of a debate – putting learners into groups to argue for or against a particular assertion such as: "Air travel should be banned". The rule is that each argument that a learner makes should be backed up by a fact or statistic to add weight to their idea. For example, "The environmental impact of air travel is too high because air travel carbon emissions are 2% of global emissions". Or "Air travel is important to let people see the world – it would take three weeks to get to Australia by sea, but only 24 hours by aeroplane." Again, this works best if related to an existing subject area.

Reinforcing it

This step lends itself well to reinforcement in the classroom:

- When asking learners to share their ideas, they should be pre-warned that they will be expected to justify their opinion or idea with a fact or statistic to back it up.
- In mathematics, when learners might be thinking about statistics, they could extend this to practising speaking about the insights that they have been able to gain through their data work.
- Learners could also be asked to prepare a talk on a particular topic, and to present a structured answer to a question that was posed.
- The debate approach could also be extended to other learning to explore issues in greater depth.

Assessing it

This step is best assessed through a structured activity. For example:

- Asking learners to prepare a talk or to participate in a debate, where they have to use facts or statistics to back up their opinions.

Speaking Step 8

Step 8: I speak engagingly by using visual aids to support my points

To achieve Step 8, individuals will be able to use visual aids to support the points they are making when they are speaking.

The focus in the last step was how to talk engagingly by using facts and examples to support the points that have been made. This step extends that by looking at how visual aids like props, drawings, or written slides can help to make speaking more engaging.

Building blocks

The building blocks of this step are:

- I understand what visual aids are and how they can help
- I know how to use visual aids effectively
- I create simple visuals and props to support what I am saying

Reflection questions

- What are visual aids? Can you give some examples?
- When have you seen someone use a visual aid effectively?
- When have you seen visual aids used badly?
- Have you had any experience of using visual aids already? What worked well and what worked less well?

What you need to know

Visual aids, and how can they help

A *visual aid* is something that helps to illustrate or show what is being said.

Examples of visual aids include:

- Images or photographs
- Written text, particularly a summary of key points (i.e. bullet points)
- Films or animations
- Props or models

There are several benefits of using visual aids when you are speaking:

- Visual aids can be particularly helpful in sharing new ideas or concepts with listeners, or if you are trying to help people imagine something that they have not seen before. It can be difficult to describe things in words only, and sometimes it is necessary also to see something for it to make sense.
- If you are speaking for a longer time, having visual aids will help people to follow and understand your talk. That is because what people remember is a combination of what they hear but also what they see or read.

- It can be tough as a listener just to concentrate on the words that someone is saying for an extended period. The use of visual aids can help to break up that period of just listening.
- If you are sharing statistics or facts to support what you are speaking about (as explored in the previous step) then sometimes a visual graph or some of the critical statistics written down can help listeners to understand that information better.
- Finally, visual aids can help to provide a context to what you are saying. For example, a short film clip of a particular country or event can help bring it to life for the listeners, who will then be ready to hear what you have to say about it.

Therefore, giving opportunities to use these other senses will help listeners to take in and recall what they have heard.

Using visual aids well

While visual aids can be hugely helpful when you are speaking, it is also easy to make some simple mistakes which stop visual aids being effective.

Some tips for using visual aids effectively are:

- *Make sure the listeners can see them*: if you are planning a longer speech, and you want to use visual aids, it will be frustrating for any listeners who can't see them.
- *Make sure the technology works*: if you're going to show slides or a video clip, then you should practice with it and make sure that the technology works before you start your presentation.
- *Make sure the visual aids are relevant:* you should always choose your visual aids to support what you are trying to say, rather than just because you think something is interesting.
- *Keep your visual aids clear and short:* visual aids should add something to what you are saying, but they should not be a distraction from it.
- *Make your visual aids attractive and appropriate:* it is worth spending some time to get these right. Slides or images that look poor quality will make your listeners feel that your whole speech is of poor quality. Similarly, pictures, diagrams, charts, or graphs that you make should be clearly and well produced. Be careful when thinking about the fonts or clip art you might choose to use, and make sure they are appropriate to the setting.
- *Think about variety:* do not just use the same visual aids over and over again. Instead, you could combine a model with a graph, and then some images at relevant points.
- *Think about the size of your audience and the context:* some visual aids will be more appropriate in some settings than others. If you are just speaking to one person, putting up a big presentation might seem strange. On the other hand, a small model will not be useful if you are presenting to a big room of people who might not be able to see it.

Visual aids: Traps to avoid

When it comes to visual aids, there are also some easy traps to avoid:

- *Do not introduce a visual aid too soon*: as soon as you have a visual aid visible to the audience – whether it is a picture, a film, some words, or anything else – they will immediately look at it so only introduce the visual aid when it supports what you are saying.
- *Do not just read our visual aids:* for longer presentations, it can be helpful to have some of the critical points or bullet points on a slide to help listeners to take in and understand what you are saying. However, you should never put the full text of what you were going to say on a slide – people can read faster than you can speak, which means they will read before you have said what you wanted to, and then stop listening to you.
- *Do not use too many visual aids:* it can quickly become overwhelming for an audience if there are too many visual aids. It means too much information for an audience to absorb, and then adds to the confusion rather than helping provide a clear explanation.

There is a lot more guidance available on how to create visual aids out there and how to use popular tools like Microsoft PowerPoint or other presentation programs.

Teaching it

To teach this step:

- The teacher can ask learners to think about how they see visual aids being used in the school day and beyond it. In the context of the school day, that might include presentation graphs, pictures, slides, posters or films. Beyond the school day, they might see people using props when talking, or posters or clips in the same way that News programmes use both a presenter and visuals to tell a story.
- Learners can create a short presentation on a topic – this might be linked to something already being studied or a subject of their own choice. They could be asked to use two different visual aids such as a picture and some bullet points, or a short film clip or similar. They should look to build that into their presentation.
- Learners can then give feedback about how to make the visual aids as useful as possible in backing up what the speaker is saying.

Reinforcing it

This step is well reinforced when learners have opportunities to present their ideas or their work. On occasion, they could be encouraged to produce some slides and to talk about their response to a question, rather than just providing a written response.

This step can also be reinforced through computing lessons when learners can practice how to create visual aids and presentations, and then take the next step in presenting them.

Assessing it

This step is best assessed through a structured observation activity. For example:

- Learners prepare a short presentation of 5-10 minutes which has to include the effective use of at least two visual aids. The topic could be linked to existing subject learning or created for the occasion.

Speaking Step 9

Step 9: I speak engagingly by using tone, expression, and gesture to engage listeners

To achieve Step 9, individuals will show that they can use their tone, expression, and gesture to engage listeners with what they are saying.

In Step 6, the concepts of tone, expression and gesture were introduced. This step goes much further than that by focusing on how to use tone, expression, and gesture to speak engagingly.

Building blocks

The building blocks of this step are:

- I know how tone, expression and gesture can make speaking more engaging
- I speak in front of others and manage my tone to be more engaging
- I use appropriate gesture and expression to make my speaking more engaging

Reflection questions

- What are tone, expression, and gesture?
- How do they work together to affect the meaning of what is said?
- How can you use tone, expression, and gesture to make your talk engaging?
- Are there things that you should avoid?

What you need to know

What are tone, expression, and gesture?

As a reminder from the previous step:

- **Tone:** We can refer to this *way* that something is said. This tone varies by several dimensions:
    - *Pitch:* This about how high or low someone is speaking
    - *Tempo:* How quickly someone is speaking
    - *Volume:* This is how loudly or quietly someone is speaking
    - *Intonation:* This is about the 'melody' of their speech
    - *Stress:* This is about where the emphasis is placed on different words
- **Expression** is how your face communicates information to whoever you are speaking to. By moving our faces in different ways, we convey a range of emotions from joy to disgust.
- **A gesture** is a movement of the body which means something.

When we are listening, we are building up an understanding of what is being communicated. This understanding is not just from the words themselves, but also how they are being said and the way someone is moving their body and their face. When we listen, we take clues from each of these to build up our understanding of what someone is communicating. The right pitch and intonation will keep your audience engaged – a monotone delivery will suggest that you are not interested in the topic.

Choosing tone:

Pitch: Try to keep your pitch from low to medium. Low pitch gives the appearance of calm and confidence, whereas a high pitch gives the opposite impression. However, some change of pitch throughout your talk can help to provide variety that makes listening more interesting.

Tempo: Try to speak at a moderate pace. Speaking slowly gives the impression of calm and control, whereas speaking too quickly makes someone seem panicked and not in control – and can also be hard to follow. It can work well to speak at a moderate pace so that the audience does not get bored, but to include pauses so that they can think about what you have said.

Volume: Speak at a volume that makes it easy for the listener to hear you, but not too loud that they are uncomfortable. You can change your volume over time. For example, if you want someone to pay close attention or lean in, you can slightly lower your volume. Sometimes speakers, particularly with larger audiences, speak more loudly at other times to show passion for what they are saying.

Intonation: Generally, a downward intonation adds gravitas and authority to what is being said – it sounds like a statement rather than an invitation for discussion or disagreement.

Stress: Emphasising different words shifts the meaning of a sentence or highlights which parts of it are more important to the speaker. Stress signposts to the listener which elements of a statement are important.

Adapting expression:

As a general rule, you should think about what emotion you want your listeners to feel and ensure that your facial expressions support that.

Normally, if you are sharing information, you will want to keep an expression of being interested and enthused.

However, sometimes you might be trying to get your listeners to have a different response – perhaps you want them to be shocked, surprised, or embarrassed. In each case, how your facial expression changes will influence how they feel about the words you are saying.

If you are speaking for an extended period, you might want to think about how to create variety through what you are saying. For example, you might want your audience to be initially puzzled by a problem you pose, then surprised by some facts that you share, then excited when you show a solution.

Using gesture:

Generally, gestures are also a way of conveying emotion, but we are often less aware of them than we are of our facial expressions.

Normally, when talking we want to show an openness and interest in what we are saying. To do so, we want to face the people we are speaking to, use open gestures with our hands, and use eye contact to show engagement.

However, as with facial expression, sometimes you are looking for a different emotional response from your audience and it can be helpful to model that with how you use gesture.

Teaching it

To teach this step:

- The teacher can model how they use tone, gesture, and expression to engage learners when they are talking. They can pause at different moments to provide a commentary of how they are using those elements to engage their listeners.
- Learners can then practice giving a short, prepared speech of maybe 1 minute, trying out different variations of tone, expression, and gesture. Working with a partner, they could get feedback on what the impact the way they have spoken has had. This could be repeated with the goal of eliciting different responses from the listener (boredom, excitement, curiosity, or others).
- Learners can then prepare a short speech of up to 3 minutes that they aim to deliver to achieve a goal around the response they want from their audience. If they feel able to, they could even seek to add variety into how they deliver the speech to achieve a different emotional response from the audience at different points in their speech.
- Other learners might observe and look to identify examples of how tone, gesture, and expression have been used through the speech.

Reinforcing it

This step lends itself well to reinforcement in the setting of a classroom. Learners can be reminded of how they might use their tone, expression, and gesture before giving presentations or speaking in front of their peers.

Opportunities like presentations, assemblies, shows or other events can help learners practice using these elements to make their speaking as compelling as possible.

Assessing it

This step is best assessed through observation of a structured exercise:

- Asking learners to prepare a short speech of 3-5 minutes, being warned in advance that they will be assessed on their ability to use tone, expression, and gesture.
- These can then be assessed by a teacher.

Speaking Step 10

Step 10: I speak adaptively by changing my language, tone and expression depending on the response of listeners

To achieve Step 10, individuals will show that they are aware of the response of their listeners, and that they can change their language, tone, and expression accordingly.

Up to now, the steps have been focused on how to speak clearly so that an individual can be understood, then how to speak effectively so that the order of words is logical and meaningful, and then thinking about how to make speech more engaging by using facts, examples, and visual aids.

The focus is now on the ability to speak adaptively, responding to the listeners in order to communicate ideas more effectively.

Building blocks

The building blocks of this step are:

- I know how to prepare for different audiences
- I identify how my listeners are feeling about what I am saying
- I know how to adjust language, tone, and expression in response to an audience

Reflection questions

- How do you know what someone listening to you is thinking or feeling?
- How can you do this when you have several people listening to you?
- How can you adapt your language, tone and expression to your audience's reaction?
- What is the value of doing so?

What you need to know

Preparing for your audience

Being able to read your audience is one of the things that distinguish good communicators. If you can read your audience, you have a way of getting instant feedback about whether you are achieving your goals as a speaker.

Before you even start communicating, you make sure you are adapting to them by thinking about some of these questions:

- *Why are they there?* Think about what your listeners want to get out of listening to you. Successful speakers are those that think about what their listeners already know and engage them (see *Step 4*)
- *How long do you have?* If someone has asked you to share an opinion quickly, then you might only have a couple of minutes. If asked to share your thoughts to a group, you might have even less time. On the other hand, you might give a presentation to a team for five or ten minutes, or to a larger audience for even longer.

- *What is the context?* Think about what the context is even before you start speaking. Should you use formal, informal, or technical language (see *Step 5*)? How loudly or quietly should you speak? Are the proceedings formal or informal?

Reading your audience

Careful preparation will help set you up for success. However, adaptive speakers are also able to react to how they see the audience is responding, and this uses lots of the skills steps that are part of Listening.

The good news is that your listeners are probably not thinking about their body language and so you can get honest insight into how they are feeling. Some of the things to look for are:

- *Speaking: Are your listeners speaking to one another?* An early sign that you might be losing the attention of your listeners is if they start talking to one another – this is a sign that you do not have their full attention.
- *Eye contact: Are your listeners looking at you?* If so, this is a sign that they are engaged, but if they are seem distracted by other things, you might be beginning to lose their attention.
- *Nods and smiles: Are your listeners agreeing with you?* Nods and smiles are a good sign that your listeners are taking in what you are saying and are in agreement with you. On the other hand, shaking of heads is a good sign that they are disagreeing.
- *Body language: Are your listeners leaning forwards?* If your listener is leaning forwards then this is another good sign that they are engaged. On the other hand, if they are leaning away or have their arms crossed this is a sign that they are not engaged with what you are saying.
- *Fidgeting: Are your listeners distracted?* If your listeners are starting to fidget or to look at phones or other distractions, then this is a warning sign that they are losing interest and need to be reengaged.
- *Applause and verbal agreement: Are your listeners enthusiastic?* This is the most obvious sign of agreement and engagement from an audience.
- *Other emotional responses: Are you seeing the response you expected?* At other points when speaking you may be looking for other emotional responses – perhaps surprise, concern, or excitement. Look at your audience's faces to see whether you are having that impact.

If you have lots of listeners, then it is important not to just read one or two of your audience members (your eyes might be drawn to those with the strongest reactions) but to keep looking at different audience members to read what they are thinking.

Responding to your audience

It is possible to change the mood of an audience quite quickly if you are able to adapt your language, tone, and expression.

- If your audience is starting to look distracted, you could add energy to your speaking by raising the pitch of your voice, talking more quickly, or using expression to convey more energy and enthusiasm for what you are saying.
- If your audience is starting to seem bored, then you might need to engage them through lowering the volume of your voice, drawing them in to concentrate more on listening to you.
- If your audience does not seem to be thinking about something as seriously as you would like, then you can introduce more pauses to help give them space to think about something properly.

In subsequent steps, we will look at how you can plan for different responses from your audience and how you adjust to changing needs. We will also look at how you adapt your content to keep your listeners engaged.

Teaching it

To teach this step:

- The teacher can lead a discussion about how they look around the classroom to understand how engaged their listeners are, and what some of the different clues are.
- The learners could then practice acting out different attitudes on behalf of themselves as listeners, so that they can look around and see what that looks like (for example, boredom, distraction, engagement, difficulties hearing, and others).
- Learners can then practice giving a short speech and trying to read what the reaction is of their listeners. They could try out some different techniques, varying their language, expression, and tone to elicit the audience response they are seeking.

Reinforcing it

This step is more difficult to practice in the day to day of the classroom. However, for extended presentations and other pieces of presented work, it would be worth reminding learners about the value of trying to read their audience and adapting their tone and expression to engage them best. Presentations in assemblies or other events also provide an excellent opportunity for this.

It is also possible at points for the teacher to pause teaching and to model how they read their audience and adapt to their reactions.

Assessing it

This step is best assessed through observation and reflection with the learner. For example:

The learner gives a short 3-5 minute talk with a live audience. They should be encouraged to think about the reactions of the audience and to adjust accordingly.

Afterwards, they can reflect with the teacher about how they read their audience and what adjustments they made as a result.

Speaking Step 11

Step 11: I speak adaptively by planning for different possible responses of listeners

To achieve Step 11, individuals will show that they are aware that their listeners might respond in different ways and develop plans for those responses.

In the previous step, the idea of speaking adaptively was introduced and how language, tone, and expression might need to change in response to the listeners. This step builds on this by anticipating what some different responses of listeners might be – this is a core part of negotiation.

Building blocks

The building blocks of this step are:

- I define what a negotiation is and explain why they happen
- I anticipate the other party's position before a negotiation
- I plan changes to my points in response to the other party's position

Reflection questions

- When is it helpful to think ahead about your audience's possible responses?
- What is negotiation?
- What do you need to know before you start a negotiation?
- How can you also anticipate what the other party might do?
- Could you give examples?

What you need to know

Introducing negotiation

A negotiation is a discussion to reach an agreement on something. Sometimes negotiations are high-profile, high-stakes events like trade negotiations or international treaties. We sometimes see negotiations in legal dramas or the news when two giant corporations are looking to merge, or one is seeking to acquire the other.

Most negotiations are much lower-key – they involve two or more parties seeking to overcome an obstacle or deciding to do something together. That includes buying a house, selling a car, dividing assets in a divorce, choosing what to have for dinner, or trying to establish a fair price for a service.

Why negotiations happen

Negotiations happen when the answer is not obvious or preordained. Good negotiations should reach a conclusion that is a good outcome for both parties – there is a mutual benefit from whatever is agreed. However, there will be differences in how the benefits are shared between the two parties. Each is interested in securing as much of the benefit for themselves or their organisation as they can.

Generally, negotiations will happen between the two or more parties who have a stake in the decision. Sometimes though, there will be a facilitator to help to reach an agreement – and this might be essential in particularly acrimonious or complex negotiations.

Thinking about your position before a negotiation

Several key concepts are essential to understand when planning for a negotiation:

- *What your goal is from the negotiation?* Plan ahead to be clear on what you want to achieve, and how you will know if you have achieved it.
- *What are your non-negotiables?* Think about which things you absolutely cannot concede in the negotiation. These are sometimes referred to as 'red lines'.
- *What are you willing to concede?* Choose those things that you are ready to compromise on if it helps to reach an agreement.
- *What are elements of mutual benefit?* Identify those 'easy wins' which will be easy to agree as you both benefit from them.
- *What happens if you can't reach an agreement?* Identify what the *Best Alternative to a Negotiated Agreement (BATNA)* is for you. This is the best thing you could do if you are unable to reach an agreement. This is your 'walk away' position and is vital to know.

Anticipating the other party's position before a negotiation

It is vital to think not only from your perspective, but also to predict what the other party is likely to be thinking about. Negotiation is often compared to a game of chess – you cannot only think about your plan, but you need to be constantly aware of the intention of your opponent too. Some things to think about in advance:

- *What is the goal of the other party?* Think about what success will look like for them and challenge yourself to be sure that this is really the case.
- *What might be their non-negotiables?* Identify what they might feel unable to compromise on at all.
- *Where might they be willing to compromise?* Think about where they might be ready to make concessions.
- *What will happen for them if you can't reach an agreement?* Trying to identify what their *Best Alternative to a Negotiated Agreement (BATNA)* is can help you work out how much the other party needs the agreement and so how much they might compromise.

Spending time on this planning means that you are best prepared to speak adaptively and to achieve your goals.

Teaching it

To teach this step:

- The teacher can start by asking learners to think about what they believe a *negotiation* is and whether they can give any examples.
- The teacher can introduce the idea of a negotiation being a route to reach an agreement, and how it links to these more advanced parts of speaking and the need to be adaptive.
- The critical questions for the learners to consider before a negotiation can be introduced here. The crucial point is that learners should not only be thinking about those questions for themselves and their position, but also from the view of the other party or parties that they are negotiating with.

- Learners should then have the opportunity to plan a negotiation. This is important because it is only in applying these concepts to a scenario that they will fully make sense. A topical issue, or something from subject learning, could be used as the focus – for example, negotiating the construction of a new development between the developers and local community.
- Learners need to have enough information or insight around the issue to engage with it and should create their plan following the key questions outlined above.

Reinforcing it

This step can be reinforced whenever there is a negotiation or conflict that emerges in the course of what learners are studying – for instance, in history, geography, politics, economics or current affairs. The critical thing to reinforce is what the views of the different parties are likely to be and so what the scope for an agreement looks like.

Assessing it

This step is best assessed through a structured activity where learners are asked to:

- Remember the five key questions that they need to think about when planning for a negotiation from their perspective, and the four questions they need to ask themselves from the perspective of the other party or parties.
- Work through a negotiation scenario to put this into practice from two different perspectives.

Speaking Step 12

Step 12: I speak adaptively by changing my content depending on the response of listeners

To achieve Step 12, individuals will show that they can adapt the content of what they are saying depending on the response of the listeners.

In the previous step, the focus was on how to plan for different responses from those listening, which is an important step before any sort of negotiation. This step builds on this by showing that the individual can change their content in the moment depending on those reactions.

Building blocks

The building blocks of this step are:

- I identify the structure of a negotiation
- I recognise the importance of listening in negotiations
- I use strategies to adapt the content of what I say

Reflection questions

- What is the difference between planning a negotiation and being in it?
- Why is listening an essential part of negotiation?
- How can you adapt the content of what you are saying in response to listeners?
- Have you had any experience of doing this?

What you need to know

The structure of a negotiation

Planning ahead for a negotiation, as we explored in Step 11 is essential. But there is a big difference to preparing for a negotiation and actually being it.

When participating in a negotiation, there are likely to be several stages to reach an agreement:

- *Build some trust:* Before you get anywhere, you need to show that you are entering the negotiations in a spirit of wanting to achieve a good outcome, and that you are going to display integrity in your approach.
- *Agree a structure:* If the negotiation is complex, it will be helpful to agree on how you will work through the different points and reach an agreement. This is the scaffolding that will support you to work effectively.
- *Understand their perspective:* Before you get too far, it is worth trying to check some of the assumptions that you made about the other party. For example, what is the goal that they are looking to achieve? What are their areas of non-negotiation, and where are they able to compromise? What will they do if this agreement doesn't work out? You might not be able to ask these questions directly.
- *Work through point by point:* Follow the structure that you have agreed, making points clearly and in turn.

- *Identify points of agreement:* Where points of agreement have been reached, make sure these are captured. At the same time, capture those points of disagreement which can be returned to.
- *Work through points of dispute:* This is where being adaptive in your speaking is particularly important so you can shift your position if necessary to reach an accommodation – this is discussed more below.
- *Reach an agreement:* Ultimately, you should be able to reach an agreement with the other parties that everyone is happy with.

The importance of listening

At this advanced level of Speaking, advanced Listening skills are also required. We cannot build trust or adapt if we are not keenly aware of what the other party is communicating and their needs and priorities.

This includes being able to:

- Demonstrate active listening and engagement to build trust (Step 6)
- Ask questions, summarise, and rephrase what is being heard (Steps 7 & 8)
- Avoid being unduly influenced by the other party (Steps 9 & 10)
- Listen critically to compare different perspectives (Steps 11+)

If those are areas that you have not yet mastered, it is worth turning to these, as it is difficult to master speaking without those Listening steps too.

Adapting your content

As a negotiation progresses, you will have to be able to adapt the content of what you say to the responses of your listeners. This will include what you want to tell them and the points that you want to make in response to their suggestions, as well as whether you are willing to change based on their arguments.

There are several strategies that individuals might take in negotiations:

- *Accommodating:* The listeners might be willing to adapt to try to reach an accommodation that you are happy with. This means that you can be open in your points and try to secure the best result for you.
- *Avoiding:* Sometimes, individuals might feel awkward about areas of disagreement and so actively avoid talking about them. In this case, you will need to lead the conversation to this area, otherwise you might never address the differences or reach an agreement.
- *Collaborating:* This is where individuals are willing to change, but they want to reach an agreement that works for both parties. The tone is positive, and you can mirror that by talking about mutual benefits.
- *Competing:* On the other hand, individuals might be keen to win for themselves, and to have the satisfaction that they got the best deal. The tone is often more confrontational, and you will have to think harder about what to concede to make the other party feel they have won, while you still achieve your goal.
- *Compromising:* Finally, individuals might be willing to 'split the difference'. This can be helpful to reach an agreement, but it can mean that the full range of options isn't fully explored. Here, you can help to slow down the conversation, and try to get it back on a more positive footing.

In each of these cases, making the step from having a clear negotiating plan to speaking adaptively depending on the context will mean thinking about the behaviour of your audience.

Teaching it

To teach this step:

- The teacher should introduce the idea that there is a big difference between planning for a negotiation and actually being in the middle of it. Learners can suggest why it might feel quite different.
- The teacher can suggest a structure for a negotiation, talking the learners through the steps, or providing the headings and asking learners to try to work out what should happen at each point.
- The teacher should emphasise the importance of listening to an effective negotiation – at this level, speaking is about being able to respond to what is heard by adapting what is said with great care.
- Learners can then be introduced to the five broad approaches others might take to negotiations and be asked to think about how they should respond in each scenario.
- Finally, for this step to come together, learners should have the chance to take part in a negotiation. This will take some planning to create a plausible scenario with sufficient information and clear parameters of what can be negotiated.
- The teacher can ask learners to reflect afterwards whether they were able to follow the suggested structure, the approach to the negotiations that the other party took, and how they reacted to that.

Reinforcing it

This step is more challenging to reinforce in class, as it relies on a carefully designed scenario. However, debate can be adapted where groups are given different perspectives on an issue and have to represent their interests to try to reach a negotiated agreement. It can be an excellent model to explore more complicated subject matter.

Assessing it

This step is best assessed through an assessment of a negotiation activity. It can be supplemented by a reflection to explore how the learners considered their interactions with their opponents in the negotiation.

Problem Solving

The ability to find a solution to a situation or challenge

Why it matters

Problem solving is the partner of creativity. While creativity is about expansive thinking and the generation of new options and ideas, problem solving is about honing those ideas to try to reach the optimal solution.

Of course, when we apply problem solving it is obvious that you need some knowledge of that subject area. Generally, you will find it quicker to solve problems if that knowledge is greater. However, it is also important to be able to break down or structure a problem in order to solve it – particularly when problems become more complex.

The ability to structure and solve complex problems is critical for advanced levels of learning, effective entrepreneurship, and employment.

How problem solving is built

This skill focuses on how to solve problems, recognising that while part of problem solving is technical know-how and experience, there are also transferable tools that individuals can develop and use.

The first steps focus on being able to follow instructions to complete tasks, seeking help and extra information if needed. The next stage focuses on being able to explore problems by creating and assessing different potential solutions. This includes more complex problems without a simple technical solution.

Beyond this, the focus is on exploring complex solutions – thinking about causes and effects, generating options, and evaluating those options. This extends to analysis using logical reasoning and hypotheses.

Finally, individuals implement strategic plans to solve complex problems, assess their success, and draw out learning for the future.

Skills Builder Framework for Problem Solving

The ability to find a solution to a situation or challenge

Step 0	I complete tasks by following instructions
Step 1	I complete tasks by finding someone to help if I need them
Step 2	I complete tasks by explaining problems to someone for advice if I need
Step 3	I complete tasks by finding information I need myself
Step 4	I explore problems by creating different possible solutions
Step 5	I explore problems by thinking about the pros and cons of possible solutions
Step 6	I explore complex problems by identifying when there are no simple technical solutions
Step 7	I explore complex problems by building my understanding through research
Step 8	I explore complex problems by analysing the causes and effects
Step 9	I create solutions for complex problems by generating a range of options
Step 10	I create solutions for complex problems by evaluating the positive and negative effects of a range of options
Step 11	I analyse complex problems by using logical reasoning
Step 12	I analyse complex problems by creating and testing hypotheses
Step 13	I implement strategic plans to solve complex problems
Step 14	I implement strategic plans to solve complex problems and assess their success
Step 15	I implement strategic plans to solve complex problems and draw out learning to refine those plans over time

Problem Solving Step 0

Step 0: I complete tasks by following instructions

To achieve Step 0, individuals will show that they can follow simple instructions to complete tasks.

This is the first step towards becoming an effective problem solver and is strongly related to some of the early steps around listening (being able to recall and follow simple instructions). The difference here is that the instructions might also be given in a written or visual format.

Building blocks

The building blocks of this step are:

- I know what instructions are
- I understand and follow simple verbal instructions
- I understand and follow simple visual instructions

Reflection questions

- What is meant by instructions?
- Can you give any examples?
- How do we best prepare to follow instructions?
- What might be we do wrong when following instructions?

What you need to know

What are instructions

Instructions tell or show us how to do something. They can help us to solve problems or learn how to do something new.

Instructions come in lots of different forms:

- A recipe is a set of instructions to tell you how to bake or cook something
- A map with directions is a set of instructions to help you find your way to somewhere
- Almost all games come with a set of instructions to help someone know how to play
- This handbook is itself a set of instructions

We might receive instructions:

- In a verbal or spoken form
- In a written form, using words
- In a visual form, using pictures and diagrams

Almost all instructions will follow an order: you have to do one thing, then the next, and then the next. If we do not follow the order of these instructions, it is unlikely that the task will be completed accurately.

How can we be sure we follow instructions

Before we get ready to follow instructions, there are things we can do to help:

- *Know what the goal is:* It is helpful to know what the end goal is – whether getting to a particular location, building a piece of furniture, or cooking something. If we can imagine what we are trying to get to, then we can better see if we are on track.
- *Having space to focus:* Following instructions takes focus and concentration. Make sure you don't have any distractions first.
- *Look over the instructions before getting started:* If you can, it is good to look at all the instructions so you understand how they fit together before you get started
- *Working through in order:* Take each instruction one at a time and try to follow that very carefully. You might want to ask instructions to be repeated if you are listening to them. If you are reading the instructions, you can read them as many times as you'd like.
- *Check as you go:* As you move through the instructions it can be challenging to undo steps that you've already completed so check you are happy before you move on.

Teaching it

To teach this step:

- The teacher can show learners examples of different types of instructions and how they vary. For instance, you could show examples of maps, visual guidance for building furniture, or a recipe book.
- The teacher can model following a simple set of instructions and show how they use the five tips above to do so.
- This can then be extended to asking learners to follow a simple set of verbal instructions to have that experience. This could start simply and then be extended further into more complicated directions.
- Learners could then be given the challenge of following a set of written or picture-based instructions. Again, they could be reminded to follow the five guidelines above.
- Finally, this learning could be consolidated by learners creating their own set of instructions to complete a simple task.

Reinforcing it

This step can be reinforced in the classroom since it's an environment where instructions are often given. At these points, the best reinforcement is to remind learners explicitly that they are about to follow instructions and to take them through the five guidelines (if appropriate). Afterwards, learners can be encouraged to reflect on whether they followed the instructions effectively.

Assessing it

This step is best assessed through observation of a structured activity. For example, giving learners simple sets of instructions in verbal, written, and visual formats, and evaluating whether they can complete the task by following those instructions successfully.

Problem Solving Step 1

Step 1: I complete tasks by finding someone to help if I need them

To achieve Step 1, individuals will be able to identify when they need help and find someone appropriate who can help them to complete the task.

In the previous step, individuals showed that they could complete tasks by following instructions. This step builds on that by introducing the idea that they might be able to seek help if they are unable to do something by themselves.

Building blocks

The building blocks of this step are:

- I know when I need help
- I explore where I might find help
- I know who I can ask for help

Reflection questions

How does it feel when you need help?

- When do you ask others for help?
- Who can you turn to in different areas of your life for help?
- How do you know who the best people are to help you with different problems?

What you need to know

When do I need help

There are times when we all find something too difficult to do by ourselves.

There might be several reasons why we might need help:

- We don't understand something
- We haven't done something before and can't work out how to do it
- We are not trained to do something that might be dangerous
- We are in a new place

Before we ask for help, it is always worth taking a bit of time to think about the problem again.

- Are there any instructions available that might help us?
- Can we remember doing something like this before?
- Can we think of any ways of solving the problem ourselves?

Sometimes when we need help, we can feel worried or upset. However, it is best not to panic – there is almost always someone who can help us.

Who can I turn to for help

We all have different people we know who can help us in various areas of our lives.

In education, we have friends, teachers and other members of staff who might be able to help us if we are struggling with schoolwork, feeling upset, or finding something too complicated.

In work, friends, colleagues, or managers might all be able to help us.

Outside school or work, we have parents and carers, wider family, and other people we know in our communities as well as friends who might be able to help us. They can help us with lots of different problems in our lives if we ask for help.

Before asking for help with a problem, it is good to think:

- Why do I think this person might be able to help me?
- Who else could I ask if they are not the right person?
- How will I explain to them what the problem is, so that they can help me?

If the first person you think of can't help you, don't give up – you could ask them who they think might be able to help you instead, or you could think of other people yourself.

Teaching it

To teach this step:

- The teacher can talk learners through some examples of problems that they might have which they need other people to help them to solve. This modelling can be extended to show how they think about some of those questions before asking for help (e.g. Are there any instructions available?)
- Learners can then talk through some ideas of the sorts of the problems that they had before with which they needed help. Are there problems in common? Who did they ask for help? These can be used to think about which people in the learners' lives they could go to for help.
- Learners can be given some problems to solve which need them to ask a different person for help (for example, finding out who the tallest person in the class is, finding out the history of their family, or solving a difficult maths problem).

Reinforcing it

This step can be naturally reinforced in class. For example, it could become a mantra that when learners are struggling with something, they have to ask themselves the three questions:

- Are there any instructions available that might help us?
- Can we remember doing something like this before?
- Can we think of any ways of solving the problem ourselves?

If they still do need help, they can be encouraged to think about who the best person to ask is, and who else could help them if they can't.

Assessing it

This step can be assessed through sustained observation – for example, observing the behaviour of a learner over a sustained time and whether they can identify those problems that they genuinely need help with, and then ask an appropriate person for that help.

Alternatively, an activity could be used as the basis of assessment, as suggested in the *Teaching it* section above with a range of problems that need different people to help (as well as potentially a couple that learners should be able to resolve alone).

Problem Solving Step 2

Step 2: I complete tasks by explaining problems to someone for advice if I need

To achieve Step 2, individuals will approach difficult problems by seeking advice from an appropriate person to help them to solve the problem.

This builds on the previous steps, which focused on being able to complete tasks by following instructions, or finding someone to help if they needed it. This step changes the focus to explaining problems and asking for advice so that the learner can then complete the task.

Building blocks

The Building blocks of this step are:

- I identify a problem I am having
- I explain a problem to someone else
- I act on advice to solve problems

Reflection questions

- How can you best explain a problem you are having to someone else – what do they need to know?
- What mistakes could you make when trying to explain a problem?
- What is meant by advice?
- How can you make sure you listen well to advice?

What you need to know

Explaining a problem to someone else

A problem is something which is causing us difficulties and which we need to fix. In many cases, we can work out how to solve problems by ourselves, but we all have times when we cannot solve a problem alone.

In the previous step, we looked at how we could find someone to help us if we get stuck on a problem. This step is about how to explain a problem we have to someone else so that they can help us.

There are a few things that we can do to explain a problem to someone else:

- *Start with the goal – what are you trying to do, and why?* It is essential that whoever is helping you knows what you are trying to achieve so they can see whether their suggestions will help to achieve that
- *The challenge – where have you got stuck?* Once the other person understands what you are trying to do, you can explain what is currently stopping you from being able to do that. For example, maybe you don't understand a particular instruction, you can't find something, there is a piece of information that you don't know, or you can't physically reach something.
- *Attempts already - what you have tried so far?* It is worth telling the other person what you have attempted previously – this will stop someone just suggesting things that you have already tried.

How to act on advice

Advice is an opinion that someone gives you about what you should do.

When we receive advice, it is crucial that we think about it fully:

- Sometimes, we are so pleased that someone is taking a problem off our hands that we just follow their advice without thinking about it. This might cause problems, particularly if we have more information or knowledge of a particular issue than they do.
- On the other hand, sometimes we feel negatively about other people's ideas because we want to come up with the solution ourselves.

Therefore, we need to get the balance right: to be open to the advice of others, while still thinking about it and checking that it makes sense before acting.

It is also essential to draw on some of your Listening skills when taking advice by making sure that you're able to understand and by asking questions to check your understanding if needed.

Teaching it

To teach this step:

- The teacher should start by modelling an example of finding a problem difficult to solve. They can invite one of the learners to be the person giving advice and show how they would share their problem, following the three suggestions above. On receiving the advice from the individual, the teacher can demonstrate what they think about that advice and whether to follow it.
- This activity can then be repeated with the learners working in pairs: one to articulate the problem, and the other to provide advice. This can be followed with a peer reflection.

Reinforcing it

This step can be effectively practised in the context of a classroom, for example, by helping learners to structure how they ask for advice if needed. Alternatively, the teacher can encourage learners to turn to one another with questions if they are stuck on a problem.

Assessing it

This step is best assessed through observation over time. For example, by observing whether learners can effectively articulate problems that they are facing and act on good advice.

It is also possible to assess this step through a structured activity where learners have to seek help from others to complete the task (for example, learners have incomplete information, so they need to ask a peer for advice to complete the task). This can be effective but needs to be carefully designed to make it necessary for a problem to be articulated and advice sought and acted on.

Problem Solving Step 3

Step 3: I complete tasks by finding information I need myself

To achieve Step 3, individuals will show that when faced with a problem, they can find the information they need themselves to complete a task.

In earlier steps, the focus was on completing tasks by following instructions, finding someone who could help if they were stuck, and articulating a problem to them. This step builds on this by encouraging individuals to think about how they can find information themselves to help them complete a task.

Building blocks

The Building blocks of this step are:

- I identify what I already know and what I need to know about a problem
- I know where to go for extra information
- I use extra information to help me solve a problem

Reflection questions

- What is meant by 'information'?
- When might we need additional information to solve a problem?
- How do we know what information we need?
- Where are some of the different places you might find extra information?
- Which are the best places for different types of information?

What you need to know

Identifying additional information needed

Information is another word for knowledge and focuses typically on facts or things that we can know to be true.

When we try to complete tasks, one of the problems we can sometimes run into is that we don't have enough information. For example, if we were going to plan a party we might need to know information like:

- Where might we be able to have the party?
- How many people do we want to invite?
- What catering might we need?

Or, if we were going to plan a trip, we would like to know information like:

- Where is good to visit?
- How would we get there?
- What transport arrangements would we need?

In these examples, and many others, when completing a task, we might want to ask questions to be clear on what information we need. Some of this information we will have already – you might already know that you want to visit a particular town and that you have a car available to you. In this case, the question that you have not resolved is the route to get there.

Where to look for additional information

Different types of information can be found in different places. For example:

Information	Where it can be found
Facts or dates	For significant events, this information can be found in an encyclopaedia or by searching online. If using an online search, it is always worth checking in a couple of places to make sure the facts you have found are correct.
Directions or routes	To plan a journey, you can use a map, although this requires some additional map-reading skills. You could also use online maps, which can suggest the best route for you. Be sure that the directions are taking you the right way, though.
Instructions	To build something, you can try to find an instruction manual. Alternatively, similar information might be available online.

There are lots of other types of information that you might need to complete a task. If there is no one to ask, a good starting point is to use an online search.

However, in some cases, the information we need is not written down anywhere. Instead, we have to ask other people for the information, or do research ourselves to find it out. This is something we look at more in later steps.

Teaching it

To teach this step:

- The teacher can start by modelling how they might think through a problem, identifying what they need to know to complete a task. They might break this down into questions that they need to be able to answer, and then answer those questions they can. This leaves the unanswered questions, and therefore the extra information that is required.
- Learners can then be taken through this process in a structured way for themselves, either working by themselves or in pairs. They might be given a task to complete like planning an assembly or writing a recipe book as a class. They should identify all the things they need to know to complete the task. They should then answer as many of those questions as they can, leaving the extra information required. They can then seek this information themselves.
- This activity can be repeated with a different task and with a lower level of scaffolding as learners become more confident at using the approach.

Reinforcing it

This step lends itself well to being used and reinforced in the classroom. For example, learners can be introduced to seeking out extra information themselves to complete tasks, and these opportunities can be structured into lots of learning.

Assessing it

This step can be assessed by setting the learners a task to complete that requires them to identify and then seek out information from a range of readily available sources in order to do so.

The assessment can focus on those who can locate the information they require to complete a task, identify what extra information is needed, and find that information.

Problem Solving Step 4

Step 4: I explore problems by creating different possible solutions

To achieve Step 4, individuals will be able to see that many problems have multiple possible solutions. They will be able to start coming up with different options to solve those problems.

In earlier steps, the focus was on completing a simple task by following instructions, seeking help, or finding extra information. The emphasis here now switches to exploring problems – understanding that, unlike simple tasks, there is not always one obvious solution but multiple options.

Building blocks

The Building blocks of this step are:

- I identify complicated problems that do not have a simple solution
- I understand why creating lots of possible solutions can help solve complicated problems
- I develop multiple potential solutions for complicated problems

Reflection questions

- What sort of problems might have more than one answer?
- Can you give any examples?
- How can you come up with lots of possible solutions?
- Why is that sometimes more difficult than it sounds?

What you need to know

When problems have many solutions

There is a difference between *simple problems* which have one correct answer, and those that we call *complicated problems* which might have different possible solutions.

Simple problems might include things like

- Where did I leave my keys?
- What is my address?
- What is the most popular car colour in 2020?

For simple problems, it is about trying to find the correct answer.

Complicated problems do not have one obvious answer, and might include things like:

- How should I travel to Manchester?
- Where should I visit in Birmingham?
- What should I do next?

For these, no answer is factually correct, and a range of options exist.

For example, for travelling to Manchester there are a range of possibilities (wherever in the world you're starting from) – car, walking, cycling, flying are all options. Similarly, there are plenty of places in Birmingham that you could visit, and the best answer to that question will be different for every individual and what they want to achieve in their visit.

In the next step, we will think about how you could choose between different options.

How to come up with possible solutions

To create lots of possible solutions to a problem, we first have to recognise that something is a complicated problem where it is helpful to have lots of possible solutions.

We then have to decide that we want to explore a problem, rather than using the first idea that we have.

Although it sounds simple, there is good evidence that humans are often quite bad at exploring problems. We tend to take the first idea that comes into our heads and to imagine that is the best answer that there could be. We become very attached to that idea and decide that it must be the right answer.

This is because it is hard to come up with lots of ideas, so it easier just to stick with the first one we create. However, there is also evidence that our first ideas are rarely our best ideas, however you feel at the time.

So, the most important thing to remember about achieving this step is that it takes commitment to create lots of possible solutions.

Teaching it

To teach this step:

- The teacher can introduce the difference between *simple problems* where there is one answer and *complicated problems* where there are a range of possible solutions. The teacher can give some examples of each of these, and then learners can be asked to come up with lots of other examples of each type.
- The teacher can then suggest some complicated problems and ask learners to come up with as many possible solutions as they can. Some example questions might be "When do we learn best?" or "What is the best way to travel to school?"

Reinforcing it

This is a good step to reinforce in a classroom setting. Learners can be reminded when a question they are being asked is a simple problem or a complicated problem.

In the case of a complicated problem, it is worth actively encouraging learners to think about the range of possible answers or solutions that they could come up with, rather than just picking the first idea that comes to mind.

Assessing it

This step is best assessed through an exercise:

- Asking learners to identify from a list of options, which problems are simple or complicated?
- For complicated problems, learners could be asked to generate a range of possible ideas or solutions.

Problem Solving Step 5

Step 5: I explore problems by thinking about the pros and cons of possible solutions

To achieve Step 5, individuals will be able to explore problems by analysing the pros and cons of possible solutions.

In the previous step, individuals developed the idea that there are some problems where there is not always one obvious answer and that there might be several possible answers or solutions. In this step, the focus is on how to be able to choose between those possible answers by thinking about the advantages and disadvantages of each.

Building blocks

The Building blocks of this step are:

- I explain and define what pros and cons are
- I identify the pros and cons of different solutions
- I apply pros and cons when evaluating solutions to make the best choice

Reflection questions

- What is meant by pros and cons?
- Why can it be helpful to use these on complicated problems?
- How can you use pros and cons to make a decision?
- What mistakes do people sometimes make?

What you need to know

Identifying pros and cons

Complicated problems are those that do not have one obvious answer or solution – there are a range of possible answers or solutions. That does not mean that we can't reach a 'best answer', though.

When we are thinking through the different possible answers or solutions, we have to find some way of choosing between them. One of the simplest approaches to this is to think about:

- *The Pros*: this is the positive side of a possible answer or solution, which could also be called the advantage of the solution.
- *The Cons*: this is the negative side of a possible answer or solution, also known as the disadvantage of the solution

As an example, we might decide that the complicated question we want to answer is how to travel on our holiday.

We can make a list of different options – we might choose to fly, to take the train or to drive. This is a complicated problem because there is no one easy answer, but we should be able to get to the best solution for us.

For each of those options, we can then identify the pros and cons. For example:

- Flying: the pros might include the speed, a reasonable cost, and some comfort. The cons would be the environmental impact and not being able to take heavy luggage.
- Driving: the pros might include being able to control the time you leave and when you stop, being able to pack more of what you want to take, and a lower environmental impact than flying. The cons might be the effort of driving and the much lower speed.
- Train: the pros might include being faster than a car, being able to relax, not having a long check-in time, and lower environmental impact. The cons might be the cost, limited baggage, and not being as fast as flying.

Other examples of complicated problems include things like building a house, navigating a long drive, or deciding how much money to save. All of these are complicated, but we can get to the best answer for us.

Using pros and cons to make a choice

The simplest way of using pros and cons is just to make a list of each and then to see which possible solution has the most pros and the fewest cons.

The problem with this approach is that it presumes that all pros or cons are equally important. In reality, we might care a lot more about some things than others.

Looking at our travel example from before:

- If you care a lot about the environment, then the environmental impact might be the factor that you care about more than anything else. So, in this case you would choose to travel by train because it has the lowest environmental impact.
- If you need to get somewhere quickly, or in an emergency, then you care more about speed than anything else. In this case, you would choose to fly because that is the fastest option.
- If travelling as cheaply as possible is your priority, you would pick whichever option is the cheapest – probably driving if you already have access to a car.

We can see, then, that pros and cons can help us to understand what the advantages and disadvantages are of different potential solutions to complicated problems but to make the right choice we need to know what we care about most.

Teaching it

To teach this step:

- The teacher can model what sort of problems are *complicated problems*. It should be made clear that these are different from *simple problems* where there usually is one correct answer. Remember that *complicated problems* differ from *complex problems* which are characterised by being much less predictable and where there are interdependencies between different parts of a system. We will explore these in the next step.
- The teacher can model some examples of complicated problems where there might be various possible solutions and generate the pros and cons of each solution. It can then be shown how to choose between different options based on what one cares about most.
- This can be extended to learners working in pairs to generate a range of possible solutions to a complicated problem. They can then create the pros and cons of each, and then present their preferred solution, justifying their choice. This would work well if it could be linked to other current subject learning.

Reinforcing it

This step can be effectively reinforced in the classroom, as complicated problems are often presented to learners. The key thing is to encourage learners to follow the structured process of generating the range of solutions and then use pros and cons to choose between them. They will often try to shortcut this process, so reinforcing will teach them that following each step is critical for them to secure this step.

Assessing it

This step is best assessed through a structured activity:

- The learners can be posed a complicated problem where they have enough prior knowledge to be able to grapple with the content matter.
- Ask them to come up with a range of solutions and then use the pros and cons of each to reach a justified choice of solution.

Problem Solving Step 6

Step 6: I explore complex problems by identifying where there are no simple technical solutions

To achieve Step 6, individuals will be able to identify *complex problems*, which are those without simple technical solutions.

In the first steps of Problem Solving (Steps 0-3) the focus was on *simple problems* with a simple correct answer and on completing those either by following instructions, finding someone to help, seeking advice, or finding the additional information themselves. The next steps (Steps 4-5) focus on *complicated problems* where there is a technical solution, but there might be a range of options which have to be considered in turn.

This step introduces *complex problems* – those without a 'correct answer'.

Building blocks

The building blocks of this step are:

- I explain and define what complex problems are
- I identify the characteristics of complex problems
- I know how to work with complex problems

Reflection questions

- What sort of problems are most difficult to solve?
- What do you think complex problems are?
- Can you give any examples?
- How can we solve complex problems?
- What should we do? What should we not do?

What you need to know

How to spot complex problems

So far, you have been introduced to two different types of problem:

- *Simple Problems:* These normally have one correct answer. The answer might be obvious to us, or we might need to use research or seek help, but there is only one answer to find.
- *Complicated Problems:* These problems might have multiple possible answers or solutions. We can come up with different possible answers, and then we need to find a way of choosing between them. Identifying the pros and cons is one simple method of doing that. Although these are more difficult than simple problems, we can normally get to the best answer.

We are now introducing a third type of problem: the *complex problem*. This is a problem where we cannot entirely know what the correct answer is, because it depends on a lot of different things, only some of which we can know.

Complex problems are much more difficult to work with than simple or complicated problems, because even when we have done lots of work on them, we might never know if we have come up with the best answer. Instead, we just have to try to come up with as good an answer or solution as we can.

Some examples of complex problems include:

- What would be the effect of banning air travel?
- How can we improve the environment?
- How can we make a business more successful?

These are complex problems because we cannot just solve one part of the problem – they all link together. For example, banning air travel could be expected to have a positive impact on the environment. However, it might also reduce the amount of fresh food that is imported from other countries. This might mean that people eat less healthily, or that we try to grow food that we used to import in our country which might require a lot more energy because the climate is not right. Banning air travel might also lead to a lot of unemployment for people working for airlines, building aircraft, or working in airports. This, in turn, will have further effects on people's incomes and happiness. It is also likely that more journeys will be made by car or by train, so there will still be some environmental impact.

Complex problems do not have easy answers, and experts might disagree (and indeed, often do) because no one has all the information they need to come to one correct answer.

Working with complex problems

Complex problems are very difficult to solve completely, but we can make some good progress if we work hard on them.

Some things that we should do when working with complex problems:

- *Accept that it is a complex problem*, and that you are not going to come to one correct answer that everyone understands
- *Take time to understand the problem*, try to build a deep appreciation of the problem, and what the different links are between this problem and other issues in the world
- *Try to break the problem down into smaller questions* so that the big, complex problem becomes more manageable

Teaching it

To teach this step:

- The teacher should first ensure that learners are secure in their understanding of what the difference is between simple, complicated, and complex problems. This might include giving some examples of different questions and asking learners to classify them.
- Learners could then look at a complex problem. Ideally, this would link to other subject learning they are carrying out, so that they have the opportunity to explore and join up that knowledge with building their understanding of their essential skills.
- This complex problem should be structured by a teacher to help them think about what the links are between different parts of a problem.

Reinforcing it

This is a step that can be reinforced through the prism of building subject knowledge. Learners could look at a subject area through the lens of a particular complex problem and use their learning as a way to answer that question. This idea is explored more in the next step.

Assessing it

This step is best assessed through an activity:

- Learners could identify the complex problems from a list of questions and justify why they think that is a complex problem.
- They can then choose a complex problem and think about how they would go about starting to solve it, and what some of the different questions are that they would need to answer.

Problem Solving Step 7

Step 7: I explore complex problems by building my understanding through research

To achieve Step 7, individuals will have to show that they can carry out research to build their understanding of complex problems.

In the previous step, the idea of *complex problems* was introduced: these are problems where links or interdependencies mean that there is no simple technical solution to the problem – no clear 'correct answer'. This step focuses on the importance of being able to carry out research to explore complex problems.

Building blocks

The building blocks of this step are:

- I identify what I know and what I need to know to understand a complex problem
- I identify the research that would be useful in exploring complex problems
- I know how to carry out primary and secondary research

Reflection questions

- Why is research an important part of exploring complex problems?
- How can we know what research to carry out?
- What are some of the different types of research?
- When is each the best to use?

What you need to know

Identifying useful research

Complex problems are those problems that do not have a simple answer. Instead, there are lots of potential answers, and there are *links* or *interdependencies* between different factors which mean that solving part of a problem might create new ones.

Complex problems do not have an easy answer, and experts will often disagree over the best solution to a particular problem. That is because experts often have different information, and sometimes this leads them to hold different views on what to do.

Sometimes there is not information that is already known and written down to answer a particular question; we have to carry out other types of research or experiments to find out the answers ourselves.

To know where to start with a complex problem, we should start by being clear on what we are trying to achieve – that is, what does a successful solution allow us to do? What are the things that we need to know to come up with the best answer that we can to the complex problem?

How to carry out research?

Research is working to increase our knowledge and understanding of a particular topic or idea. Broadly there are two types of research:

- *Primary research:* This is using new information that you collect yourself. For example, you might carry out a survey, interview people, carry out an experiment, or observe what is going and collect data.
- *Secondary research:* This is about using existing information that you find. For example, looking at existing books, articles or studies, or data that is published by different organisations like the government.

When looking at a complex problem, individuals normally start with secondary research. That is because this is often easier and less expensive than primary research. It means that you can find out whether your question has already been answered and what is still unknown.

Primary research can be helpful because it can use an experimental approach to answer the particular problem that you want to solve or give a more direct answer to your question. However, it is often more challenging to set up, takes longer, and is more expensive, particularly for big, complex problems.

Teaching it

To teach this step:

- The teacher can reinforce the difference between simple, complicated, and complex problems, and demonstrate that complex problems are often made up of lots of smaller questions. Carrying out research is a key part of exploring complex problems.
- Learners can be asked to identify whether different examples of research are primary or secondary research (e.g. surveys, reading reports, looking at government data, interviews).
- Learners could be asked to think about a particular complex problem – ideally something derived from other subject learning – and think about what some of the component questions are that they would want to answer to solve that problem. They can also think of examples of primary and secondary research that they would use to help to solve that complex problem.

Reinforcing it

Some elements of this step are straightforward to reinforce in the classroom setting. For example, introducing how we know something and whether that is from primary or secondary research.

Other elements would need slightly more organisation, e.g. using complex problems as a focusing lens for covering subject content.

Assessing it

This step is best assessed through a worked activity:

- Asking learners to define and identify some examples of primary and secondary research.
- Posing a complex problem to learners, based on a subject area that they have some understanding of, and asking them to identify some of the questions they would need to answer to solve the complex problem. They should then come up with some examples of primary and secondary research they could carry out to answer those questions.

Problem Solving Step 8

Step 8: I explore complex problems by analysing the causes and effects

To achieve Step 8, individuals will show that they can understand that complex problems often have causes and effects.

Earlier, in Steps 6 and 7, individuals have been exploring complex problems by being able to recognise them and then carry out appropriate research to understand them better. This step builds on this by breaking down complex problems into causes and effects.

Building blocks

The building blocks of this step are:

- I explain and define 'causes and effects'
- I know why causes and effects are important in understanding complex problems
- I identify causes and effects and how they might join up into chains or circles

Reflection questions

- What are causes and effects?
- Why are causes and effects a critical part of understanding complex problems?
- How can causes and effects join together?
- Why does that matter?

What you need to know

Causes and effects

One of the key things about complex problems is that they are not *self-contained*. Instead, there are links between those problems and other problems – that one thing might affect something else – sometimes quite unexpectedly.

A key part of understanding complex problems is, therefore, to think about causes and effects:

- *Causes:* the factor, or factors, that lead to something happening
- *Effects:* the result of the causes – the thing that happened as a result

For example, a cause of litter in a park might be that the park has picnic benches that encourage people to eat their lunch in the park, but there are no litter bins available, so people leave their rubbish out. A further effect of the litter in the park might be that wildlife sometimes eats some of the rubbish which can be harmful, or it encourages rats who eat the remaining scraps of food.

So, if our complex problem was how to make the park better for wildlife, we might see one of our goals as reducing litter in the park. This would then lead to us trying to identify what the causes and effects were of things that caused litter in the park. So, part of the solution might be to have more litter bins, to remove the picnic benches, or to make people more aware of what the impact of littering was to discourage them from doing it.

However, that is likely only to be part of the solution. Making the park better for wildlife might also be about providing habitats that wildlife can live in, reducing nuisances like too much noise, or providing more staff to look after the park. Each of these is likely also to have further causes and effects.

We need to think carefully about all of these causes and effects, or we could just go for a simple solution that turns out to be a mistake. For example, if we just put in more bins, the effect of this might be to encourage more people to use the park and scare away wildlife through more noise. We need to think through how causes and effects join together if we're going to be able to solve complex problems.

How to join up causes and effects

Causes and effects can join together in a range of different ways. The main three are:

- *Static:* One cause leads to one effect, which is self-contained, e.g. more watering leads to the grass to grow faster.
- *Linear:* The causes and effects join together in a line – one thing causes something else which causes something else. In this way, we can follow one line of thinking all the way through. For example, more rainfall might lead to higher rivers which leads to flooding.
- *Circular:* The causes and effects are circular, and so become self-reinforcing. For example, cheaper technology leads more people to want to buy that technology which means that more of that technology is produced, which makes it cheaper for the manufacturer. This lowers the prices again so increases the demand further. Sometimes this cycle eventually reaches an *equilibrium,* i.e. it's not possible to reduce the price any further, or everyone who wants the technology has bought it.

To understand complex problems, we need to think about what the causes and effects are that help to make sense of what we see. If we just fix one part of linear or cyclical causes and effects, we might have a different overall effect than we expected.

Teaching it

To teach this step:

- The teacher can introduce learners to the concept of causes and effects and why it is important to understand how they link together if we want to be able to solve complex problems.
- Starting with a simple starting point – for example, closing school for the day –learners can think about what a variety of possible effects that would have (parents or carers having to stay home to look after their children, missed learning, lower traffic, etc.). This can be repeated for a few different examples.
- Then one can look from a different angle, starting with an effect such as a shop closing and thinking about what the different causes might have been. Additional examples can be brought in.
- Once learners are secure in understanding causes and effects, the ways that they interlink can be introduced by talking through *static, linear,* and *circular* causes and effects. Learners can be asked to create one example of each of these.

Reinforcing it

This is a step which can be usefully introduced in many different aspects of learning. For example, when talking about scientific concepts, a series of events in literature, or historical or geographical phenomena. Learners can map out what the different causes and effects are around these.

Skills Builder Handbook for Educators

Assessing it

This step is best assessed through a structured assessment:

Asking learners to define cause and effect, and to outline three different ways that causes and effects might interact

Asking learners to show the causes and effects linked to a complex problem they are given and to share their ideas and rationale

Assessing it

Problem Solving Step 9

Step 9: I create solutions for complex problems by generating a range of options

To achieve Step 9, individuals will show that they can approach complex problems by creating a range of possible options.

In earlier steps, individuals showed that they could identify and explore complex problems through research and looking at causes and effects. This step builds on this by extending this into creating options for addressing complex problems.

Building blocks

The building blocks of this step are:

- I generate a range of solutions for complex problems
- I understand what feasibility is and why it is important
- I know how to assess if solutions are feasible

Reflection questions

- Why is it important to consider a range of solutions for complex problems?
- How can we come up with a range of solutions?
- What does feasible mean?
- How do we know whether our solutions are feasible?

What do you need to know

Generating a range of solutions for complex problems

In *Step 5*, we looked at the importance of generating multiple options to consider when trying to solve *complicated problems*, those problems where there is an optimal solution, but it is not an obvious one or there is more than one answer which is correct.

Since then, the focus has been on *complex problems*, where interdependencies and links between problems mean that even experts might not agree on the optimal solution. In the last couple of steps, we have explored how to build up an understanding of these types of problems through using research and looking at causes and effects.

To build on this, we need to create a range of possible solutions to evaluate. Doing so is particularly important with complex problems because often solving these problems is about a combination of different actions or activities. In essence, no one thing answers or solves the problem.

The most important thing to remember here is that, as with *Step 5*, we have to take the attitude of *trying* to create lots of possible alternatives. It is far too easy for the human brain to think that whatever idea if first came up with is good enough and therefore to stop trying to create more. To help overcome that, we can set ourselves a goal such as coming up with at least ten or twenty possible solutions to the problem. I've seen organisations looking at complex problems where they try to create up to fifty or even a hundred ideas.

Checking solutions are feasible

Feasibility is about whether something is possible and at what cost or level of difficulty.

When generating a range of solutions, it is essential to check that they are feasible by considering these key questions:

- Does the solution have the potential to answer part of the complex problem we have explored?
- Does the research that we have carried out suggest that the solution might work in solving part of the complex problem?
- Thinking about the causes and effects, would the solution have further effects that might be problematic?
- If relevant, does the solution have the potential to be delivered within the required time, or would it take far too long to be considered?
- If relevant, would the cost of putting the solution into practice be far too high?

It is crucial to start by generating lots of ideas and possible solutions if we are going to have the best possible chance of solving a complex problem successfully. However, once we've done this, we should focus our energies on those with the highest likelihood of success.

Teaching it

To teach this step:

- The teacher can talk through why it is essential to come up with lots of potential solutions of complex problems, and how we need a good attitude towards trying to come up with as many possible answers as possible. The teacher could model this by taking a complex problem, ideally related to an area of study, and working with the learners to generate as many possible solutions as they can.
- The teacher can then model how, having produced lots of possible solutions, learners need to work out which ones are feasible. Together, you could review the list of possible solutions and work out which ones are feasible, according to criteria you agree.
- The learners could then be set a similar challenge, working by themselves or in small groups to generate ideas and then discuss them to create a shortlist of feasible alternatives. This could be extended further as an individual exercise with another problem, potentially linked to other subject learning.

Reinforcing it

This step lends itself to reinforcement in some aspects of broader learning such as when discussing more complex phenomena. The complex problem that learners are investigating could also be related to a variety of subject matter, from religious education, influences on an artist, or understanding a natural phenomenon.

Assessing it

This step is best assessed through an assessed activity:

- Learners could be posed a complex problem, related to subject content with which they are familiar. Learners could be encouraged to generate as many possible solutions as they can and then to assess their feasibility and come up with a justified shortlist of 3-5 solutions to a complex problem.

Problem Solving Step 10

Step 10: I create solutions for complex problems by evaluating the positive and negative effects of a range of solutions

To achieve Step 10, individuals will show that they can create a range of solutions for complex problems and then evaluate their positive and negative effects.

In the previous step, individuals looked at how to create a variety of solutions for complex problems and decide which of them were feasible to create a manageable shortlist. In this step, individuals evaluate those solutions to choose the optimal solution or combination of solutions.

Building blocks

The building blocks of this step are:

- I know how to evaluate possible solutions to a complex problem
- I understand that implementing solutions will have secondary effects
- I evaluate potential solutions by considering secondary effects

Reflection questions

- How might you choose between different solutions to a complex problem?
- Why is it important to know what you want to achieve?
- What do we mean by secondary effects?
- Why is it important to consider these when working on complex problems?

What you need to know

Evaluating possible solutions

When considering how to choose between possible solutions to a complicated problem in *Step 5* we used the pros and cons to think about the positive and negative effects of a potential solution.

For complex problems, it is essential to start by thinking about what the *primary goal* is that one is trying to achieve, but also what some of the *secondary goals* are:

- The *primary goal* is the main thing that you are trying to achieve, e.g. how to improve the range of wildlife in a park. This is usually posed as the main problem or question.
- The *secondary goals* are those things that also matter. These are things that our solution also has to be able to do. For example, while we want the range of wildlife in a park to increase, our secondary goals might be that we do not want to spend any more money, or that we also want there to be more visitors to the park. These secondary goals, therefore, also act as constraints on what the solution will do.

One of the things that make complex problems challenging to deal with is that sometimes the secondary goals are not always known at the outset. Instead, they emerge as the complex problem is explored, and some of the trade-offs between different choices emerge.

It is also important to remember that not everyone will see the strengths and weaknesses in the same way, depending on their diverse perspectives and whether they have other goals that they are trying to achieve from the solution. Something which is an advantage to one person might be a disadvantage to another, i.e. more parking might make it easier to travel to the park but, for the local resident, the additional pollution and traffic from more people driving to the park is a significant disadvantage.

How to think about secondary effects

When we think about complex problems, we have probably already done some research, and thought about causes and effects and how they link together.

Another challenge of complex problems is that solving part of them might lead to *secondary effects* which can negative impacts that we do not initially expect. For example, trying to increase wildlife in a local park through hiring more park wardens might lead to a budget shortage for the council, so they then reduce spending on something else like street cleaning. This makes the town dirtier and more polluted and reduces wildlife across the town.

Therefore, it is important to evaluate potential solutions not just in terms of whether they help to achieve the primary and secondary goals, but also whether they will have any secondary effects that could be damaging.

Teaching it

To teach this step:

- The teacher can introduce a model of a complex problem that the learners can work through together. For example, how to help learners do better in their exams (it is essential to pick a model that learners will be able to relate to and have some prior knowledge they can deploy).
    - In this way, teachers can help to highlight in conversation with the learners what the *primary goal* might be – to see an improvement in exam grades.
    - There can then be a discussion of *secondary goals* – what are the constraints on what is possible. For example, it might not be possible to hire new teachers, or to extend the length of the school day.
    - Learners can then generate a range of possible ideas to solve this complex problem, shortlisting them to those that seem feasible.
    - Working in pairs to support conversation and reflection, learners can evaluate the advantages and disadvantages of their different solutions and to propose their recommendations.
    - They should also talk about any of the secondary effects that might emerge from their proposed solution. For example, stopping doing any learning that isn't linked to the exam might have the negative secondary effect of stopping learners developing skills that help them to learn better or to stay positive in difficult situations. Only thinking about exams might also make the learners less employable in the future if they don't have any other experiences to draw on.
- This structured exercise could be extended by giving learners another complex problem to grapple with – perhaps something which is a challenge in their community.

Reinforcing it

The key concepts here that lend themselves to regular reinforcement across other learning are those of *primary goals, secondary goals,* and *secondary effects*. These ideas can be revisited in lots of areas of education.

Assessing it

This step is best assessed through posing a complex problem to learners and asking them to work through solving that problem. This might also take the form of an extended project linked to subject learning. You might want to use this as an opportunity to see evidence of Step 6-10 looking to see that learners can:

- Differentiate between simple, complicated, and complex problems
- Build their understanding of complex problems by carrying out relevant primary or secondary research
- Explore the causes and effects of complex problems
- Create a range of options, and filter those down according to what is feasible
- Make a recommendation based on an explicit review of the primary and secondary goals, the advantages and disadvantages of the options, and an appreciation of secondary effects

Problem Solving Step 11

Step 11: I analyse complex problems by using logical reasoning

To achieve Step 11, individuals will show that they can work through complex problems by using logical reasoning.

In the last couple of steps, the focus was on complex problems, where there is no obviously correct answer. Those steps explored how to create potential solutions for such problems, and how to evaluate them. Step 11 and Step 12 focus on more in-depth analysis of the issues to try to come to better conclusions where information is unclear.

Building blocks

The building blocks of this step are:

- I explain and define what logical reasoning is
- I understand the differences between inductive and deductive logic
- I use logic trees as a tool for logical reasoning to arrive at a conclusion

Reflection questions

- What is logical reasoning?
- What is deductive logic?
- What is inductive logic?
- What are logic trees, and how can we use them?
- Do you have any experience of using logical reasoning?

What you need to know

Logical reasoning

Logical reasoning is about using a series of rational, systematic steps to go from known information to a justifiable conclusion.

It is crucial when trying to analyse a complex problem where we do not have perfect knowledge and we want to try to understand the links between different events. Logical reasoning can also support planning a sequence of events and how they might link together.

There are two main types of logical reasoning:

- Deductive reasoning
- Inductive reasoning

Deductive reasoning

Deductive reasoning is about how we can *deduce* or *predict* specific outcomes through rules that we know to be true.

This is sometimes known as 'top-down' logic because we start with rules and reach conclusions from rules.

For example, we know that all rabbits are mortal. Therefore, if something is a rabbit, it must be mortal. However, that does not mean that everything that is mortal must be a rabbit.

In the context of the working world, we might be trying to plan a marketing campaign. We know that for most goods, demand for the good will increase when it is less expensive. Therefore, reducing the price of a product is likely to increase the demand.

As another example, we might know that the quality of a service is related to how much time a customer gets with a customer services operative. Therefore, if we make more time available with customer service operatives, then the customers will get a higher quality of service.

In summary, *deductive reasoning* is what we can predict based on what we know.

Inductive reasoning

Inductive reasoning takes the opposite approach to deductive reasoning. It is about how we can *induce* or try to create general rules based on a situation.

This approach is known as a 'bottom-up' approach to logic. We make observations, and we strive to use those to learn lessons and make rules that make sense of those observations.

For example, we see that lots of rabbits die, and we are unable to find a rabbit that is older than 18 years old, so we might conclude that rabbits must be mortal.

In the context of the working world, we might see that lots of young people have started wearing hats, so we might induce that hats have become fashionable. Or our customer support number might have started receiving a lot more calls, thus we might induce that there is a problem with the service we are providing.

However, inductive reasoning is about reaching *probable* conclusions, rather than the certainties that deductive reasoning works towards.

In summary, *inductive reasoning* is what we can learn from what we see in the world.

Logic trees

A logic tree is a problem-solving tool that uses a tree-like visual to help us lay out the different parts of a problem and the consequences of making different logics.

The logic tree can either be:

- A *diagnostic* logic tree: understanding *why* something has happened
- A *solution* logic tree: understand *how* to address a problem

Of course, it might also be possible to combine these, as in the example given below:

- A logic tree starts with a root, which is often the problem itself.
- This leads to the main branches, which are the potential causes of the problem.
- These can then be explored further through sub-branches.

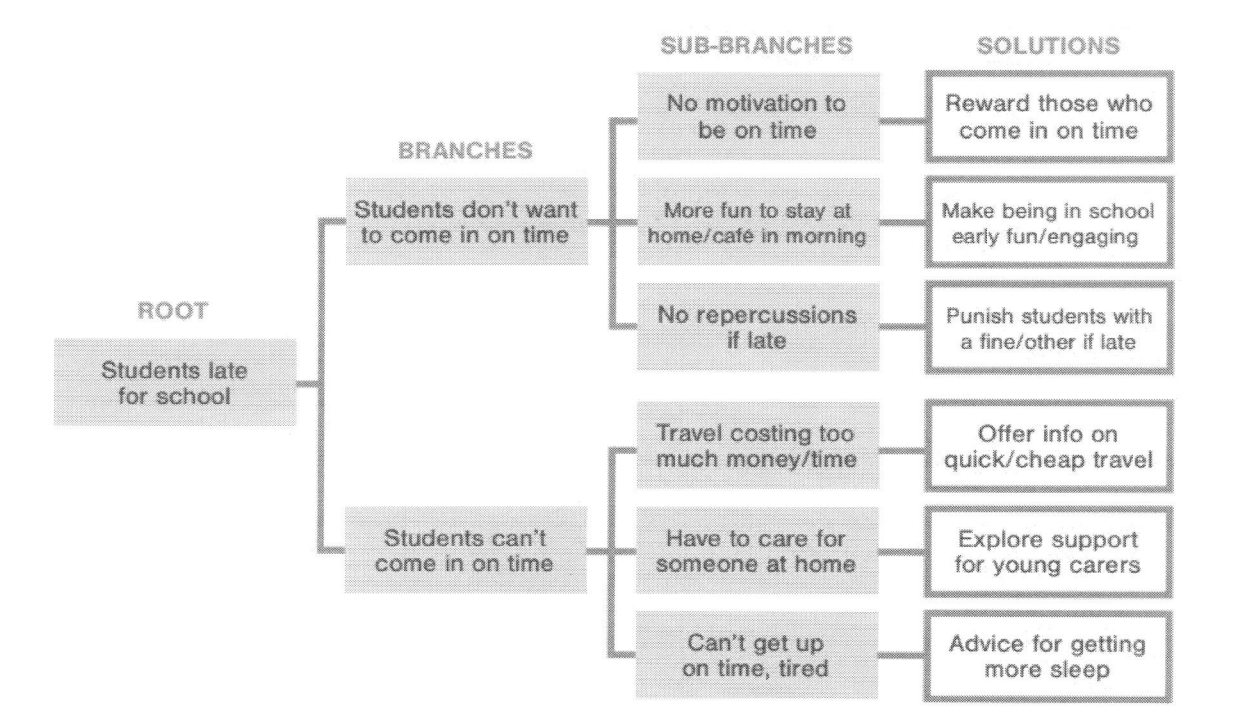

```
ROOT                BRANCHES                    SUB-BRANCHES              SOLUTIONS

Students late ──┬── Students don't want ──┬── No motivation to ──── Reward those who
for school      │   to come in on time    │   be on time            come in on time
                │                         │
                │                         ├── More fun to stay at ── Make being in school
                │                         │   home/café in morning   early fun/engaging
                │                         │
                │                         └── No repercussions ──── Punish students with
                │                             if late               a fine/other if late
                │
                └── Students can't ───────┬── Travel costing too ── Offer info on
                    come in on time       │   much money/time       quick/cheap travel
                                          │
                                          ├── Have to care for ──── Explore support
                                          │   someone at home       for young carers
                                          │
                                          └── Can't get up ──────── Advice for getting
                                              on time, tired        more sleep
```

Teaching it

To teach this step:

The teacher should be ready to spend some time ensuring that learners can understand the theoretical difference between *deductive* and *inductive logic.* This can be quite a difficult concept, but a powerful one so it is worth persisting.

Learners can be given examples of how deductive logic builds from what is known to apply those rules to new problems, while inductive logic looks at the world and then tries to work out rules from that. Learners could then try to distinguish whether examples given by the teacher are examples of deductive or inductive logic, before coming up with their own examples.

The teacher can then introduce the idea of logic trees, and how they can be used for understanding why something is the case, or for exploring how to fix a problem. The teacher can talk through an example like the one above, and then ask learners to create their own.

At the end of the session, a short quiz should be used to check understanding and consolidate learning.

Reinforcing it

This step can be reinforced in the classroom when there are opportunities to think through how theories are induced from what is seen in the world such as how some scientific theories were induced.

Alternatively, the logic tree could be used to explore the causes of historical events or topics that are covered in geography. Finally, the logic tree can be used to identify the causes of social or environmental problems which would link well to youth social action projects.

Assessing it

This step is best assessed through:

- Testing whether learners understand and can explain deductive and inductive logic, with examples.
- Asking learners to prepare a logic tree to explore the causes of an issue.

Problem Solving Step 12

Step 12: I analyse complex problems by creating and testing hypotheses

To achieve Step 12, individuals will show that they can create and test hypotheses to help them to understand complex problems and develop theories.

In the previous step, logical reasoning was introduced, including both deductive and inductive logic. Inductive logic is about deriving general rules from what is observed, and so this step builds on that by turning those proposed rules into hypotheses that can be tested. This is important for grappling with complex problems.

Building blocks

The building blocks of this step are:

- I explain and define what a testable hypothesis is
- I create testable hypotheses to be used to solve complex problems
- I test hypotheses using sample data

Reflection questions

- What is a hypothesis?
- Why are hypotheses helpful to us in solving problems?
- How can we test hypotheses?
- Why are hypotheses particularly important in entrepreneurship and innovation?

What you need to know

Hypotheses

A hypothesis is a proposed explanation for a phenomenon that has been observed in the world, or a prediction.

It is linked to inductive reasoning, as we explored in the previous step. Inductive reasoning is how we try to make sense of the world through what we observe, and create rules that we think are probably true. However, they inherently have a great deal of uncertainty.

For instance, to extend a previous example, we might see a lot of people wearing hats and decide that hats have become fashionable. However, before we decide to get into hat production, we would be advised to test that idea. If we don't, we might not realise that they are wearing hats because of World Hat Day, or as a temporary response to a flock of aggressive pigeons in a small part of town. Without testing our hypothesis, we might have opened that hat factory in vain.

Creating a good hypothesis

The heart of the scientific method is the idea that a useful theory or hypothesis must be testable. It is impossible to prove that any hypothesis is absolutely true – we can only say that it has not yet been disproved so that we can operate as if it is true.

For instance, a testable hypothesis is that all rabbits are mortal. We cannot be absolutely sure that it is true because there are plenty of rabbits that are still alive, and one of those might live indefinitely. However, until that happens, our working hypothesis can be that rabbits are mortal.

As an example, if we are interested in whether to open that hat factory, our hypothesis might be that there is a nationwide increase in demand for buying hats. Then we can test that hypothesis.

When we create a hypothesis, we should be sure that existing facts or insights have not already disproved it.

Testing a hypothesis

To test a hypothesis, we want to see if we can disprove it.

To stretch that exciting hat example further, we could test the hypothesis by asking:

- Is there any data that shows an increase in hat purchases?
- Could we survey a representative sample of customers to see if their attitude to hats has changed?

If there is no evidence of either an increase in hat purchases or a shift in customer beliefs, we might be able to disprove the hypothesis that there has been a nationwide increase in demand for buying hats. This has saved us all the bother and expense of setting up that hat factory.

A reasonable hypothesis must be specific and testable, or it is of little use to us.

Hypotheses and agile development

Entrepreneurship is increasingly interested in how we can use hypotheses to develop and test products for customers quickly. This is sometimes called *lean innovation*. It works particularly well for technology or website development where small changes can be made (e.g. rearranging a page, or even changing a colour) and then seeing what the difference in user behaviour is.

For this approach, something called *A/B testing* is often used, where a proportion of users ('A') experiences the website or product in one way, and the other users ('B') experience a minor change. This change is a hypothesis. It can be tested to see if the switch has an impact on user behaviour.

Teaching it

To teach this step:

- The teacher should lead learners to review what is meant by a hypothesis – this is probably a concept that they are familiar with from science, but which they might not have thought of as relevant beyond those experiments.
- The teacher can lead a conversation about how hypotheses, and testing them, can be valuable beyond science experiments. It would be good to explore application to solving social challenges, business challenges, and a range of complex problems.

- The learners could reflect on what a reasonable hypothesis looks like and the need for it to be testable. They can come up with good and bad examples of hypotheses.
- Ultimately hypotheses have to be testable to be useful – learners could reflect on how they would test out the hypotheses that they created.

Reinforcing it

This step can be effectively reinforced in science learning, but also in other subject areas. Learners could be asked, before embarking on a topic, to give their hypothesis in response to a particular topic such as the drivers of the Repeal of the Corn Laws in history.

Learners could review their hypotheses as they learn more and try to disprove their original ideas.

Assessing it

This step is best assessed through:

- Testing learners on their understanding of what a hypothesis is, and what makes a good hypothesis (i.e. that it is clear, specific, and testable).
- Asking learners to develop hypotheses around a particular question, and then come up with ideas for how they would test those hypotheses.

Creativity

The use of imagination and the generation of new ideas

Why it matters

Creativity sits alongside problem solving and focuses on expansive thinking, generating more options, ideas and innovations.

Sometimes we assume that creativity is all about the arts, including singing, drama, painting, or performing. While these are an important way of expressing creativity, creativity can also be applied in many different areas.

The skill of creativity, as outlined in the Skills Builder Framework, helps to provide structures and tools to help stimulate and focus creative thinking and innovation.

With a widely acknowledged increased pace of change in the working world, individuals who can innovate creatively will be in demand.

How creativity is built

Creativity is the complement to problem solving and is about generating innovations or ideas which can then be honed through the problem solving process.

The first few steps focus on the individual's confidence in imagining different situations and sharing their ideas.

The focus is then on generating ideas using a clear brief, making improvements to something that already exists, and combining concepts. Individuals then apply creativity in the context of their work and their wider life. They can build on this to develop ideas using tools like mind mapping, questioning, and considering different perspectives.

The most advanced steps focus on building effective innovation in group settings and by seeking out varied experiences and stimuli. Finally, individuals support others to innovate, by sharing tools, identifying the right tools for the situation, and through coaching.

Skills Builder Framework for Creativity

The use of imagination and the generation of new ideas

Step 0	I imagine different situations
Step 1	I imagine different situations and can say what I imagine
Step 2	I imagine different situations and can bring them to life in different ways
Step 3	I generate ideas when I've been given a clear brief
Step 4	I generate ideas to improve something
Step 5	I generate ideas by combining different concepts
Step 6	I use creativity in the context of work
Step 7	I use creativity in the context of my wider life
Step 8	I develop ideas by using mind mapping
Step 9	I develop ideas by asking myself questions
Step 10	I develop ideas by considering different perspectives
Step 11	I innovate effectively when working in a group
Step 12	I innovate effectively by seeking out varied experiences and stimuli
Step 13	I support others to innovate by sharing a range of tools
Step 14	I support others to innovate by evaluating the right creative tools for different situations
Step 15	I support others to innovate by coaching them to be more creative

Creativity Step 0

Step 0: I imagine different situations

To achieve Step 0, individuals will have to be able to imagine different situations.

This is the first step in Creativity – the ability to imagine things that do not currently exist. It provides the foundation for everything that follows.

Building blocks

The building blocks of this step are:

- I understand the difference between imaginary and real
- I give examples of where imagination has been used
- I show how I have used my imagination

Reflection questions

- What does imagination mean?
- Why do you think imagination is useful?
- When do you use your imagination?
- Can you give examples?

What you need to know

What is imagination?

Using your imagination is about being able to think about something and being able to see it in your head. You might imagine an event that hasn't happened, something that is impossible, or a place that doesn't exist.

Sometimes we use imagination by ourselves, and what we imagine is only in our heads. At other times, we use our imagination with other people such as when we talk or act things out together.

As you get better at using your imagination, you might be able to explain what you imagine in a way that someone else can understand. You might also be able to act out or draw what you are imagining. For now, just focus on whether you can imagine things in your head.

How do we use imagination?

Our imagination is crucial because it allows us to think about new ideas and to go beyond what exists today.

Everything man-made in the world started in somebody's imagination – it didn't exist yet, but someone thought that it might be a good idea, and they used what they imagined to make it.

We might use our imagination at lots of different times, but normally our mind has to be relaxed and not trying to think about other things.

Some of us find that we use our imagination best when we're with other people, and some of us find it easiest to use our imaginations alone.

Teaching it

To teach this step:

- The teacher can ask learners what they think imagination is, and where they have used imagination. Do they enjoy using their imaginations?
- The teacher can model how to imagine an object or creature. For example:
    - Model how to imagine an object or creature: "Let's use our imagination. Can you close your eyes and imagine you are looking at a dog? What colour is it? How big is it? Can you stroke it? Is it friendly or snappy? We're pretending there's a dog, but there isn't one really."
    - Model how we can imagine a familiar setting. "Now let's use our imagination to pretend we're at the seaside. Close your eyes and imagine you are stood on a beach by the sea. What can you see? What can you hear?"
    - Explain how we can use imagination to pretend to be someone or somewhere else, and that this is called role-play. "Imagine you are paddling in the sea, let's pretend to take off our shoes. Can you pretend to splash about in the sea?"
- To encourage learners to use their imaginations, the teacher could provide a stimulus for imaginative role-play by introducing dressing up costumes or props from familiar settings. Model how learners might use the props and encourage learners to join in with imaginative role-play.
- Learners could also play 'Let's Pretend' where someone pretends to be an animal, and the others have to guess which animal they are trying to be.

Reinforcing it

There are several ways to reinforce this step across other learning. For example:

- When reading, stop to ask learners to use their imaginations to think about what might happen next
- Introduce simulations or role-play where appropriate to engage learners' imaginations in wider learning

Assessing it

This step is best assessed through observation and discussion. For example:

- Asking learners to explain what they are pretending to be or do in a role-play activity. Do they show awareness of an imaginary object or setting?
- Use teacher observations to watch how learners interact with one another. Can they join in imaginative activities with other learners?

Creativity Step 1

Step 1: I imagine different situations and can say what I imagine

To achieve Step 1, individuals will be able to imagine different situations and be able to say what it is that they are imagining.

In the previous step, the focus was on being able to imagine different situations. This step builds on this by adding the ability of individuals to be able to say what it is that they are imagining.

Building blocks

The building blocks of this step are:

- I know why it is helpful to explain what I imagine
- I know how to talk about what I have imagined
- I describe what I have imagined

Reflection questions

- What does imagination mean?
- Can you think about examples of when you have used your imagination?
- Why is it helpful to be able to explain what we imagine?
- How can we talk about what we imagine?
- What are some simple mistakes that we could make if we get it wrong?

What you need to know

Why explain what we imagine?

Imagination is about being able to think about something and being able to see it in your head. There are lots of different times that we might use our imagination:

- When thinking about what we might do in the future
- Thinking about somewhere we haven't been but might like to
- When thinking up new ideas or ways of doing something better
- When acting out situations that haven't happened yet

If you imagine something, it starts in your head. However, everything in the world has started in someone's imagination. If it had only stayed in that person's imagination, then it would never have turned into something real in the world.

One of the best ways of sharing what we imagine is through talking about it.

How to talk about what you imagine

When we use our imaginations, we have to remember that no one else knows what is in your head until you tell them.

Therefore, you have to use lots of detail to help bring what is in your head to life for them – they will not know anything that you don't tell them. If there are gaps in what you describe, they will use their own imaginations to fill in the other details, and so they might end up thinking about something entirely different.

When describing what you imagine, it is helpful to give *context* – start by telling them what situation or thing you were broadly imagining. For example,

- I imagined that I was making a trip to the moon.
- I imagined that we got a new puppy.
- I imagined what to do at the weekend.

You can then start to give some of the detail of what you were imagining:

- I would have to travel in a huge rocket, and to wear an astronaut suit. When I left the earth, it would feel like there was no gravity so I would have to learn how to travel around without being stuck to the floor.
- I would like a small one, with brown fur and bright eyes. I would take it for walks every day and teach it how to chase a ball.
- I would go to my favourite coffee shop and get a croissant and an orange juice, then read a magazine. I make sure to get a seat by the window, so it is nice and bright, and so I can watch other people walking by.

Without giving the *context* first, none of these second examples make any sense.

- You might also want to explain how you *feel* – this can help people you are talking to be more interested in what you are sharing.
- Finally, you have to decide how much detail you want to give – you cannot describe everything, so you have to choose what is essential.

Teaching it

To teach this step:

The teacher can model imagining an answer to a challenge they set the class. For example, what would you do today if school was cancelled? They should structure how to give context and then think about the amount of detail to share to make sense of what they are imagining.

Learners can practice this in several ways, for example:

Taking a well-known story or routine and then thinking about hypothetical questions about what might happen next if that story or routine was broken. What would have happened if all the buses were cancelled?

Creating a scenario to get started: what if your house was at the bottom of the sea, how would you get there?

Reinforcing it

This step can be effectively reinforced in the classroom setting. For example:

- The teacher could create a routine for introducing tasks where learners are going to use their imaginations. For example, "We are now entering the imagination zone".
- During teaching, the teacher could use "What if...?" or "What do you think...?" questions to explore imaginative answers across different ideas.
- The teacher can talk about when they are using their imaginations themselves.

Assessing it

This step is best assessed through verbal discussion. For example:

- Learners can explain what imagination is and when they use their imagination
- Ask learners questions about what they can see in their head when you encourage them to think about different scenarios.
- Use teacher observation to watch how learners play and pretend with one another.

Creativity Step 2

Step 2: I imagine different situations and can bring them to life in different ways

To achieve Step 2, individuals will show that they can bring what they imagine to life in different ways, including through role-play or acting out their ideas, and through pictures or diagrams.

In the previous step, individuals focused on how to say what they could imagine. This step builds on this by exploring other ways of communicating ideas to others.

Building blocks

The building blocks of this step are:

- I know different ways to share what I have imagined
- I draw or record what I have imagined
- I act out or model what I have imagined

Reflection questions

- How can you share what you imagine through acting it out?
- When can this be helpful?
- How can you share what you imagine through drawing pictures or diagrams?
- What are the advantages of this?
- Can you give examples of where you have done this?

What you need to know

Sharing imagination through acting it out

When we imagine something, it is in our heads. Imagining things in our heads can help think about new ideas or what we might want to do in the future. However, some of the things we imagine are useful to share with the world.

One method of doing this is through acting it out or by using role-play. Acting or role-play is helpful when you are trying to share a conversation or behaviour with someone else and for them to join you in being part of your imaginary world.

For example, all drama – whether in films, in theatres or on video clips – comes from imagination and then it is made real by being acted out to you. If this done well, it can be so convincing that you feel that you are part of the action and understand very clearly what is in someone's imagination.

Another example is the use of role-play – when someone, or multiple people, play different roles. This can help build an understanding of what someone is thinking or for playing out different scenarios. For this reason, role-play is often used in creative play and also in learning so that you have to think about what someone else was thinking and feeling at a certain point. It can be good for building *empathy* and understanding how someone else is feeling and why they make certain decisions.

Sharing imagination through drawing pictures or diagrams

Alongside talking about ideas or acting them out, the other big way that people share what they imagine is through pictures or diagrams.

Most artists use their imagination to create their works of art. They imagine a situation, or how they feel about it, and bring that to life through their artwork. That might use materials like paint, pencil, metal, stone, or many others. In every case, they have taken something that was in their mind and turned it into something physical to share what was in their imaginations. However, we don't need to be brilliant artists to get across our ideas – sometimes a quick *sketch* can be enough.

Alternatively, lots of things people imagine turn into *diagrams*. Diagrams are designed to be a way of getting crucial technical information to other people. They can be simple such as showing where in a room a picture should be put up, or more complicated like a set of architectural plans. Diagrams can also show instructions for other people to follow to build something or make something happen. Diagrams do not have to be perfect to be useful.

Teaching it

To teach this step:

- The teacher can show how *role-play* can be a useful way of bringing imagination to life by asking learners to imagine that they were two well-known figures or acting out a familiar scenario like a shopkeeper and a demanding customer. Learners could explore what they learnt through having to act out this scenario – that might include empathy for the characters, and also ideas about how they would deal with that scenario if it happened.
- The teacher can show how *acting* can be a useful way of bringing imagination to life by asking learners to create a short sketch in response to a stimulus like "when the aliens landed". Learners can explore how acting can help share the feelings and emotions that they imagine.
- Learners can then take on the challenge of sharing what they imagine through art using a stimulus if they need, e.g. "When it wouldn't stop raining".
- Finally, learners can create a diagram, e.g. how they would rearrange the classroom if they could, or an invention that would help do something in their day.

Reinforcing it

This skill step can be reinforced in other parts of learning. This can be done by encouraging learners to engage their imaginations during learning. They can then express what they imagine through the appropriate methods from above.

Assessing it

This step is best assessed through a series of structured activities. These can be based on the *Teach It* section above, using a sequence of different challenges that can be used to assess learners' abilities to use the various methods of sharing what they imagine.

Creativity Step 3

Step 3: I generate ideas when I have been given a clear brief

To achieve Step 3, individuals will show that they can generate ideas when given a clear brief.

In earlier steps, the focus was on the use of imagination, and how to share what learners can imagine through speaking, role-play, and drawing pictures or diagrams. This step shifts now to think about idea generation rather than just imagining.

Building blocks

The building blocks of this step are:

- I explain and define what a creative brief is
- I know how to generate ideas for a creative brief
- I explain and define what success criteria are

Reflection questions

- What is meant by a brief?
- How can a brief be helpful?
- Can you give examples of where you have been given a brief?
- How can you create ideas to fulfil a brief?
- What are some things that you should do, and some things that you should avoid doing?
- Have you got any examples of having done this?

What you need to know

What is a brief

A *brief* is a problem or challenge that we have to come up with ideas to solve. The brief might be short or long; it might be in a written form, or it might be spoken.

A brief will normally have *success criteria* attached to it. The success criteria will tell you what your idea needs to be able to do or answer to be judged successful:

- the success criteria for a lunch box might be that it needs to big enough to hold a sandwich, waterproof, and not too heavy to carry
- success criteria for a school trip might be that learners can learn something that links to their school work, that it is not too far away, and that the whole class goes together

If it is not clear what the success criteria are, you should either ask the person who is setting you the brief or think about what you think they should be if they cannot tell you.

Success criteria are critical because knowing what we are working towards and what needs to be included means we can focus our imagination rather than creating ideas that will not work for the brief. There is also good evidence that people come up with better ideas when they are constrained or limited.

How to generate ideas to a brief

When you are creating ideas, the most important thing is to try to create as many as possible at the beginning. If you only come up with one idea, then it is unlikely to be your best idea.

You can then think about which of those ideas fulfils the success criteria that you have been set. This might get rid of quite a few of the ideas.

There might also be other things that mean an idea becomes unrealistic, such as it depends on events, materials, or inventions that do not exist. Again, at this stage, these ideas should be removed from your list.

Of the ideas that are left, you might combine different elements of those ideas to create the best plan that you can to fulfil the brief that you have been set.

Teaching it

To teach this step:

- The teacher can model what a brief might look like and identify the success criteria from it.
    - For example: You need to design a new form of transport for travelling underwater. It must be made of something waterproof, fit at least 20 people, and be shaped like a fish or some other sea creature.
- Encourage learners to generate as many ideas as possible for what they could create and then remove those that would not fulfil the success criteria or are too unrealistic.
- This approach could also be explored in other ways, for example:
    - Using simple story writing to help learners practise generating good ideas. These could be linked to something you are working on or learning about more widely. Create different constraints and success criteria for learners to work towards. For example: learners need to tell a story using only ten words; using words that start with a limited set of letters; or where they must include certain familiar characters.

Reinforcing it

This step lends itself to being reinforced in lots of different aspects of learning, when you are encouraging learners to engage with a particular topic or subject area. Some further strategies can be used by a teacher include:

- In other areas of teaching and learning, asking learners to identify the success criteria provided, or challenging them to produce their own.
- Explicitly praising learners for thinking about success criteria.
- Encouraging learners to create lots of ideas before filtering them down according to the success criteria – this is a crucial discipline so that they do not always just think that their first idea is the best one.

Assessing it

This step is best assessed through a structured activity. This can include giving them a simple brief with clear success criteria. Try to structure the activity so that there is space for learners to generate lots of ideas, and then go through the process of filtering that list down.

Sharing their final idea might draw on any of the methods of speaking, drawing, or acting that were highlighted in Steps 1 and 2.

Creativity Step 4

Step 4: I generate ideas to improve something

To achieve Step 4, individuals will show that they can generate ideas to make something better.

In the previous step, individuals focused on how to generate ideas when given a clear brief and success criteria. This step continues to focus on creating ideas but without the brief and success criteria being given. Instead, to improve something individuals have to be able to identify what the success criteria are for themselves.

Building blocks

The building blocks of this step are:

- I explain why success criteria are important
- I use success criteria to identify what something is supposed to be able to do
- I use success criteria to generate ideas for improving something

Reflection questions

- What are success criteria?
- How can we work out what they are for different things?
- How can we come up with lots of ideas?
- How do we know if an idea will make something better or not?

What you need to know

Understanding success criteria

In the last step, we looked at success criteria, which we said were what will tell you what your idea needs to be able to do or answer to be judged successful.

If you don't have success criteria, it is impossible to come up with great ideas because you have no way of knowing whether an idea is a good one or not. This means that if we are not given success criteria, then we need to work some out for ourselves.

Some questions that we might ask ourselves to develop those success criteria are:

- *What is this thing trying to do?* It might be that the thing is a physical product like a car, or it might be a service like repairing a car.
- *What does the thing do well?* For example, the car might be good at not using too much fuel when it is driven. It might also be reliable and not break down often.
- *What could it do better?* For example, it might be that the car could be made bigger, or a better colour, or have bigger windows so people can see out better.
- *Which of the improvements matter?* In the end, we have to think about which of those potential improvements really matter. For example, if it a sports car then perhaps it is not worth making it bigger because the success criteria are that it is as light as possible and can seat two people. On the other hand, if it is a car that is used as a taxi, then being bigger might be helpful.

We can use this thought process to work out what the success criteria of the product or service are, what is it trying to achieve, and for whom? Once we know the success criteria, we can work out how to make something better.

Making something better

When thinking about improving something, you might start from a problem that you have experienced in using the product or service:

it took a long time to do your shopping, or you couldn't find what you were looking for.

a machine broke or cost more money than you thought it should have done.

This gives you a success criteria to work towards. You will be successful in improving something if it can do it better.

However, it is really important that we think about whether your idea might solve a problem but accidentally make something else worse.

To take our car example from earlier, adding some overhead storage on a sports car might mean that it can carry more luggage. However, the downside of that might be that it would ruin the aerodynamics of the vehicle, and also make it heavier so it would be slower which might be working against an important success criteria.

The other important test for improvements is that they should be *feasible*. We looked at what it meant to be feasible before, but essentially it means that something is achievable in terms of cost and being real. These should also be success criteria but can easily be overlooked.

Teaching it

To teach this step:

- The teacher can model taking a product or service that will be familiar to the learners and thinking about how it can be improved. First, this means modelling how to identify its success criteria.
    - Analysing the whiteboard, some of its success criteria might be that it can be seen by all learners, that it is easy to clean, that it is within certain size limits, and that it can be safely attached to the wall.
- The teacher can then take the learners through an exercise thinking about what is good about the product or service and what could be improved.
    - For example, the whiteboard is visible to everyone in the room, was cheap, and is securely fastened to the wall. However, it might be challenging to clean, and hard to read when the sun is shining on it.
    - Learners can then think about what they could do to fix those problems – for example, by putting a surface on that was easier to clean, or to put up shades to stop the sun shining directly on the whiteboard.
- It is essential then to circle back to ensure that none of the ideas would have adverse effects in other areas.
    - For example, making the surface easier to clean might make it more difficult to write on in the first place, or stopping the sun shining on the whiteboard might make it harder to see on a dull day.
- Having modelled this for learners, they can then be encouraged to go through this process themselves, using some scaffolding to ensure they follow step by step. As they grow in confidence, it should be possible to remove some of this structure.

Reinforcing it

This step can be reinforced in the classroom, and learners can also be encouraged to think more widely across their experience at school and at home to identify things, whether products or services, that they could improve. The teacher can take the lead on sharing examples of where they personally have changed something or come up with new ideas to make things better. This encourages learners to realise that they probably all have areas of their lives where they can come up with ideas to make things better.

Assessing it

This step is best assessed through a structured challenge. For example, by setting learners a challenge to improve something that they are familiar with and providing them with some cues to think through the logical process to ensure they really are making improvements, not just changes.

Creativity Step 5

Step 5: I generate ideas by combining different concepts

To achieve Step 5, individuals will show that they can generate ideas by combining different concepts.

In earlier steps, individuals thought about creating ideas when given a clear brief and success criteria, and then when they had to create their own success criteria to improve something. In this step, individuals build on this by exploring how they can combine different concepts to generate new ideas.

Building blocks

The building blocks of this step are learning:

- I explain and define what a concept is
- I identify the different components of an idea or concept
- I know how two or more ideas can be combined

Reflection questions

- What are concepts?
- What are components?
- How can you break an idea or concept into components?
- How can we combine the components of ideas to create new ones?
- What are the advantages of doing this?
- What are the risks of doing this?

What you need to know

Components of ideas and concepts

A *concept* is a type of idea that is usually quite general or big. For example, if we were decorating a classroom, we might say that the concept was 'bright and colourful'. This gives a vague direction, but there is a lot more detail that would need to go into this to make it helpful.

A *component* is a part of a whole thing or idea. For example, components of a bright and colourful classroom concept would include the positioning of the furniture, the colours on the walls, and the size of the windows.

When we respond to a brief (as in *Step 3*) or try to improve something (as in *Step 4*) we might come up with a complete concept or set of ideas to try to answer that brief or make an improvement. However, we might have more than one concept or lots of different ideas. Sometimes we will want to choose between them, but at other times we might be able to pick the best bits of each and put them all together.

How to combine components of ideas

When we combine ideas, it is helpful to think of the components of those ideas and the success criteria that each of those components helps to fulfil:

Continuing our classroom decorating example, we might have two concepts which look quite different: One has a circular classroom, with the furniture arranged around in a semi-circle with bright orange walls and windows set in the ceiling. The second has a rectangular classroom, with the furniture arranged in rows, big glass doors along two sides of it, and sky blue walls. Both of these ideas fulfil the same broad criteria that they are 'bright and colourful', but in very different ways.

Rather than picking one of these, we might break down both concepts into their component parts. Both concepts include room shape, furniture layout, wall colour and window positioning. We can then pick our preference for each of these component parts.

In this way, we might end up with a circular classroom, with furniture arranged in a semi-circle but with blue walls and big glass doors all the way around.

If we get it right when we combine ideas, we can end up with the best of both worlds. It can give us the chance to see different ideas for each of the components of the concept and then pick the best one for each of those.

However, it is important to be aware of the risk here too. We could end up spoiling the idea if the component parts need to be linked together or can't be separated.

- In our example, it might not be possible to build big glass doors into a circular wall. In the same way, you might not be able to combine a circular room with furniture arranged in rows.

Therefore, it is always important to review whether the combination of components really is better, or whether some components can't be separated from one another.

Teaching it

To teach this step:

- The teacher can model this process of combining ideas by asking learners to develop an idea for how they could redesign part of the school – for example, the playground area. Learners should be encouraged to work alone initially, capturing their ideas as diagrams.
- Learners can then share their different ideas. The teacher can highlight components that they like from the ideas. Learners can then work in small groups, or as one facilitated group, to identify the components of the playground and the success criteria to put together their favourite components.
- It is important that the teacher models reviewing whether the idea is better for combining parts or whether further changes are needed. For example, it might be that combining all the components of learners' ideas would overfill the playground area.
- This activity could be repeated with a lower level of structuring and with a different challenge – for example, how to create the ultimate school bag.

Reinforcing it

This is a step that can be reinforced in other areas. For example, learners could be encouraged to explore two characters who they have been reading about by thinking what would happen if they were combined.

Equally, when learners come up with ideas, you could give them another idea which they have to combine with it or ask them to combine ideas as a group. During group activities, learners can be asked to explicitly identify where different components of group ideas have come from.

Assessing it

This step is best assessed through a structured, assessed task as laid out in the Teaching it section above. The critical thing is that the focus should be on a topic area that is familiar to the learners so that they are demonstrating their ability to combine ideas rather than their subject knowledge.

Creativity Step 6

Step 6: I use creativity in the context of work

To achieve Step 6, individuals will understand what creativity is and see how they can use it in the context of doing their work.

In earlier steps, the focus was first on imagination and how to share those imaginings, and then on how to generate ideas against a brief - or by combining different concepts - to improve something. This step shifts into thinking about creativity more broadly and its relevance across various aspects of learners' work.

Building blocks

The building blocks of this step are:

- I define and describe what creativity is
- I see the value of creativity for supporting work
- I know how creativity can be used across different types of work

Reflection questions

- What is creativity?
- Why is creativity important?
- How is creativity useful in doing your work?
- Can you give examples of how you use creativity in your work?

What you need to know

Creativity and its value

Creativity is made up of three different aspects:

- *Using imagination:* this is all about thinking of something that does not exist, and being able to capture and share it in some way. This was explored in *Steps 0-2*.
- *Generating new ideas:* this is about being able to harness imagination to create something new, or to improve on an existing thing
- *Turning those ideas into something*: this final step is about enacting those ideas and turning them into something, whether an action or a product

Importantly, creativity is not just about art or performance. We can find it in all different areas of work – anything from engineering to medicine.

Creativity is important because we need it every time that we want to do something new, or to make something better, or to imagine something that someone is telling you that you cannot directly see for yourself.

Using creativity in your work

We all need creativity in different parts of our work. For example, when we are:

- Trying to develop new ideas to solve a problem
- Trying to combine different ideas to create new things
- Responding to a brief that we have been given
- Imagining an experience that we have not yet had

Without the skills of creativity, we would not be able to plan ahead for what might happen in the future because we have no way of knowing beyond what we learn and then imagine.

Teaching it

To teach this step:

- The teacher can start by modelling lots of the different areas of teaching where creativity is important:
    - Developing interesting lesson plans
    - Planning for what might happen in the future
    - Creating teaching resources and things that you can do as a class
    - Learning from other teachers and their experiences
- Learners can then think of all of the different times that they use creativity in their work, such as:
    - Creative writing
    - Thinking about what might happen when they do experiments
    - Imagining places or events that they are learning about
- Learners can then write down as many different jobs or professions as possible in one minute. Learners can identify when these individuals may use creativity. They can be challenged to think of examples for each of the three elements of creativity:
    - How do they use imagination?
    - What new and original ideas do they come up with?
    - What are they turning those ideas into?

Reinforcing it

There are several ways of reinforcing this step across learning in school. The most significant part of this is to help learners to recognise and be able to articulate when they have used creativity in their work.

This could be supported by a 'Creativity Champion' each week who is responsible for acknowledging when others have been creative and give them a call out, sticker, or reward (as appropriate!).

In praise and feedback, the teacher can be explicit that creativity is being used, especially when it is not as obvious – for example, in science, history, ICT, or geography.

Assessing it

This step is best assessed through conversation or a written reflection, asking learners to define the different aspects of creativity and to reflect on when they have used creativity in their work.

Creativity Step 7

Step 7: I use creativity in the context of my wider life

To achieve Step 7, individuals should be aware and reflect on how they use creativity in the context of their wider life.

In the previous step, individuals showed that they were aware of how they use creativity to complete their work. This step builds on this by expanding thinking about creativity into wider life as well.

Building blocks

The building blocks of this step are:

- I identify the aspects of creativity
- I explain when I have used creativity in my wider life
- I recognise the benefits of using creativity in my wider life

Reflection questions

- What is creativity?
- How can creativity be used in different areas of life?
- Why is it helpful to see when you are being creative?
- How can you learn from being creative in different areas?

What you need to know

How creativity is relevant in wider life

Creativity has three parts to it, as we saw in *Step 6*:

- *Using imagination:* this is all about thinking of something that does not exist, and being able to capture and share it in some way. This is what we explored in Steps 0-2.
- *Generating new ideas:* this is about being able to harness imagination to create something new, or to improve on an existing thing
- *Turning those ideas into something:* this final step is about enacting those ideas and turning them into something, whether an action or a product

Creativity has uses in lots of different areas of life:

- When you plan on going somewhere, you imagine what it would be like to go there, and whether you would enjoy it or not
- When you think about something you want to make, you imagine what it will look like when it is finished, and steps you will take to get there
- When you change a routine that you have at home, you are generating new ideas and working towards making things better
- You might also have hobbies or other interests which draw on creativity like drama, art, music, crafts, or even gardening

The benefits of using creativity

It is helpful to know when we are being creative so that we can make links between different areas of our work and lives.

We often treat our work and our wider lives as two completely different parts of our lives, without any overlap. However, when it comes to creativity, this is a great waste. Often, inspiration can cut across both those areas if we spot it.

It is important to remember that good ideas often come from unexpected places. By recognising when we are creative, we can take ideas from one area of our lives and use them in other areas as well.

Teaching it

To teach this step:

- The teacher can start by modelling lots of the different areas of their wider lives where they use their creativity:
    - In hobbies
    - In making home improvements
    - In travel plans
- Learners can then think of all of the different times that they use creativity in their wider lives. This could include:
    - Activities that they do outside of school
    - When they come up with plans
- Learners could then be asked to reflect on how using creativity in one area of their life has helped them in another area of their life, such as between work and life.

Reinforcing it

There are a variety of things that can be done to support and reinforce learners' understanding of how they use creativity across different aspects of their lives. For example, the teacher could:

- Create a reward system that values creativity, explicitly recognising the importance of using imagination and generating something original.
- Be explicit about when they have used creativity recently in their own personal or professional life: when creating the session they are delivering, when cooking dinner or planning what to do last weekend.
- Encourage learners to draw on what they already know and to use their memories and previous experiences to spark creativity. Be explicit that this is a way of using creativity.
- Ask learners for reflections on what they have done outside of school to use their creativity

Assessing it

This step is best assessed through learners' reflections. For example, getting them to complete a journal or reflection on times when they have used creativity in lots of different areas of their lives.

Creativity Step 8

Step 8: I develop ideas by using mind mapping

To achieve Step 8, individuals will show that they can use mind mapping as a way of further developing their ideas.

In earlier steps, individuals explored what it means to use imagination in different situations and how to generate ideas. They also explored how creativity can be useful in the context of both work and their wider lives. These next steps are about using different techniques to develop and refine more sophisticated ideas, starting with mind mapping.

Building blocks

The building blocks of this step are:

- I explain and define mind mapping
- I create mind maps to explore ideas
- I share mind maps to explain how ideas are linked and related

Reflection questions

- What is a creative tool?
- What is a mind map?
- When are they helpful?
- When are mind maps less useful?
- What other visual creative tools have you come across?

What you need to know

How to create a mind map

As we develop our creativity, we want to be able to not only generate lots of ideas but to start to link them and expand our thinking. *Creative tools* are methods that support creativity. That is, they support you to use your imagination, generate something new, and work towards an outcome.

A *mind map* is a simple creative tool to explore a particular idea:

- It starts with a single theme or question in the middle of the page, called the stimulus
- Initial ideas then fan out from that stimulus
- Lines are drawn between the ideas and the stimulus to show they are linked
- There might also be further ideas or connections that come from those ideas, and links between them can also be linked with arrows

How mind maps can be helpful

Mind maps can be helpful for a few different reasons:

- *Speedy:* They are quick to create and can be made using a pen and paper or using mind mapping software to organise thoughts.
- *Adaptable:* Unlike writing in sentences, they allow for more flexible thinking because ideas can be arranged and linked in different ways, and it is easy to add more thoughts later.
- *Sharable:* Because mind maps are widely used, they can be easily communicated, and it is possible to use a mind map as a visual aid to support an explanation to someone else (See *Speaking Step 8* for how visual aids can help communication)
- *Support working together:* Since mind maps are not linear, they are a great collaborative tool as several people working together can all write their ideas onto a single mind map. This can be a great way of getting a lot of different ideas quickly.

Other Visual Creative Tools

While mind maps are useful tools, they have their limitations because they only focus on one stimulus or idea and work out from there.

An alternative is *concept maps* which take different ideas and then look at connections between them. They might include labels on their linking lines to explain what the connection is between those ideas.

At other times it will be useful to think about *flow charts*, for how ideas link together, or *circular diagrams* if there is a cycle. Again, these help to add clarity about what the connection is between different ideas (these are explored more in *Problem Solving Step 8*)

Finally, while mind maps are helpful for *identifying and organising* ideas, they are only a starting point. Eventually, we are likely to want to create other things to help explore those ideas further, like diagrams, charts, or fuller explanations.

Teaching it

To teach this step:

- The teacher can model how to create a mind map for a particular theme or stimulus – this can initially be something simple, perhaps related to subject knowledge.
- Learners can then have the opportunity to create a mind map for themselves, again linked to a different simple stimulus that relates to recently acquired knowledge. The focus is on how they arrange and expand their thinking about ideas by following through on creating a mind map.
- The teacher can then work with the class to create a mind map for exploring a creative question, to generate as many ideas and alternatives as possible. This should be an expansive question like 'How can we combat climate change?' or 'What would make the classroom a more pleasant place?'.
- The teacher can illustrate through this how effective use of mind mapping can help to capture and explore ideas collectively, as well as being a useful tool for individuals.

Reinforcing it

This is a step which can be regularly reinforced in the classroom setting, and which supports learning. For instance, it can be used regularly as a way for learners to reflect on what they already know about a new subject, or as a tool for gathering notes as they listen.

Assessing it

This step is best assessed through an exercise. This could be through setting the learners a question or stimulus challenge and asking them to gather and organise their ideas through a mind map. The question or stimulus should be something accessible and familiar for learners so that the assessment is focused on the mind map, not the underlying knowledge.

This assessment could be extended to include an observed group task (linked to *Teamwork* skills) where the focus would be on whether learners can use a mind map as a tool to support effective group working.

Creativity Step 9

Step 9: I develop ideas by asking myself questions

To achieve Step 9, individuals will demonstrate that they can develop ideas by asking themselves questions.

In the previous step, the focus was on developing ideas through mind mapping. This step continues to think about how to develop ideas, this time through the use of effective questioning.

Building blocks

The building blocks of this step are:

- I recognise the role of questioning in developing ideas
- I identify what sort of questions to ask
- I use answers to questions to develop my ideas

Reflection questions

- Why is questioning a vital part of developing ideas?
- Why do we need to redraft and revise our ideas?
- What sort of questions are likely to help to improve your ideas?
- What do you need to know to ask good questions?

What you need to know

The role of questioning

No idea is ever created fully formed and ready to go. All ideas evolve and are developed, refined, and improved. This process of improvement is often called re-drafting.

Even the greatest masterpieces weren't created in one go – they were planned, refined, and improved. For instance, many of the paintings that we think of as masterpieces have signs of earlier versions underneath the paint we see today. Similarly, many sculptures are preceded by smaller experimental models.

Almost all engineering designs are changed and substantially improved before they make it to being built. Famously, after his idea of a lightbulb, it took Thomas Edison hundreds of revisions and attempts to make the idea come to reality.

One of the best ways of helping ourselves to go through the process of improving our ideas is through asking good questions. These questions help us to pre-empt the response that others will have to our ideas and will help us to consider whether there are other ways of reaching our goals too.

A big difference between those who have mastered creativity and those who are at an earlier stage is the willingness to ask challenging questions and be open to changing the idea to make it better.

The questions to ask

There are two broad types of questions, as you might be familiar with from Listening (See *Listening Step 7*):

- *Closed questions:* those which can be answered with a 'Yes' or 'No' response. For example, 'Is that...' or 'Did...' They are useful for confirming or denying facts.
- *Open questions:* those that cannot be answered with a 'yes' or 'no' response. For example, they tend to start with words like 'who', what', 'why', 'when' and 'how'. Sometimes these questions can still be answered with short factual answers, but they have the potential to be much broader.

There is a place for closed questions when questioning your ideas, but mostly around whether you have achieved particular *success criteria*. If your ideas don't achieve the success criteria, then these sorts of questions will help you to identify that.

However, open questions are much more useful – for example, if you haven't hit one of the success criteria, the obvious question is 'How could this be adapted to meet the success criteria?' Other open questions that you might find useful include:

- How does this idea fit in with the brief?
- What could make this idea better?
- What would make this shorter / easier to use / more engaging / simpler to understand / more enjoyable?
- How will I know if this is an idea that will work in practice?
- How will other people react to this idea?
- What makes me think that this is the best idea I can come up with?

Teaching it

To teach this step:

- The teacher can share examples of how ideas develop and change. For example, looking at how the car evolved from a horseless carriage to where we are today, or how mobile phones evolved. The critical point is that no idea reaches perfection, and a core attitude around creativity is the willingness to challenge oneself to keep developing ideas and improve on them. Learners could be encouraged to come up with some examples themselves.
- Learners can then be presented with a stimulus or challenge to come up with ideas for. Learners will work individually to come up with some initial ideas (this could be a good chance to reinforce the previous step about mind mapping). Then ask them to come up with 5-10 questions to challenge their work. They can ask these to themselves or their peers.
- Learners should then use those questions to help them to redraft and to improve their ideas further.

Reinforcing it

This step lends itself well to being reinforced across other learning, because it is healthy for learners to build a positive attitude to redrafting and reworking their ideas. This concept could be used across lots of different subject areas too.

Assessing it

This step is best assessed through discussion. For example, by starting with an exercise similar to that laid out above for *Teach It and then,* after that, asking learners to produce and discuss a redraft, demonstrating how they questioned themselves and how these questions led to improvements in their ideas.

Creativity Step 10

Step 10: I develop ideas by considering different perspectives

To achieve Step 10, individuals will show that they can actively seek out and consider different perspectives.

In recent steps, the focus has been on how to develop ideas, going beyond just creating them to exploring them further through mind mapping and other tools, and then interrogating them through questioning. This next step introduces the importance of looking at ideas from different perspectives to improve them further.

Building blocks

The building blocks of this step are:

- I define and describe what perspectives are
- I outline factors that might cause a different perspective
- I recognise how different perspectives can be used to improve ideas

Reflection questions

- What do we mean by perspectives?
- Why might there be very different perspectives on the same idea?
- Where can we get different perspectives from?
- How can you make sense of different perspectives?
- Can you incorporate every perspective?
- If not, how do you prioritise them?

What you need to know

Different perspectives

A *perspective* is a point of view that someone has of something. The term perspective is also used in art and design, referring to how a three-dimensional landscape looks different depending on where one stands relative to it. This is a helpful idea to bear in mind – we might be looking at the same thing, but from our two different viewpoints it ends up looking very different.

Creativity and Problem Solving are intertwined, and if you've started to look at the Problem Solving steps, particularly Step 10, you will have seen that there are sometimes effects that come from an idea which are unexpected. These are called *secondary effects*. These secondary effects might be positive, or they might be negative. In any case, they are certainly worth consideration.

As we develop our Creativity skills, we need to be more challenging of our own ideas and considering different viewpoints is an important part of that. For instance, a tall person might have a very different view from a shorter person of lowering ceiling heights of rooms to improve energy efficiency . Someone with longer legs will be less enthusiastic about airlines saving money by putting seats closer together. In these cases, it is important to think about different perspectives and different needs when developing ideas.

When we develop ideas, we do it mainly from our own perspective. You can find different perspectives in a variety of ways, by thinking about these questions:

- Who else might end up being a user of your idea?
- In what ways might those individuals vary?
- Do they have different needs or success criteria?
- Are there changes that are needed to make an idea feasible for them?
- What changes might other people suggest to your idea, and why?

These questions should give you a view of who your different *stakeholders* are. *Stakeholders* are those groups of individuals who might share a common perspective on your idea.

Making sense of different perspectives

It is one thing to gather lots of different perspectives, but it is quite another to try to make sense of the results. This brings us on to the critical concept of *trade-offs*: we are unlikely to be able to fully satisfy everyone, all of the time.

To extend those examples from before: For a shorter person, lower ceilings are worthwhile because they lower heating costs. For a taller person, they want higher ceilings so that they don't feel constrained. In this case, *compromise* becomes important. What is the ceiling height that achieves the best trade-off of being high enough so that even tall people can feel comfortable, but as low as possible to be energy efficient?

For someone with shorter legs, they will be pleased that their seat price is lower as a result of the airline being more efficiently filled with paying passengers. The individual with longer legs would probably pay more to be less comfortable. In this case *differentiation* might be possible – that is, having different options for different passengers. This is why some airlines have seats available with more leg space at an extra cost – only those passengers who need the space would be willing to pay extra, which means that everyone gets closer to what they are looking for.

These are two examples of how to reconcile different perspectives: *compromise* and *differentiation*.

There is a third important point though, which is that sometimes you need to *prioritise*. Perhaps ultimately your idea can't be for everyone, and you have to choose what the most important priority is. For example, if your intention was to help a particular marginalised or disadvantaged group, then you might prioritise their perspective over others. To be able to prioritise, you need to have a clear view of what your focus and success criteria are.

Teaching it

To teach this step:

- The teacher can introduce the idea that we need to take different perspectives by sharing a plan – for example, lengthening the school day. Together with learners, the various *stakeholders* in this idea can be identified, potentially including teachers, learners, parents, and others.
- Learners are divided into different groups to represent each of these stakeholder groups and challenged to come up with their perspective on the idea. These different perspectives can be shared as a fuller group

- Carefully supported by the teacher, learners can then be challenged to think about how they would balance these different perspectives, thinking about the concepts of:
    - Compromise – is there a middle ground that would satisfy most perspectives?
    - Differentiation – could we create options that work for different stakeholders?
    - Prioritisation – which perspectives matter the most?
- This exercise can then be repeated by thinking about a different challenge. For example, banning learners from being dropped off at school by car. This time, learners are given less scaffolding and have to identify the stakeholder, perspectives, and approach to managing those different perspectives themselves.

Reinforcing it

The idea of different perspectives lends itself well to many different areas of learning. For example, considering historical events from different perspectives, or the perspectives of different characters in literature.

Some of the trade-offs that have to be made in coming up with development policies could be considered in geography, for example, or how businesses try to compromise, differentiate, and prioritise could well be captured in business studies.

Assessing it

This step is best assessed through a structured challenge, giving learners an idea as a starting point and then asking them to bring different perspectives to that idea, and then to reach some way of reconciling or making sense of those perspectives through compromise, differentiation, or prioritisation.

Creativity Step 11

Step 11: I innovate effectively when working in a group

To achieve Step 11, individuals will show that they can innovate effectively as part of a group, not just when working alone.

In earlier steps, the focus was on how to develop ideas individually, using tools like mind mapping, questioning, and considering different perspectives. This step builds on this by looking at what changes when other people are involved in the creative process.

Building blocks

The building blocks of this step are:

- I identify the advantages and risks of innovating as a group
- I know how to avoid a group reaching a consensus too quickly
- I know how to broaden a group's perspective

Reflection questions

- What can the advantages be of innovating as a group?
- What are the risks of innovating as a group?
- Why is there a risk of a group reaching consensus too soon? How can this be avoided?
- Why is it essential to take on broad perspectives when innovating? How can a group achieve this?
- When do people feel safe and confident to contribute to a group?

What you need to know

The advantages of innovating in a group

Creativity is all about the use of imagination and the generation of new ideas. We've seen already that ideas can start from many places and then need to be honed and improved by considering lots of perspectives.

Working as part of a group has some significant advantages here:

- More people trying to generate ideas is likely to lead to a higher number of ideas to start with (see *Steps 3 and 4*)
- This, in turn, leads to more opportunities to combine concepts, which can be an effective way to generate better ideas (see *Step 5*)
- Ideas can also be refined more effectively through questioning, because there are individuals actually present who can ask those questions; they do not have to be created by the same person coming up with the idea in the first place (see *Step 9*)
- Finally, if the group is diverse to start with, it gives you a head start on ensuring that your ideas benefit from multiple perspectives (see *Step 10*)

For all these reasons, working in a group to innovate should have significant advantages over trying to innovate alone.

The risks of innovating in a group

However, there are often significant risks to working in a team which are frequently overlooked. Effective group innovation relies on being able to identify and mitigate risks:

- *A rush to consensus:* This is sometimes referred to as *Groupthink*. It is a phenomenon often observed where groups put too much value on reaching an agreement quickly. In this scenario, individuals do not raise concerns, express disagreement, or share alternatives because they feel this would undermine group cohesion. (See *Leadership Step 6* for more)
- *Lack of diversity:* Where groups lack diversity, they will not benefit from the full range of perspectives of different stakeholders. Instead, they might take false comfort from the idea that because there are several of them in the room, they cannot have missed any views.
- *Not a safe space:* Depending on the group's norms, it might not feel safe to group members to propose ideas or to question those of others. This might be because there is a power imbalance in the group, or because ultimately decision-making power is concentrated in a small sub-group. In this case, the less risky approach for group members is not to suggest ideas that contradict the decision-makers.
- *Risk aversion:* A group can sometimes be more risk-averse than an individual if there is a perceived risk that there will be blame for ideas that go wrong. In this case, group members will only make very low-risk suggestions.

Some useful creative tools for groups

These risks of group work show that for group innovation to achieve its potential, it needs to do several things:

- resist reaching a consensus too quickly
- encourage a wide range of perspectives, including beyond the group
- provide a feeling of safety for individuals to contribute ideas
- reduce the feelings of risk

Several approaches can help to address these risks:

Ways to avoid reaching a consensus too quickly

To avoid a premature consensus, you could:

- Designate one member of the team to challenge emerging consensus actively, and to provide an alternative perspective. In some settings, this is called being the 'devil's advocate. This forces ideas to be thought through in greater depth.
- Another approach is to set a goal for the number of ideas generated by the team (maybe 20 or 50), which will force the group to consider a much broader range of options than they otherwise would.
- The group could also commit to taking several options through to a final decision where the merits and drawbacks of each approach will be considered. This gives time for multiple opportunities to be fully explored, rather than rushing too quickly to only pursue one idea.
- The group could also be split into smaller sub-groups to champion different ideas, leading to a better final debate about the options.

Broaden perspectives

To broaden the perspectives, you could:

- Widen the membership of the group to include stakeholders who will be affected by the ideas that you are developing. For instance, if you are trying to improve some aspect of community life, you would want to have a diverse range of community members involved. If you are creating a new customer product, it is helpful to include some of those customers in the thinking, as well as suppliers and other partners. In an education setting, some institutions now make an effort to include learners in decision-making bodies alongside other leaders.
- If it is not possible to have other stakeholders in the room, there might still be a value in allocating different roles to individuals or asking them to approach the problem from that particular mindset, such as that of a loyal customer or a concerned parent.

Creating a feeling of safety and reducing fear of risk

- The leader of a group has a vital role in making the group feel like a safe space where individuals can contribute ideas without fear. This might include making clear that they welcome a full range of ideas, or that they don't want to reach the final answer too quickly.
- Other tools, like generating ideas anonymously before sharing any of them could help here, so individuals feel that they will not be judged for what they come up with.
- At other times, it might be helpful for individuals to have space without a leader or with a neutral external facilitator so they can share their ideas without worrying as much about perceptions of themselves.

Teaching it

To teach this step:

- The teacher can start by asking learners to reflect on the opportunities that come from working to innovate in a group, and some of the risks.
- This conversation can be expanded to think about how some of those risks can be mitigated by thinking about three broad areas: avoiding reaching consensus too quickly; broadening perspectives; creating a safe, low-risk environment.
- Learners can contribute strategies and tools that can be used in each of these areas. This is a good place for consolidating learning across Creativity so far.
- It would then be good to give learners a practical exercise to apply these ideas by asking them to work as a group to come up with an innovation that would improve their experience of some aspect of school or college life like the canteen, or changes to the library.
- Depending on the experience of learners, the teacher can structure this activity by asking them to reflect at different points on putting into practice some of the tools already shared. In a subsequent lesson, learners could repeat the exercise without the same teacher support to consolidate their understanding of the step.

Reinforcing it

This step can be effectively reinforced whenever there is a chance for group innovation or idea generation. Learners should be reminded of some of the key tools before starting the exercise. At the end, they can then reflect as to whether they managed to use those strategies in practice.

Assessing it

This step is best assessed in combination:

Firstly, an assessment of whether learners can suggest tools that could be used to support group innovation, perhaps using the broad categories above as a structure.

Secondly, to see whether learners can practically apply those ideas to innovating effectively as a group. A reflection afterwards can help to identify whether learners were aware of the tools they were using.

Creativity Step 12

Step 12: I innovate effectively by seeking out varied experiences and stimuli

To achieve Step 12, individuals will show that they actively seek out a range of experiences and stimuli to support them to be creative and innovative.

In the previous step, the focus was on how to be innovative while working as part of a group. This step builds on this by looking at how individuals can bring ideas back to the group.

Building blocks

The building blocks of this step are learning:

- I define experiences and explain their role in the creative process
- I reflect on my own experiences and use these to create new ideas
- I define creative stimuli and explain their role in the creative process

Reflection questions

- What are experiences?
- What role do experiences play in the creative process?
- What are stimuli? Can you give some examples?
- Why are stimuli also essential in the creative process?
- Can you give any examples of how you have used these in your work or life?

What you need to know

Experiences and stimuli

It is near impossible to be creative in a vacuum. When we think back to some of the earliest steps of Creativity, which focused on using imagination, that imagination came from combining ideas and events that had happened in real life.

There are no truly unique ideas in the world, they are all about combining concepts and components of other ideas or things that exist. To have more raw material to innovate, we should seek varied:

- *Experiences:* These are things that we have happened to us or which we have observed, which leave an impression that we remember.
- *Stimuli:* These are things which spark activity or energy in someone, and which act as a spur or an incentive.

The power of experiences

Our experiences give us the limits of what we can imagine. That might seem strange because imagination is about going beyond what currently exists. However, the reality is that most of what we imagine is about taking something that already exists and changing the:

- Goal to be achieved
- People involved
- Place or context
- Scale
- Speed or timeframe

For instance, although it has had a tremendous effect, the internet is the development of lots of communication technologies that have built upon each other. Of course, there are new inventions too, like fibre optic cable, but even the ideas behind this come from previously existing technologies – like the way that lighthouses use pulses of light to communicate to ships combined with sending signals down a copper wire.

The broader our experiences, the more raw material we have to draw on to create new ideas. It also means that we need to be open to drawing across that full range of experiences. Too often, as we explored in *Steps 6 and 7,* we don't see how experiences across our working and home lives can support creativity. Making these connections is critical.

Using stimuli

If experiences are the raw material for innovation, stimuli are those things that spark our motivation to do something with that raw material.

A stimulus might be seeing a new technology, art or performance, or an exciting article in a magazine or newspaper. Each of these things can spark engagement in our minds and help encourage us to join together different experiences to make something new.

Individuals who excel at creativity seek out a range of stimuli and look to go out of their comfort zone. They are not content to simply do the same thing every weekend, or to read only the same content. Instead, they look to try something new, and are open-minded about whether they will enjoy it or what they think they will get out of it.

Together, experiences and stimuli will lead to new innovations and ideas when coupled with some of the tools that have already been explored in Creativity.

Teaching it

To teach this step:

- The teacher should first ensure that learners are clear on what we mean by the core definitions of experiences and stimuli.
- This can be expanded by asking learners to think about why each of them plays a very different but essential role in the creative process.
- The conversation can be expanded to learners thinking of ideas that they have had, or innovations they had seen. They should identify what experiences and stimuli they think led to those innovations. These will be guesses in most cases, but helpful for consolidating the ideas.
- The teacher can then set learners a challenge to stretch themselves by seeking out a new experience that could support them to be more innovative.

Reinforcing it

This step lends itself well to being reinforced across school life, because it is often attuned to the values of a school or college. Learners can be encouraged to think about building their experiences and pushing themselves out of their comfort zone, as a way of developing their thinking and ideas.

Assessing it

This step is best assessed through a quick reflection:

- Learners can be asked to define what is meant by experiences and what is meant by stimuli, and to explain why both are important.
- They should then be asked to share examples of when they have used both to support themselves to be creative. This can be delivered as a presentation, a conversation, or a written piece.

Staying Positive

The ability to use tactics and strategies to overcome setbacks and achieve goals

Why it matters

Staying Positive is about being able to adapt to the inevitable changes and setbacks that emerge over time. Individuals who are effective at staying positive will be able to respond to these changes and challenges without giving up.

This is a fundamental skill to support being able to learn effectively in the classroom and then to be able to succeed in the workplace or in entrepreneurship beyond education too.

The focus in the Framework is on learnable strategies that help learners work through setbacks, barriers, or mistakes, while making the most of what they learn along the way.

How Staying Positive is built

This skill is all about individuals being equipped to manage their emotions effectively and being able to remain motivated, and ultimately to motivate others, even when facing setbacks.

The early steps focus on identifying emotions, in particular feeling positive or negative. Building on that is the ability to keep trying, staying calm, thinking about what went wrong, and trying to cheer up and encourage others.

The focus then turns to identifying new opportunities in difficult situations, sharing those, and adapting or creating plans accordingly. At more advanced steps, individuals identify and manage risks and gains in opportunities.

Finally, individuals support others to stay positive by managing their own response, helping others to see opportunities, and creating plans to achieve them.

Skills Builder Framework for Staying Positive

The ability to use tactics and strategies to overcome setbacks and achieve goals

Step 0	I can tell when I feel positive or negative
Step 1	I can tell when others feel positive or negative
Step 2	I keep trying when something goes wrong
Step 3	I keep trying and stay calm when something goes wrong
Step 4	I keep trying when something goes wrong, and think about what happened
Step 5	I keep trying when something goes wrong and help cheer others up
Step 6	I keep trying when something goes wrong and encourage others to keep trying too
Step 7	I look for opportunities in difficult situations
Step 8	I look for opportunities in difficult situations, and share these with others
Step 9	I look for opportunities in difficult situations, and adapt plans to use these opportunities
Step 10	I look for opportunities in difficult situations, and create new plans to use these opportunities
Step 11	I identify risks and gains in opportunities
Step 12	I identify risks and gains in opportunities, and make plans to manage them
Step 13	I support others to stay positive, by managing my own responses
Step 14	I support others to stay positive, by helping others to see opportunities
Step 15	I support others to stay positive, by helping others to see opportunities and creating plans to achieve them

Staying Positive Step 0

Step 0: I can tell when I feel positive or negative

To achieve Step 0, individuals will be able to recognise when they are feeling positive or negative.

This is the first step in the skill of Staying Positive – the ability to identify emotions that are mainly positive and those that are primarily negative in themselves.

Building blocks

The building blocks of this step are:

- I understand what emotions are
- I know that emotions might feel positive or negative
- I know why understanding emotions is important

Reflection questions

- What is an emotion?
- What do we mean by feeling positive?
- What do we mean by feeling negative?
- Why do we have emotions?
- How can we use our emotions to help us?

What you need to know

Emotions: positive and negative

An emotion is a strong feeling that is caused by something that is happening. There are broadly two different types of emotions:

- *Positive emotions:* These emotions make us feel good, and that we want to continue to feel like this. We might describe ourselves as being happy, excited, or calm.
- *Negative emotions:* These emotions make us feel bad, and we want to stop feeling like this. We might describe ourselves as feeling sad, angry, or scared.

Lots of different things cause our emotions, and here are some examples of emotions that we might feel (of course, there are many more):

Positive emotions	Negative emotions
Happy: • Joy • Grateful • Optimistic Excited: • Amused • Energetic • Inspired Calm: • Kind • Loving • Relaxed	Sad: • Disappointed • Tired • Fed up Angry: • Irritated • Angry • Upset Scared: • Nervous • Anxious • Frightened

Do you think you can recognise when you feel these different emotions? Sometimes it can help to talk to someone else you trust when you feel positive or negative but can't work out exactly what it is that you are feeling.

Why emotions are important

In life, we will feel different emotions at different times. This is a normal part of how we think about what is going on around us. Sometimes our feelings change quickly, and other times we might feel the same way for a longer time.

It can be confusing and challenging if we feel negative emotions without understanding what we are feeling. However, if we can work out what the cause is, then we can often do something to change that feeling. For example:

- If we feel tired, then we can rest.
- If we feel disappointed, then we can either try to fix the situation or look for something exciting to do instead.
- If we feel angry, we might need to take some time to calm down, and then we can talk to the person who has made us angry or help to fix the situation.
- If we feel scared, then we might be able to speak to someone about what we are afraid of, and we find some ways of making that better.

If we take the time to think about how we are feeling, we can start working out how to change our feelings from negative to positive.

Teaching it

To teach this step:

- The teacher can introduce the idea of emotions and ask learners to think about occasions when they have felt positive or negative emotions. If it doesn't come up naturally in the discussion, introduce the three broad types of feelings for each of positive and negative:
    - Positive: Happy, Excited, Calm
    - Negative: Sad, Angry, Scared
- Ensure that learners understand what each of these means. They could then be asked to come up with ideas of when they might feel those different emotions.
- This activity could be extended to a set of different hypothetical scenarios with learners identifying the feelings that they might feel in each of those.

Reinforcing it

This step can be reinforced in different ways, depending on the age and context of the learners. In a primary school setting, learners could regularly check in on how they are feeling at different times throughout the school day.

In a secondary school setting, the use of a reflective journal or other personal space for reflection on learners' feelings might be appropriate.

Assessing it

This step is best assessed through discussion. For example, asking learners to identify different positive or negative emotions that they might feel, and in what situation they might experience them. This sort of assessment has to be managed carefully. The focus should remain on whether learners can identify when they feel positive or negative.

Staying Positive Step 1

Step 1: I can tell when others feel positive or negative

To achieve Step 1, individuals will be able to recognise positive and negative emotions in others.

In the previous step, the focus was on individuals being able to identify positive and negative feelings in themselves. For this step, the extension is to recognise them in others too.

Building blocks

The building blocks of this step are:

- I explain what positive and negative emotions look like
- I know what events might lead to positive and negative emotions
- I recognise and name emotions in others

Reflection questions

- How can you tell when someone is feeling positive or negative?
- How can you tell what emotions other people are feeling?
- Aside from how someone looks, what else might help you to understand how someone is feeling?
- How can you use your understanding of the situation to help work out how someone is feeling?

What you need to know

How to spot positive emotions

In the previous step, we looked at the range of different emotions, which we can think of as being broadly positive or negative.

It is not always easy to tell what emotion someone is feeling, and some people might choose to try to hide how they are feeling for different reasons. However, we can also pick up some clues about how people are feeling:

Positive emotions	How you might be able to tell
Happy: • Joy • Grateful • Optimistic	Happy people tend to smile, and to look at you directly. They might also laugh and seem comfortable.
Excited: • Amused • Energetic • Inspired	People who are excited tend to be very active and look like they have lots of energy, like they want to get on and do something.
Calm: • Kind • Loving • Relaxed	Calm people are likely to have a more neutral facial expression, although they might smile a bit. They seem to be content to stay where they are, rather than having lots of energy to use.

How to spot negative emotions

We might also pick up clues for negative emotions that people might be feeling. For example:

Negative emotions	How you might be able to tell
Sad: • Disappointed • Tired • Fed up	People who are feeling sad are unlikely to be smiling and might have downturned mouths. They are unlikely to laugh and might cry or look like they could cry.
Angry: • Irritated • Angry • Upset	People who are angry tend to have a lot of energy. They might shout or talk loudly and look red-faced. They might frown or clench their teeth together.
Scared: • Nervous • Anxious • Frightened	People who are scared might not look directly at you but look around. They might seem twitchy and are unlikely to laugh or smile.

Over time, you might well be able to get better at recognising emotions in other people by looking for some of these signs.

What events cause different feelings

As well as seeing how someone looks, we can also use our understanding of a *situation* to help us to guess how someone might be feeling. This is another vital source of information to help us to work out someone else's emotions.

This is because in most cases, emotions are linked to what is going on. By understanding events, we might be able to understand how someone else would be feeling. This ability to think about the feelings of someone else is called *empathy*.

As some examples:

Positive emotions	What might cause this
Happy: • Joy • Grateful • Optimistic	Things are going well, someone has got good news or is having an enjoyable day doing something that they like doing, with people they like.
Excited: • Amused • Energetic • Inspired	Something is going to happen, which is likely to mean something good for that person, or they are doing something which is using a lot of energy but for a positive outcome.
Calm: • Kind • Loving • Relaxed	Things are relaxed, and there is no pressure. Someone is having a pleasant time with people they like or love.

Events might also lead to negative emotions for people. For example:

Negative emotions	What might cause this
Sad: Disappointed Tired Fed up	Something bad has happened, which might have been expected or unexpected. Alternatively, someone has been working too hard or has not had enough rest.
Angry: Irritated Angry Upset	Something bad has happened to that person that they do not feel was fair. They might blame someone or something for what has happened and might want it to be made right.
Scared: Nervous Anxious Frightened	Someone feels that something bad might be about to happen - either they know that something bad is coming, or they think that it could happen. People are often scared when faced with uncertainty.

Of course, it is essential to remember that not everyone will react in the same way to different events and that not all emotions that people feel are linked to what is happening there and then. Feelings can be complicated and can sometimes be affected by mental health difficulties.

However, thinking about what is going on for someone, as well as how they look, can help to give a better idea of their feelings.

Teaching it

To teach this step:

The teacher could start by reminding learners about what different emotions might look like and how they can be identified, using some of the content from Step 0.

The teacher could start with the three main categories of emotions for each of positive and negative and ask learners whether they can recreate what those facial expressions might look like for each emotion. This can be extended to draw or write down what those look like – for example, learners could create a poster.

The teacher can ask learners to think about what situations or scenarios might lead to the different emotions and write down some ideas. The learners could be posed a series of hypothetical scenarios and asked to imagine what the emotional response of someone else might be to those events.

Reinforcing it

This step lends itself to being reinforced in different areas of learning. For example, learners might occasionally reflect on how they are feeling and how they think other people might be feeling depending on what is going on.

At other times, when events are described in history, literature, or geography, learners could be asked for their reflections on how the individuals involved might have felt at those times and why.

Assessing it

This step is best assessed through discussion or a reflective exercise. For example, learners could write about how individuals involved in events they are familiar with felt at different times. They might also identify how they think individuals in pictures are feeling and why. Reflection with learners during individual tasks might also be helpful here.

Staying Positive Step 2

Step 2: I keep trying when something goes wrong

To achieve Step 2, individuals will show that they can keep trying when something goes wrong.

In earlier steps, the focus was on identifying emotions in themselves and others. This is an essential precursor to being able to manage the emotional response to give up when something goes wrong, and to keep trying instead.

Building blocks

The building blocks of this step are:

- I know typical emotional responses to something going wrong
- I explain the downsides of giving up
- I know different strategies to motivate myself to keep trying

Reflection questions

- How do you feel when something goes wrong?
- Can you give any examples?
- Why might negative emotions make you want to give up?
- How can you try to keep going instead?

What you need to know

How we feel when something goes wrong

None of us ever want something to go wrong for ourselves. Unfortunately, in life there is a huge amount that is far beyond our control, and so it is inevitable that somethings things go wrong.

These might be small things such as a cancelled train or bus, a letter getting lost in the post, or losing something. Or they might be much more significant things such as the death of someone we know, the loss of a job, or becoming ill.

When something goes wrong, we swing into feeling negative emotions that we have been looking at already:

Negative emotions	The effect
Sad: • Disappointed • Tired • Fed up	It is normal to feel deflated when something bad happens. We might want to give up or that we have lost the energy to continue to try at something. We might feel that there is now no hope of success.
Angry: • Irritated • Angry • Upset	We might feel angry if we feel that it was unfair that this setback happened. Perhaps we feel that someone else was to blame, or that we are being unfairly punished for something. We feel the need to try to put it right or get some sort of justice or fairness back.
Scared: • Nervous • Anxious • Frightened	Alternatively, we might feel scared. Perhaps we now don't know what to do next, or feel that if something bad has happened once, then more bad things might happen soon.

It is important to recognise that it is very natural and normal to have a strong emotional response to something going wrong. Sometimes, we will have a combination of all of these emotions, or feel them at different times, particularly in response to something which has gone very wrong – like the death of a loved one.

However, we also need to avoid letting our emotional responses overwhelm us.

Overcoming the urge to give up

We all feel like giving up sometimes. If you feel sad, angry, or scared, the natural response can be to take yourself out of the situation and do something else.

In some cases, for example if you are in danger, then that is the right response.

At other times though, we need to think about how to be *resilient*. That is, how do we keep going despite feeling negative emotions?

There are a few things which might help you:

- *Recognise your emotions and why you feel like that:* It can be valuable to see your feelings and explore them. Naming your feelings can be very helpful in understanding and eventually managing them.
- *Focus on what has been going well:* While there might be a setback, there are probably also lots of things that have been going well. It's important not to lose sight of the positive things when something has been going well.
- *Put the setback in perspective:* For smaller setbacks, there are probably alternative ways to achieve something. A late train probably just means being a bit late for something, a lost letter can be resent. Even more significant setbacks will not be as overwhelming as they might first appear, even if they are rightly things that will cause great sadness.
- *Think about taking positive action:* When you feel ready to, think about what you could do next which would be a positive way forward.

These ideas are all explored further in the following steps. The focus for now is on not immediately giving up on what you are doing. Instead, it is about recognising those emotions and that the emotional feeling of stopping is not necessarily the right call.

Teaching it

To teach this step:

- The teacher can introduce a discussion of when things have gone wrong for them and how they felt in response.
- They can then pose other hypothetical or real scenarios that learners will be familiar with and ask them how they think the individuals involved felt as a result of those events.
- This can be expanded to learners reflecting individually on small setbacks they have experienced and how they felt as a response.
- The teacher can then open up a discussion about how when we face setbacks and negative emotions, we can sometimes think that the best way of stopping those negative emotions is to stop what we are trying to do. However, negative emotions almost always pass. Instead, we should try to take positive action.

Reinforcing it

This step can be effectively reinforced in several ways. Sometimes when learners are facing setbacks themselves, a teacher can play an influential role in helping them to identify negative emotions they are feeling in response, and coach them to continue to persist even in the face of setbacks.

Learning about other world events, communities, or characters in literature can also provide a range of scenarios with setbacks, which can be useful for framing a discussion about overcoming the urge to give up.

Assessing it

This step is best assessed through discussion and sustained observation, as learners face setbacks in their studies. It might also be explored through discussion, talking to learners, about how they respond to setbacks in their wider lives beyond school.

Staying Positive Step 3

Step 3: I keep trying and stay calm when something goes wrong

To achieve Step 3, individuals should react to setbacks by staying calm and continuing to try hard at the task, if appropriate.

In the previous step, the focus was on individuals continuing to work at something when something goes wrong. This step builds on that by focusing on not just persisting but staying calm to allow for a measured response.

Building blocks

The building blocks of this step are:

- I know typical actions people take to emotional responses
- I know different strategies to help me stay calm
- I know how staying calm can help me to keep trying

Reflection questions

- How do you feel when something goes wrong?
- When might you feel angry? When might you feel upset?
- How do you behave if you are angry or upset?
- How can you stay calm when something goes wrong?
- Why is this important?

What you need to know

Managing an emotional response

In the previous step, we explored how things going wrong can often lead to a negative emotional reaction.

Sometimes when something bad happens, we might feel sad. However, sometimes we have a stronger negative emotional response of feeling angry or scared:

Angry: • Irritated • Angry • Upset	We might feel angry if we feel that it was unfair that this setback happened. Perhaps we feel that someone else was to blame, or that we are being unfairly punished for something. We feel the need to try to put it right or get some sort of justice or fairness back.
Scared: • Nervous • Anxious • Frightened	Alternatively, we might feel scared. Perhaps we now don't know what to do next, or feel that if something bad has happened once, then more bad things might happen soon.

When we have one of these emotional responses, we might take actions which end up making things much worse:

- When we are *scared*, we try to protect ourselves. This can be a sensible step if we are in danger and need protection. However, sometimes we want to run away from something when we are not really in danger, we are just worried. If we run away in this situation, we might end up being unable to continue with what we are doing. Essentially, we end up giving up.
- When we are *angry,* we behave quite differently. Being angry makes us feel like we have energy, but we might end up taking actions which are poorly thought through. There is a term, 'red mist descending', which describes what happens when we are very angry. It means that when we have a strong emotional response, we stop being able to see clearly what is going on. Instead, we look to blame someone or to try to fix an injustice. We might end up being aggressive to other people or situations and behave in ways that are not appropriate, damaging relationships in the process.

For these reasons, we need to think about how to avoid these emotional responses when something goes wrong.

How to stay calm

Calmness is a positive emotion which is when we are settled and content with a situation. It is not a strong positive emotion like happiness, or an energetic, positive emotion like excitement.

It is challenging to move from a setback to strong positive emotions, but with practice it is possible to neutralise strong negative emotions, to get back to a state of calm.

Being calm is helpful because it gives space to think about a setback or a problem to think through what could be done instead. It is tough to make good plans or develop new ideas if you are not feeling calm first.

There are a few steps to calm down if you feel angry:

1. It is essential to make a *choice* to calm down. It will take thoughtful effort to be able to calm down and will take energy.
2. You might need some *space*. Particularly if you have just got the bad news or feel upset about someone's actions, you should try to take yourself out of that situation so you have time and space to think. Combining this with fresh air works well.
3. You could *think* about something that calms you down, like people you love, happy memories, or something you are looking forward to.
4. Sometimes people focus on *breathing slowly* as there is some evidence that this helps you to focus.
5. Some people find *counting* in their heads an effective way of avoiding an immediate adverse reaction.
6. *Talk* to someone who you trust and who is supportive. Sometimes talking about something can help you to feel less angry or upset by it.
7. Sometimes *physical activity* can help, as can trying to relax your body. If we are tense, it often causes us to tense our shoulders, for example.

Some of these different approaches will be more or less effective for different people and you might find your own methods that work particularly well for you. However, always remember that the critical step is to recognise when you are feeling angry or upset and make the *decision* to become calm.

Teaching it

To teach this step:

- The teacher can introduce this step by reminding learners about the broad different positive and negative emotions they might feel at different times: happy, excited, calm, sad, angry, or scared.
- The teacher could talk learners through thinking about different setbacks that might lead them to feel angry or scared, and then what the subsequent consequences might be. Learners could reflect on a time they have felt angry or scared and what they then did and how that made the situation worse.
- The teacher can then ask learners for any suggestions that they might have about how to reduce their feelings of anger or fear in the face of a setback. This list can be compared to the advice given here and discussed.
- Learners could consolidate this learning by producing a list of tips or poster to share this insight with others.

Reinforcing it

This step can be reinforced in a classroom setting. It might be worth having a visual reminder of what an individual can do to stay calm in the face of setbacks which can be referred to if learners are scared or angry in the context of the classroom or elsewhere in the school.

It might also be possible to provide learners with regular reflective opportunities for them to think about their emotions of the week, and how they have managed any setbacks.

Assessing it

This step is best assessed through observing how learners respond to setbacks in the classroom or things going wrong – including how they interact with their teachers, parents, and peers outside of learning.

Staying Positive Step 4

Step 4: I keep trying when something goes wrong, and think about what happened

To achieve Step 4, individuals will show that they can persist at a task but also respond to setbacks by thinking about what they can learn from when things go wrong.

In earlier steps, the focus was on how to keep trying and stay calm when something goes wrong, with a focus on managing their emotional response. The development here is to introduce some analysis of what caused the problem, and how to learn from it.

Building blocks

The building blocks of this step are:

- I manage my emotional response to something going wrong
- I take a positive approach to learning from something going wrong
- I analyse when something goes wrong and learn lessons

Reflection questions

- How can things going wrong also be chances to learn something new?
- What emotional response do you need to learn from something going wrong?
- How can we learn lessons when something goes wrong?
- What are some of the important questions we should be asking ourselves?

What you need to know

Taking a positive approach to learning from setbacks

In previous steps, we have explored how we might have a negative emotional response when things go wrong. We looked at how these emotions might include sadness, anger or fear.

However, when something goes wrong, there is often learning that we can take from that experience. This learning might come from several places:

- We might have made a mistake ourselves, and this is what led to something going wrong. We can learn not to make the same mistake again in the future – for example, if we missed a train, we can learn to allow more time in the future. If we did not do as well as we hoped in a test, we could learn the need to revise more in the future.
- The thing that went wrong might have been beyond our control, but looking back we can see that we could have done something to have been ready in case it had happened. This is called being *aware of risk,* where *risks* are things that could go wrong.

- We might learn something new about ourselves – for example, we might see that when we are late, we get upset or angry. In this case, we can recognise these emotions better in the future and take steps to calm ourselves down (see *Step 3*).
- Something not working might teach us something. In science, the process of learning is driven as much as by things that do not work, as things that do. Science is all about creating ideas and then testing them through lots of different experiments. Most of the ideas that people come up with are wrong but they test them to find out.

Along with science, lots of businesses and other organisations also take the attitude that it is good to try things out even if they end up going a little bit wrong, because we learn useful information through trying them out. This testing of hypotheses is explored a lot more in *Problem Solving Step 12*.

Learning lessons when something goes wrong

The most important part of learning lessons when something goes wrong is about having the right attitude and *wanting* to learn those lessons.

For us to be ready to learn lessons, we must first get into an emotional state where we can think clearly and *rationally* about what has happened. Being able to think *rationally* means being able to think in a sensible and logical way.

In previous steps, we looked at how to move from natural reactions of being sad, angry, or scared to be in a state of calm. This is important to do if we are going to be ready for learning.

Then, learning is about asking ourselves a series of questions:

Firstly, analysing the situation itself:

- What happened?
- Why does it feel that something has gone wrong?
- What is the effect of that happening?
- What role did I play in the events, and what was out of my control?

Secondly, thinking about what could have prevented that happening:

- Could I have predicted that would have happened?
- What could I have done to have prevented that happening?

Thirdly, thinking about what lessons to take into the future:

- What do I know now that I did not know before?
- What would I recommend that others do or don't do based on my experience?
- How will I make sure I put what I have learned into use to help me?

This sort of analysis, once calm, means that even when something goes wrong, we can take something positive out of it, some useful learning that we can use in the future.

Teaching it

To teach this step:

- The teacher can introduce the step and the question of how we might learn something when things go wrong. Each of the four main types of learning opportunities can be introduced, and the teacher could model an example of each in turn. Learners could share their own examples from their experience at school or from their wider lives.
- The teacher can remind learners of the importance of getting back into a positive, or at least neutral, emotional state before they can think about what happened and review it.
- Learners could contribute their ideas of questions that they could ask themselves to review a situation and make improvements. The teacher can organise them into the three broad categories of:
    - Analysing what happened
    - Understanding if anything could have prevented it
    - Consolidating what learning to take into the future
- Learners could then reflect on a real incident from their own lives, or analyse a created scenario either alone, or in groups.

Reinforcing it

This is a step that lends itself well to the classroom as it can be a powerful tool for turning setbacks into more positive learning experiences. It can be applied to events that are being learnt about – natural disasters, historical events, scientific experiments, events in literature – or to events in learners' own lives.

Assessing it

This step can be assessed through a discussed hypothetical task, but a key part of mastering this step is the learners' ability to control their own emotional response first, and then to be able to look at a situation reasonably objectively. For this reason, discussion of events from learners' own lives might make for a better assessment approach, but this will need to be supplemented with a sustained view of how learners really react to things going wrong.

Staying Positive Step 5

Step 5: I keep going when something goes wrong and help cheer others up

To achieve Step 5, individuals will show persistence in the face of setbacks, and also be able to influence the emotional reactions of others positively too.

In earlier steps, the focus was on how individuals focus on their emotional response to things going wrong – persisting where appropriate, staying calm, and being able to analyse and take learning out of a situation. This next step focuses on engaging with others and supporting them to manage their emotional responses too.

Building blocks

The building blocks of this step:

- I identify clues to recognise others' emotional responses
- I understand why cheering others up is helpful
- I use appropriate strategies to cheer up others when something goes wrong

Reflection questions

- When something goes wrong, how do you sometimes react?
- How do you think other people feel when something goes wrong?
- How might you be able to tell?
- Why is it helpful to cheer people up?
- How can you cheer other people up when something goes wrong?
- How does it depend on what emotional state they are in?

What you need to know

How others might react when things go wrong

In the early steps of this skill, we looked at how we sometimes react when things go wrong. We explored three broad categories of negative emotions:

- *Sad:* Including feeling disappointed, tired, or fed up
- *Angry:* Including feeling irritated, angry, or upset
- *Scared:* Including nervous, anxious, or frightened

Since our immediate natural reaction to things going wrong is often one of these, or a combination of them, we should expect that other people might have a similar set of reactions to something going wrong.

We might be able to use clues from their facial expressions, behaviour, or things that they say to help us to understand what combination of emotions they are feeling. This is explored more in *Step 1*, but as a reminder:

Negative emotions	How you might be able to tell
Sad: • Disappointed • Tired • Fed up	People who are feeling sad are unlikely to be smiling and might have downturned mouths. They are unlikely to laugh and might cry or look like they could cry.
Angry: • Irritated • Angry • Upset	People who are angry tend to have a lot of energy. They might shout or talk loudly and look red-faced. They might frown or clench their teeth together.
Scared: • Nervous • Anxious • Frightened	People who are scared might not look directly at you but look around. They might seem twitchy and are unlikely to laugh or smile.

There are a couple of other essential things to consider when thinking about the reactions that individuals have when something goes wrong:

- They might react not just to the thing that has gone wrong but to what they fear the *consequences* of that might be – that is, what will happen next as a result. In some situations, individuals will be worried about whether they will be in trouble themselves or whether it will cause them more problems in the future.
- They might also look to *blame* someone or something else for what went wrong. This can sometimes be a negative result of working in a team, an idea which is explored more in the *Teamwork* skill.

It is helpful to be aware of these additional influences on people's reactions when you try to understand how they are feeling.

Cheering others up

In the previous steps, we have thought about what the impact of being in a negative emotional state can be on us as individuals. We saw how being angry or scared stopped us from wanting to continue with a task even if we really should, and how it stops us from being able to think logically about what happened. (See *Steps 3 and 4*)

We also saw that it is possible to calm ourselves down in a variety of ways (See *Step 2*).

When thinking about what will cheer other people up, we should start by thinking about how they are feeling. The right thing to do will depend a lot on their emotions and choosing the wrong approach might end up making things worse.

Negative emotions	What you might be able to do
Sad: • Disappointed • Tired • Fed up	• Listen to them and show that you understand how they are feeling – they might feel better for talking about it. • Talk to them about the things that have been going well, or other setbacks you might have faced in the past, and how you overcame these.
Angry: • Irritated • Angry • Upset	• Give them a chance to calm themselves down if they are trying to do this. You might give them some space or let them go for a walk if they want to. • If they want to talk about it, then you can listen to them and show you understand how they are feeling. You do not have to agree with everything they say. • When they are calm enough, you can focus the conversation on some of the positives of the situation. • Try to avoid talk of blame or retaliation.
Scared: • Nervous • Anxious • Frightened	• Reassure them that although the thing going wrong might be disappointing, that the other things that they fear might happen as a result are unlikely. • Talk about some of the positive things that are going on and how similar problems have been overcome before.

The better you know the other individuals who are involved, the easier it usually is to think about what will be most effective in getting them back into a positive emotional state.

Remember not to rush it. Some people will take different amounts of time to get back to that positive emotional state than others, depending on them as individuals and the size and nature of what went wrong.

Teaching it

To teach this step:

- The teacher can remind learners about the different emotional responses that individuals might have when things go wrong. It is worth reminding learners that if they have those reactions, then it is reasonable to expect that others might have those reactions too.
- The teacher can facilitate a conversation about why it is important to support others to return to a positive emotional state, and then think about some of the different approaches depending on whether the other individual or individuals are sad, angry, or scared.
- Learners might share some of their experiences that help to illustrate these different approaches and what did or didn't work for them.
- This could be built upon through simulation or role-play where learners take on different roles and try out techniques for cheering up others acting out different emotional states.

Reinforcing it

This step lends itself well to reinforcement in the classroom setting, where there are opportunities for learners to work together. In these cases, there will inevitably be setbacks or things that go wrong, and these provide opportunities for learners to apply their skill of being able to cheer others up.

Reflection after such events will help learners to capture those experiences for themselves and make it more likely they can perform the skill step effectively in the future.

Assessing it

This step can be assessed through a hypothetical exercise where learners are presented with different characters displaying different behaviours and either discuss or write about how they might cheer them up after something has gone wrong.

It might also be assessed through a team exercise where a setback is deliberately introduced to identify where learners are able to quickly stabilise their team and cheer others up.

Staying Positive Step 6

Step 6: I keep trying when something goes wrong and encourage others to keep trying too

To achieve Step 6, individuals will show that when faced with a setback, they can cheer others up and then encourage them to keep trying.

In the previous step, the focus expanded from the individual managing their own emotions to thinking about others' feelings too. This step builds on this by focusing not just on how to cheer others up, but to keep them focused on persisting with a task.

Building blocks

The building blocks of this step are learning:

- How motivation can change when something goes wrong
- How to encourage others to remain motivated and keep trying

Reflection questions

- I define and describe what motivation is
- I recognise how motivation can change when something goes wrong
- I encourage other to remain motivated and keep trying

What you need to know

The Role of Motivation

Motivation is your desire to do something – in this case, to continue with a task. Motivation is affected by several things, including:

- *How much we feel we need something:* If something is essential for our survival (for example, finding water in a desert), then we will be highly motivated because the cost of not getting it would be disastrous. However, we can also see things in terms of high reward. We are more likely to be motivated to do something where the positive reward is high.
- *How high the likelihood of success is:* When we think about what reward we are likely to get from something, we adjust that according to the *probability* or *likelihood* that we are successful. If we think something is likely to be successful if we work at it, then we tend to be more motivated. However, if it feels like it will be just luck whether we achieve the reward or not, then there is lower motivation.

We have already looked at how things going wrong, or setbacks, can affect our emotions. These emotions can have a significant effect on how we feel about continuing something – and we saw that other people are likely to feel similarly.

There is also another effect, though, which is on our *motivation*. If something bad happens, we might feel that either the potential reward has been reduced, or that the likelihood that we are successful has been reduced. In simple terms, we might not get what we wanted from what we were doing any more.

If we lose motivation, we are much less likely to stick at something.

Encouraging others to remain motivated

Before we can get motivated again, we need to be able to manage our emotional response to a setback, which is what we explored in some of the earlier steps. In *Step 5*, we also looked at how to cheer up others when something goes wrong.

This is an essential first step. Then we can focus on how to rebuild the motivation of other people to keep going with something.

It might be that, once the emotional response has weakened, people can see there has been little change in the reward for their efforts, or the likelihood of success. In this case, showing people this might help them to be motivated again.

However, if this doesn't work, there are some other ways of motivating others, by getting them to think about:

- How much work they have already put in
- How much progress has already been made
- How much other members of the team, or in the wider world, are relying on them to get the task done
- Other examples of individuals who have been through similar adversity and come out of it positively and been successful in the end
- How it is possible to adapt to overcome the setback

It is often important to appeal both to the *rational* side and to the *emotional* side of how people think.

Finally, it is important to maintain *positivity* – focusing on what is going well, encouraging people to see progress, and recognising their efforts. This is likely to be much more effective than being *negative* about them not putting in enough effort, needing to get a grip or similar.

Teaching it

To teach this step:

- The teacher can remind learners about what they already know about how to manage their own emotional response to setbacks and how this can be extended to support others to cheer up in the face of something going wrong.
- This can be extended to a discussion around motivation. It is worth highlighting that the rational basis for motivation is the focus here, but there are other reasons why people might persist too, including their values. The teacher could model what motivates them – what they (or others) get out of their efforts.
- The teacher can then ask learners to reflect on what they think would motivate them to continue with something in the face of a setback, and gather these ideas.
- Finally, learners could use role-play based on hypothetical or real examples to practice applying some of these ideas.

Reinforcing it

This step is best reinforced when there are group activities already taking place, where learners might need to face setbacks together. Here, the teacher can help to scaffold learners in thinking through how motivation might have changed in response to something going wrong and facilitate them thinking through some of the motivating questions together. Over time, learners can take more of a lead in motivating one another, a process which will be supported by opportunities for reflection and feedback along the way.

Assessing it

This step is best assessed through observation in a structured activity. For example, learners might be working together on an activity where something happens to reduce the likelihood of a successful outcome. It can be identified through the assessment where learners were able to maintain the motivation of others in their team to complete the task.

Staying Positive Step 7

Step 7: I look for opportunities in difficult situations

To achieve Step 7, individuals will have to be able to identify where opportunities exist, even in difficult situations.

In earlier steps, the focus was on how individuals respond to something going wrong. The focus now moves on to how to find opportunities in difficult situations.

Building blocks

The building blocks of this step are:

- I identify the challenges or risks in a situation
- I recognise that opportunities exist even in difficult situations
- I know how to start identifying opportunities in difficult situations

Reflection questions

- What do people mean when they say to 'look on the bright side' of something?
- What does it mean to say that 'every cloud has a silver lining'? Can you give some examples?
- How can you get a good view of a difficult situation?
- How can you identify opportunities in difficult situations?

What you need to know

There are always opportunities

We may be familiar, depending where in the world we are, with phrases like 'every cloud has a silver lining' or to 'look on the bright side' of something. What these clichés are getting at is the idea that very few situations are so absolutely terrible that it is not possible either to make something a bit better, or to use an opportunity that has emerged.

Of course, there are certainly incidents in world history or even closer to home where it feels that a situation has been bleak. Most difficult situations we deal with in our day-to-day lives, however, are much more balanced; they might be miserable, but they are rarely catastrophic.

On a small scale, something like missing a train might mean more time to read a book, to prepare for a meeting or to spend with friends. Being unable to get tickets to something you want to attend means you have saved some money and can use it for something else you would enjoy. An unsatisfactory test result has taught you that there is an area of your learning that you need to focus on more.

More widely, there are often upsides to a situation, but we need to understand that situation a bit better first.

Identifying opportunities

In order to find the opportunity in a situation, we have to first try to understand the situation and what has happened fully.

We then want to understand what the positive and negative sides of that situation are.

If we are dealing with an *existing situation,* then we can force ourselves to think about both what the positive and negative sides are. If you are feeling upset, then it is easy to feel that there is only a negative side to the situation. However, over time you might begin to see some positives. It is worth writing these as two lists, side by side:

Positives	*Negatives*
What is good about this situation – this is likely to be harder to write	What is bad about this situation – this is likely to be easier to write

To do this, it is sometimes helpful to try to take yourself out of a situation and imagine that you are there as an observer. This helps to put some separation between you and the emotional response you have to the events. You could ask yourself the question, if I were someone else, what would I tell me were the positives in this situation?

Alternatively, we might be dealing with *a situation that is not yet fixed but is still unfolding.* In this case, we have to think slightly differently. We cannot just think in terms of positive or negatives, but we can think in terms of threats and opportunities. Threats are things that might happen with negative effects, whereas opportunities are things that might happen with positive effects.

Again, writing these down side-by-side is a good way of forcing a balanced approach to thinking about these:

Opportunities	*Threats*
Things that might happen with positive effects	Things that might happen with negative effects

Having identified the positives or negatives in a situation, or the opportunities and threats, we can choose to focus on the positives or the opportunities. This means thinking about not just how to avoid the negatives or threats, but how we can take action to achieve a positive outcome for ourselves.

As with much of staying positive, the crucial part is deciding to do so.

Teaching it

To teach this step:

- The teacher should start by being sensitive about setting the context for learners around this step. The difficult situations that learners have faced in their own lives are likely to be extremely varied across a group, and it is important to be sensitive to that fact and to make learners aware of that possibility.
- This step can be explored through discussion, asking learners to reflect on the notion that there can be a positive side to tricky situations and asking them to draw on examples from their own lives if they wish to contribute them. The teacher can model this with some examples from their own lives too.

- The critical point to emphasise is the importance of being able to try to take an objective view of a situation by trying to get some distance between the reality and their emotional response to it.
- Different examples can be used for learners to think about the positive and negative, or opportunities and threats that arise from them. They could do this in groups initially, and then work individually once they have had a chance to build their understanding.

Reinforcing it

This step is one that can be reinforced in several ways in a school setting. For example, when discussing difficult situations in history, geography or literature, learners could be encouraged to think not just about the negatives or threats, but also the positives or opportunities. This is particularly helpful because it can lend itself to more dispassionate analysis.

There will also be setbacks for individual learners, and here a coaching role can support learners to identify for themselves what some of the opportunities or positives are in situations and focus on those.

Assessing it

This step can be assessed through an exercise such as giving the learners a situation to analyse to draw out the positives and negatives in it.

There may also be an element of assessment through observation, where learners can discuss a particular setback or difficult situation and the positives that they can identify in that situation.

Staying Positive Step 8

Step 8: I look for opportunities in difficult situations and share these with others

To achieve Step 8, individuals will show that they can identify real opportunities in challenging situations and then articulate them to others.

In the previous step, the focus was on how to look for opportunities in difficult situations. This step expands on that by also thinking about how to communicate those opportunities to others.

Building blocks

The building blocks of this step are learning:

- I identify appropriate language to express the positive side of a difficult situation
- I effectively share the positive side of a difficult situation
- I involve others in identifying a positive side for themselves

Reflection questions

- What can be the risk of sharing the positive side of a difficult situation?
- How can you avoid making the situation worse?
- What do you need to do so that your suggestions will be well received?
- How can involving others with identifying the positive side be helpful?
- How could you do this effectively?

What you need to know

Sharing the positive side

In *Step 5* and *Step 6* of this skill, we explored working with others when facing setbacks. We particularly highlighted a couple of things:

- Firstly, the need to ensure that others are in the right emotional state to be able to respond appropriately to events. This means moving them out of a state of being angry, scared, or upset and trying to support them to be in a more neutral place by cheering them up (See *Step 5* for more)
- Secondly, the need to focus on others' motivation and some of the ways to boost their motivation. For instance, by focusing on what has already been achieved and other positive reinforcement.

It is essential not to forget these previous steps, because if you do not put these building blocks in place, then you will struggle to communicate opportunities in difficult situations, as people will not be in well-placed to hear them.

If you *do* put these foundations in place, though, then you can bring people with you to think about the opportunities. A key part of that is not to forget the negative side of the situation and to acknowledge what the difficulties are.

If you don't do this, then people will think that you have misunderstood the reality of the situation, or that you are overly optimistic. For them to take you seriously when you present your ideas about the opportunities, they need to believe that you take the situation itself seriously first.

Once you do this, you can then take them through the journey that you went on thinking about what some of the positives or opportunities might be. Give them time to digest what these are because they will need the time to change their thinking only about the negative side of the situation to taking in the positive in the same way that it might have taken you time to make this change too.

Ultimately though, people are motivated by the idea of positive outcomes from a situation. So, if they believe that it is possible to find a positive result, even in a difficult situation, or at least make the situation slightly better, then they are likely to take you seriously.

Involving others in identifying the positive side

Even more effective than telling people about the positive side of a difficult situation is getting them to work this out for themselves.

This is a common trait of humans that you might have touched on already in some of the other skills. People are more invested in an idea when they feel that they came up with it themselves; this is having a *sense of ownership*.

When we own anything, we feel a greater sense of wanting to protect and look after it, and this is the same with ideas.

In this case, you can work through the same approach as you did in Step 7, thinking about the negatives and positives in a situation, or the threats and opportunities in a situation. If you can do this together, though, you will find that you will probably have more ideas than you did when you just did this alone. Just as importantly, by taking part in the exercise collectively, individuals will have more of a *sense of ownership* over the opportunities that come out at the other end, and more likely to act on them as a result.

Teaching it

To teach this step:

- The teacher should take care when introducing this topic to be sensitive to the fact that learners are likely to have considerable variations in life experiences some of which are likely to be much more challenging than others.
- It is worth spending some time to review the critical insights of *Step 5* and *Step 6*, as these are the building blocks of being able to work with others to work through something that is a setback or challenging together.
- Learners can then be taken through an exercise of sharing with peers opportunities from a difficult situation. This would work well as a hypothetical exercise (for example, the collapse of the gym block - without injuries - and the positives and negatives in that situation.)
- They could then repeat a similar exercise, but this time working as a group to develop those positives and negatives to demonstrate how they can generate more insights by working that way.

Reinforcing it

This is a step which can be deployed in the classroom through the objective assessment of a particular situation as a group, whether the scenario comes from geography, history, literature or any number of other subjects. This is a safer way of building learners' confidence in being able to analyse a situation.

It might also be expanded to group projects, working on a particular scenario. Eventually, there might be real-life occasions where it is helpful to deploy this step to analyse a situation and work through it.

Assessing it

This step can be observed through an assessed activity, for example, by building on subject learning when analysing the positives and negatives of a seemingly bad situation. Learners could be observed to see whether they are able to influence the group to find opportunities in a difficult situation.

Staying Positive Step 9

Step 9: I look for opportunities in difficult situations, and adapt plans to use these opportunities

To achieve Step 9, individuals will show that they can adapt their plans in response to challenging situations to keep going.

In the two previous steps, the focus was on how to identify opportunities in difficult situations, first as an individual, and then in the context of working with others. This step builds on these by introducing the need for action as a result of this analysis.

Building blocks

The building blocks of this step are:

- I analyse a difficult situation to review strengths and weaknesses
- I analyse a difficult situation to identify opportunities and threats
- I adapt plans to make the most of opportunities

Reflection questions

- How can we make sure we fully understand a difficult situation?
- What do we need to think about if we're going to change our plans as a result?
- How can we use our understanding of ourselves and the situation to adapt our plans?
- What should we change, and what should remain the same?

What you need to know

Analysing the situation

In *Step 7* and *Step 8*, we looked at how to try to identify opportunities in the middle of difficult situations. We saw how there are almost always positive sides to events, or at least things to do to make a difficult situation slightly better. We also saw that it is possible to help other people spot those opportunities too if we are careful about how we take them through that journey with us.

If we are going to be adapting our plans, we must get as full a view of a situation as possible. One tool that we will also see in *Aiming High Step 13* is called a SWOT analysis, which stands for:

- Strengths
- Weaknesses
- Opportunities
- Threats

The first two elements are about us, or our team, or our project so far. It is about taking an *internal perspective* on what we are already good at. We can identify strengths as those things that are going well, or that we are good at doing. Weaknesses are those areas which are not going so well, or which we do not feel we are as good at doing, or perhaps that we have less experience in doing.

The final two elements are about the situation that we are in. These are about taking an *external perspective* on the situation, both identifying the opportunities and also the threats.

When we think about adapting our plans, it is valuable to take the time to have both *internal* and *external perspectives*. Always remember, that you can ask other people for their ideas and suggestions too. Someone who is outside of the situation might have a clearer view on it than someone who is in the middle of it.

Adapting plans

If we are adapting our plans, we are assuming that there were already plans in place for what you wanted to do. These might be extensive plans for a big project, or rougher plans for a smaller undertaking.

In either case, we want to start by reminding ourselves of what we are trying to do and *what we are trying to achieve*. If we are in a situation where we have to adapt plans, it is particularly important that we don't lose sight of what the *goal* of the activity is.

For example, a postal strike might disrupt your sending a gift to a friend or relative for their birthday. However, you have to remember that the goal is to make that person know that you are thinking of them and appreciate them on their birthday – there might be lots of other ways to do that, from a thoughtful phone call or visit to arranging something nice for you to do together in the future.

Once we are clear on our goal, or goals, then we can think about how we can change our plans to adapt to a difficult situation. This is where we can bring out the threats and opportunities this gives us. For example, the postal strike means that we can't send a physical present or gift, but the opportunity is that we can use that time and effort to arrange something nice to do, and that we save some money that we can use on something else.

We can then go back to the strengths and weaknesses we identified for ourselves. If a strength is that you and the relative have a shared love of art, or dance, or music, then you could think of something you could do together to share that thing you enjoy. If you have a talent for creativity, you could make them something. However, if these were weaknesses, then best to be avoided.

Teaching it

To teach this step:

- The teacher can start by reminding learners about some of the building blocks that have got them to this stage, particularly the need to manage one's emotional response to be able to look at a situation objectively and to be able to see opportunities. This could be reviewed as a class discussion.
- The concept of thinking about strengths, weaknesses, opportunities, and threats can then be introduced as a useful tool for taking internal and external perspectives. The group could complete one analysis together of a particular situation, ideally one where all learners have enough context to be able to contribute meaningfully.
- Using this insight, learners could think about how they would recommend that someone adapts their plans accordingly. You might want to draw on other subject learning here – for example, thinking about a historical event, a scenario in literature, or a development challenge in geography.

Reinforcing it

This step can be reinforced in the classroom setting, and also applied to learners' own efforts such as when working on a project or preparing for examinations or similar. It can also be used as a tool to support analysis of difficult situations that learners might encounter when studying other subjects. They should be encouraged to think of ways that the plans of the protagonists could be adapted to respond to a difficult situation.

Assessing it

This step can be assessed through a reflection if learners are applying their skills to a particular project. The reflection could be discursive, or it could be a written reflection from learners themselves.

Alternatively, learners could complete an analysis of a situation from their studies and use this to propose how the protagonist's plans should adapt in response to that situation.

Staying Positive Step 10

Step 10: I look for opportunities in difficult situations, and create new plans to use these opportunities

To achieve Step 10, individuals will show that they can explore a situation and use their analysis to create new plans to use the opportunities they identify.

In the previous step, the focus was on how to look for opportunities in difficult situations and then adapt their plans accordingly. This step expands on this, but by looking at the creation of new plans as a result.

Building blocks

The building blocks of this step are learning:

- I review a difficult situation and identify viable opportunities
- I identify the goals we want to achieve
- I work through set stages to create a viable plan

Reflection questions

- How can we find opportunities in difficult situations?
- How can we turn analysis into new plans?
- Where should we start?
- What do we need to keep thinking about?

What you need to know

Reviewing a difficult situation

It is important to remember that almost no situation in life is ever entirely good or entirely hopeless. Instead, opportunities exist in all situations and often solving a problem is how the best ideas come about. These might be scientific discoveries, new inventions, or new businesses that turn a difficulty into an opportunity.

Strengths and weaknesses

In the previous step, we introduced the idea of the SWOT analysis. As a reminder, this is about taking two different perspectives on a particular situation.

Firstly, we want to think about ourselves, our teams, or our organisations:

- What *strengths* do we bring to a situation that might be valuable? These might include our experiences, our skills, our attitudes or knowledge, and *assets* that we have. For example, a computer, experimental equipment, or access to a factory.
- What *weaknesses* do we want to avoid? These might be gaps in any of the areas that we have already talked about. It is important to remember, though, that strengths and weaknesses are not fixed; we can learn new skills, build our experiences, or purchase equipment if we need it.

Opportunities and threats

Secondly, we want to think about the situation itself:

- What are the *threats?* That is, those things that might go wrong, risks that we face, events that might unfold, or others who might end up blocking the solution the problem that we are working on. Sometimes we avoid thinking about threats because we want to stay positive but being aware of the risks is very important for us to make the right decisions.
- What are the *opportunities*? That is, those chances that might be positive for us. These might come from new technology, more resources becoming available, or the chance to do something new. These are not always obvious, so we need to think widely about these and perhaps talk to others with different perspectives too.

If we do this exercise well, then we should end up with a clear view on a situation and see what we can bring to it as well.

Turning analysis into new plans

Creating a new plan - being able to start with a blank sheet of paper and creating something new - is an exciting thing.

The biggest trap that people fall into when creating plans is to start thinking immediately about the activity that they want to do and not thinking about what they are trying to achieve. It is essential to begin by identifying what the *goals* are of what you are trying to achieve. This is similar to thinking about the *success criteria* in *Creativity*.

In the same way that we cannot come up with really great ideas if we do not know what we are trying to solve, we cannot come up with plans if we don't know where we are trying to get to.

Different types of goals

Normally, people think in terms of two types of goals:

- *Primary goal*: The main thing to achieve. For example, it might be to find a new material that is fire resistant or to create a much more fuel-efficient engine. Wherever possible, it is good to put a number on this, so you can see how success looks. Perhaps the material should resist a temperature of 400°c, or the engine achieve more than 100 miles per gallon of fuel.
- *Secondary goals:* Additional goals that we also want to achieve and are similar to success criteria. For example, it might be that the new material must not be a risk to health or must not cost too much. Perhaps the engine needs to be easily recyclable.

These goals give us our aim, what we are working towards achieving.

Building a plan

We can then work backwards from here. The normal stages of a plan include:

- *Scoping and research:* Understanding the problem more fully.
- *Idea creation:* Developing different ideas for how the problem could be addressed or the opportunities used.
- *Testing ideas:* Putting ideas into practice and seeing how they work.

- *Reviewing and improvements:* Seeing whether the ideas worked in practice and how they might be improved. The cycle of testing ideas, reviewing, and making improvements is likely to continue until you feel confident that you are getting towards your goals.
- *Putting into practice or production:* Putting the idea into production, completing the experiments, and solving the problems.

There are lots of different approaches to creating plans depending on the situation. If the environment is predictable, then we might be able to make detailed plans with dates and times when different things will be completed, and by whom.

If the situation is changing quickly and is unpredictable, we might set goals but need to be more flexible in what we do to achieve those goals.

Teaching it

To teach this step:

- The teacher can introduce the step and how developing new plans is a step forward from simply adapting plans. It is helpful to emphasise to learners how almost all situations have elements of challenge in them, and these challenges can also lead to opportunities to resolve the challenge.
- Learners can then be introduced to a particular challenge which might emerge from some other area of their studies or a new project idea.
- The teacher could work with learners to complete a SWOT analysis together, or to work on it in smaller groups and compare approaches to check understanding.
- The teacher can then introduce learners to thinking about primary and secondary goals. This can sometimes be a difficult concept for learners to grasp, so it is helpful to provide some examples (along with numerical targets) and then ask learners to develop their own too.
- Finally, the different stages of a plan can be introduced. This can be worked on as a group.

Reinforcing it

This step is best reinforced through a sustained project or piece of work that learners develop from inception through goal planning and finally developing a plan. Even better if they then put the plan into practice so that they can see some of the challenges in reconciling their ideas and the reality.

Assessing it

This step is best assessed through a project. Learners could be given the opportunity to reflect regularly throughout the project, whether in discussion with a teacher or through written self-reflections to help them to consolidate their understanding of how to create new plans in difficult situations.

Staying Positive Step 11

Step 11: I identify risks and gains in opportunities

To achieve Step 11, individuals will show that they can assess opportunities to identify the risks and gains that they might achieve from them.

In earlier steps, the focus was on how to look for opportunities in difficult situations, and then to adapt or develop plans in response. This step builds on this by thinking about the risks and potential gains in those situations, and how to identify them.

Building blocks

The building blocks of this step are:

- I identify potential risks in opportunities
- I identify potential gains in opportunities
- I know how to compare risks and potential gains

Reflection questions

- What do we mean by risks?
- What are the potential gains of an opportunity?
- What is the value in identifying both risks and potential gains?
- How can we compare the risks and potential gains?

What you need to know

Identifying risks

Risks are those things that might happen which would have an adverse (or negative) effect. These are sometimes thought of as dangers or threats to life – and such things are certainly risks. Most risks though are more mundane like financial losses, or the loss of the opportunity to do something else.

Risks might come from the activity itself, or the broader environment. For instance, a project might be affected by events outside of its control, like a natural disaster or a pandemic. Both are worth capturing when thinking about a plan.

When we think about risks, there is a level of uncertainty – they *might* not happen. This means that we often think about risks in two dimensions:

What the impact would be: That is, what would happen if the risk came to be realised. We might look at this in financial terms, or we might simply consider whether the impact would be low, medium, or high in terms of the overall viability of what we're seeking to do.

What the likelihood is of the risk happening: That is, what is the probability that the risk will happen. In a more sophisticated model, we might be able to assign percentage probabilities to different outcomes.

Identifying potential gains

Potential gains are those things that might happen which would have a positive effect. These are the intended positive outcomes as a result of undertaking the project.

These gains might be captured in a financial model. This sometimes means that we have to attach values to certain outcomes. For instance, the UK Government's Green Book helps to show what the value of certain outcomes of a project might be, from the value of reducing a decibel of aeroplane noise for a household to cleaning up a river.

In order to calculate the potential gains, we also have to take out the direct costs of the project so that we are left with the net gain as a result of the project. For instance, a project that creates £10 of value, but costs £8 to implement has a net gain of £2 before we introduce the risk considerations.

At other times, we might simply identify the positive outcomes that we are trying to achieve without trying to attach financial values.

Balancing gains and risk

The trick then, is to make sure that we have considered the potential risks when making a decision about whether to pursue a project.

If financial values have not been attached, then this is likely to be about having a discussion and making a judgement. This is probably appropriate for small decisions, where participants have a good understanding of what they are doing.

For bigger decisions and major projects, there is normally an expectation that risks - and returns - will be considered in financial terms to make sure the project is worth doing before it is started.

Teaching it

To teach this step:

- The teacher can introduce this step by asking learners to define what is meant by risks and potential gains. This conversation can be expanded by the teacher leading a discussion about whether we should avoid all risks? This can open up the idea that almost everything in life contains some risk; the focus should be on how to evaluate whether the risk is worth it for the potential gain.
- The teacher can build on this by asking learners to identify the risks and potential gains in different scenarios (for instance, climbing a mountain, starting a business, applying to university, abseiling). This can then lead to a discussion of how you would decide whether to do each. The point is that the potential gain might be different to different people.
- The teacher can then introduce the idea that for big decisions, we might attach monetary values to risks and gains to make decisions. This might be a complex idea for some learners, so the teacher can work through an example of how to attach values to outcomes and probability-adjusted risks and then balance a decision on whether to go ahead with something.
- Finally, learners can reflect on a decision that may have coming up and analyse the risks and potential gains associated with that decision.

Reinforcing it

This step can be effectively reinforced in several subject areas, particularly business studies, economics, geography, and history. Current affairs can also be a great source of timely examples of the importance of weighing up gains and risks when making decisions.

Assessing it

This step is best assessed in combination:

- Firstly, check that learners understand the key concepts and definitions of risk and potential gain.
- Secondly, ask them to complete an analysis of these for a scenario, and to find a method of reaching a justifiable conclusion about whether the project should be undertaken.

Staying Positive Step 12

Step 12: I identify risks and gain in opportunities, and make plans to manage them

To achieve Step 12, individuals will show that they can identify risks and gains from opportunities, and then develop plans to mitigate those risks and deliver the gains.

In the previous step, the focus was on how to identify risks and potential gains from a project. This step expands on this by also considering how to create plans to manage those risks and gains.

Building blocks

The building blocks of this step are learning:

- I define and explain how to mitigate risks
- I define and explain how to manage risk aversion
- I make plans to realise gains

Reflection questions

- What does it mean to mitigate risks? Can you give any examples?
- How can we ensure we realise the gains of a plan?
- What is risk aversion? How can careful planning help to overcome risk aversion?
- Have you got any examples of having done this?

What you need to know

Mitigating risks

In the previous step, we identified risks as those things that which could happen which would have a negative effect if they did.

Identifying potential risks is important, and it can be helpful to identify the probability of them occurring as well as the strength of effect that they would have if they occurred. In the previous step, we saw that this could be done in a couple of ways:

- Either as a financial calculation of the impact in financial terms multiplied by the probability of that happening
- Or scored according to the likelihood of happening multiplied by the impact, perhaps with each scored out of 5 giving a total score of 25

This sort of calculation is important so that we can prioritise which are the most important risks to *mitigate*.

Mitigation is what actions you can take to either:

- *Reduce the likelihood that the risk event will happen:* This might include planning or training for team members or putting in additional safeguards.
- *Reduce the impact if the risk event happens:* This might include by creating back-up options which reduce the level of loss because you can switch more quickly to an alternative.

Risk registers and risk aversion

For bigger projects or organisations, there is normally something called a *risk register* which is where the project manager keeps a record of:

- The main risks that the project faces
- The probability of each of those risks happening
- The likely impact if they do happen
- The mitigating actions that are being taken

This document is something that should be reviewed regularly as the project develops or circumstances around the project change. This is a good way of ensuring that we keep thinking about what could go wrong; this can easily be forgotten about if we are busy putting a project together.

The other use of it is that we tend to be *risk-averse*. That means that we avoid risks even where, on balance, the expected gain outweighs the expected risk.

A good risk register can help to understand these risks more clearly, and so support a rational balancing of risk and potential gain rather than just a 'gut feeling'.

Realising gains

The other side of a project, and the main motivator to undertake it, is the gain that is expected. In the previous step, we explored how to identify and value the gains that might accrue to a project.

However, as a project runs it is likely that we will learn more new things and will therefore have an evolving view about the gains of the project and what we expect to happen. It is important that, as a project evolves, there continue to be regular points where we check in to see that we are still on track to make the gains that we expected.

New opportunities might also come up which make it worth adapting our approach to realise as well. Therefore, as we progress we should not only be keeping an eye on the evolving risks but also ensure that we are capturing the gains as well.

Teaching it

To teach this step:

- The teacher should start by reminding learners of the key definitions of risk and potential gains.
- The idea should be built that we can affect both the probability of a risk coming to pass, and the impact of that risk. The actions that we take to reduce the probability and impact are called mitigating actions.
- Learners can contribute ideas for different scenarios about what sort of mitigating actions might work for different risks.

- The teacher can then introduce the idea of a risk register and how that is used to record a project's key risks, impacts, likelihoods, and mitigating actions.
- Learners could apply this to their own studies or a project of their own, developing an appropriate risk register for themselves. These can be shared and discussed as a group to consolidate learning.

Reinforcing it

This step can be reinforced through wider studies where there is a discussion of risk and potential gains. This includes subjects like economics, business studies, and humanities as well as looking at examples from current affairs.

Assessing it

This step is best assessed through a practical exercise where learners are given a scenario and create a risk register in response to it. This should demonstrate their ability to identify appropriate risks, come up with a reasonable judgement of the severity of the risk and its likelihood, and then suggest some mitigating actions too.

Aiming High

The ability to set clear, tangible goals and devise a robust route to achieving them

Why it matters

Aiming High sits alongside Staying Positive. They are both self-management skills. Aiming High is about having ambitious goals for the future, but also ensuring that those goals are grounded in reality and that there is a realistic plan for achieving them.

When learners are young, we tend to structure more of their time and learning for them. Aiming High for them is about how effectively they navigate the tasks and challenges that are given to them.

As learners get older, they will need to take more responsibility across their lives, and structure and plan more for themselves. If they can master this skill, it will support how they approach learning in school, preparation for examinations, and how they navigate life beyond school too.

How Aiming High is built

This skill is about being able to plan effectively both to achieve organisational goals and also to set their own personal development targets. Initially, this is about knowing when something is too difficult, and having a sense of what doing well looks like for a learner.

The focus is then on working with care and attention, taking pride in success, and having a positive approach to new challenges. Building on this, learners set goals for themselves informed by an understanding of what is needed, and then order and prioritise tasks, secure resources, and involve others effectively.

At the higher steps, the focus is on creating plans with clear targets, informed by an individual's skill set, and then building on external views. At the most advanced level, individuals develop long-term strategies. These are informed by an assessment of internal and external factors, structured through regular milestones and feedback loops.

Skills Builder Framework for Aiming High

The ability to set clear, tangible goals and devise a robust route to achieving them

Step 0	I know when I am finding something too difficult
Step 1	I know what doing well looks like for me
Step 2	I work with care and attention to detail
Step 3	I work with pride when I am being successful
Step 4	I work with a positive approach to new challenges
Step 5	I set goals for myself
Step 6	I set goals informed by an understanding of what is needed
Step 7	I set goals, ordering and prioritising tasks to achieve them
Step 8	I set goals and secure the right resources to achieve them
Step 9	I set goals and plan to involve others in the best way
Step 10	I create plans that are informed by my skill set and that of others
Step 11	I create plans that include clear targets to make progress tangible
Step 12	I create plans that are informed by external views, including constructive criticism
Step 13	I develop long-term strategies, taking into account strengths, weaknesses, opportunities, and threats
Step 14	I develop long-term strategies that use regular milestones to keep everything on track
Step 15	I develop long-term strategies that include feedback loops to support flexibility and adaptability

Aiming High Step 0

Step 0: I know when I am finding something too difficult

To achieve Step 0, individuals will be able to identify when they are finding something too difficult.

This is the first step in Aiming High, and the focus is first on individuals recognising the limits of what they can do.

Building blocks

The building blocks of this step are:

- I understand that some activities can be more difficult than others
- I know when something is too difficult or dangerous
- I know when to keep going and when to seek help

Reflection questions

- How do you know if something is too difficult for you?
- Why might something be too difficult?
- Why is it important to think about the safety of what you are trying to do?
- What do we mean by danger?
- Why is it important to think about danger?

What you need to know

How do you know if something is too difficult?

When we first do things, we might find them difficult. This is a normal part of learning to do something, and over time it will get easier as we get better.

However, sometimes we might be in a situation where we find something too difficult to do. We might find something too difficult for different reasons:

- We do not have the knowledge to be able to complete something
- We have never done something before, and don't know what we need to do
- We are not sure what needs to be done
- We see that something is dangerous

We might know that something is too difficult if we cannot work out what to do next, or how to do it, or we cannot answer something. When something is too difficult, we might also feel some negative emotions. For example, we might feel sad, disappointed, angry, or scared.

Thinking about how to manage these emotions is important, and we explore this in *Staying Positive*. It is important that if something is too difficult, then we don't just keep going because that might place us in danger.

What to do if something is too difficult

It is important to think about the danger that is present in a situation to know whether it is something that we should keep trying at, or whether we should stop because it is too dangerous:

- If something is *not dangerous,* then it might be worth trying again, and persisting in case we can work it out by ourselves. We might be able to find something out or ask someone to help us.
- If something is *dangerous,* then we absolutely should *not* attempt it if we do not feel completely confident that we know what we are doing. For example, if we are doing anything that needs expertise, qualifications, or training that we do not have.

If something is dangerous or feels dangerous, then we should never attempt to do it ourselves.

In this case, we should ask someone who has higher expertise to help us, or a qualified person if required (for example, for repairs or anything involving gas, electricity, or water). If that person isn't available, then we should stop and wait, or come back to it later.

Teaching it

To teach this step:

- The teacher should highlight that new things often feel difficult, and ask for learners for examples of things that they have found difficult initially and then been able to get better at and find less challenging. The teacher could model this with some cases from their own life.
- The teacher could also structure a conversation about how learners feel when they find something too complicated, and how to manage those emotions (drawing on Staying Positive)
- The critical point to emphasise is that when something is difficult, it can be useful to keep trying but only if the task learners are attempting is not dangerous. If it is dangerous, then learners must stop and seek expert help.
- The teacher can capture some ideas of things that might be too dangerous to attempt and who they should ask for help – usually a responsible adult.

Reinforcing it

This step can be reinforced in the classroom context, where learners can be asked to identify whether they are struggling with something that they will be able to get better at with practice, or whether it is too complicated and they need help. Any dangerous situations should be highlighted so that learners understand the limits of what they can sensibly do.

Assessing it

This step can be assessed through discussion or through a reflective exercise where learners are given different scenarios and asked to consider whether the situation is one where they should persist or whether they should stop because there is danger.

Aiming High Step 1

Step 1: I know what doing well looks like for me

To achieve Step 1, individuals will be able to explain what doing well looks like for them.

In the previous step, the focus was on individuals identifying when they were finding something too difficult. This step takes a different angle, which is encouraging individuals to identify what doing well looks like for them.

Building blocks

The building blocks of this step are:

- I understand what doing well means
- I recognise when I have done good work
- I know when I am making a good contribution

Reflection questions

- How do you know when you have done good work?
- How does it feel when you have done something well?
- Aside from your own work, what else might doing well mean?
- Why is it important to build good relationships with others?
- Can you give examples of where you have done this?

What you need to know

Recognising good work

In the previous step, we looked at what it felt like to find something too difficult. This is the other side, which is knowing when you are doing something well.

There are two parts to explore. The first is how you feel when you are doing something well, as it will normally give as a positive emotional response. This might feel like:

- *Calm*: when you feel relaxed because you know that you don't have to worry about something, you are not feeling too challenged.
- *Happy*: A sense of joy, gratefulness, or enthusiasm because you are getting satisfaction out of the work that you're doing.
- *Excitement:* A feeling of energy and drive because you are seeing that your efforts are paying off.

Other signs of good work

There might also be other signs that you are doing well. This might be:

- *Feedback:* Other people might tell you that you are doing well
- *Personal satisfaction:* You might feel that you are learning and getting better, perhaps because you know that you are now finding something easier to do well than you previously did.

This combination of how you *feel* about the work you are doing, and the other signs that you are *doing* good work are both important.

It's important to remember that doing well rarely comes from just doing the easiest possible tasks or doing as little as possible. Over time, that will stop being very satisfying and will just feel boring. You will also stop improving at things, and people will eventually stop giving you positive feedback if they don't think you are trying very hard.

Working well with others

Although it is important, doing well is not just about our work. A part of doing well is also about how we contribute to wider tasks and support others to do well too.

Once again, we usually feel a positive emotional response from helping others and the satisfaction of seeing them do well. However, the difference is that sometimes we might not get the credit for that work because we have just supported someone else. In this case, we might not get positive feedback from other people, or see it leading directly to achieving a goal.

If you are not careful, this might lead to negative emotions like disappointment, anger, or envy. In these cases, you might look for feedback from those people that you have helped to see whether they feel that you did well. In many cases though, you will do best to take satisfaction from knowing that you helped someone else to do well, and that you have learnt something worthwhile in the process.

Teaching it

To teach this step:

- The teacher can introduce the idea of what it looks like to do well, and the associated idea of 'trying their best' which might work well with younger learners. The teacher can model an example for the learners and then ask them for their examples.
- The teacher can open a discussion about what it feels like to do well, and the emotions that individuals might feel. These ideas can be shared and recorded.
- The teacher can introduce other ways that we can know that we have done well which are outlined in the sections above.
- Finally, the teacher can ask learners to talk about the importance of helping other people do well too, and how that helps them to do well even if they don't get as much recognition for it.

Reinforcing it

This step lends itself to easy reinforcement in the class, by putting the focus on when learners have been pushing themselves to try something that stretches them, and which achieves a good result. Learners can be encouraged to take satisfaction in their own immediate achievements, and when they have supported others to achieve something too.

Assessing it

This step is best assessed through observation of learner behaviour and whether they are able to take satisfaction in their achievements. This can be explored further through reflective conversation with learners.

Aiming High Step 2

Step 2: I work with care and attention to detail

To achieve Step 2, individuals will be able to work with care and attention to detail.

In earlier steps, individuals considered how they knew when they were finding something too difficult, and when they were doing something well. In this step, the focus shifts to how to work well, starting with how to take care and pay attention to detail.

Building blocks

The building blocks of this step are learning:

- I understand what working carefully means
- I take my time when working
- I pay attention to detail

Reflection questions

- What does it mean to work carefully?
- How should we prepare and what should we do during the task?
- Can you give examples of when you have done this?
- When do you pay attention to detail?
- Do you find it easy or difficult?
- Can you give examples of when you have done this well, and when you have not?

What you need to know

Working carefully

Working carefully is an essential part of doing a good job. It is the only way of ensuring that we do a task as well as we can and that we make as few mistakes as possible.

It means that before we start on a task:

- We decide that we will do the best job we can
- We understand what we are trying to achieve
- We have a good idea about how we will achieve it
- We have the right equipment available to us to complete the task

During the task itself:

- We maintain focus by avoiding distractions
- We check that we are following our plan
- We look for possible mistakes so that we spot them quickly
- We ask for help if we need it
- We keep an eye on the time so that we are not late

When finishing the task:

- We look back over our work and think about whether we could make it better
- We might ask someone else to check our work to give us feedback
- We make any corrections or improvements that we need to
- We share our work in the best way we can

If we follow these steps, then we will be well set up to do the best we can do.

Paying attention to detail

Something that sits alongside working carefully is paying attention to detail. This means thinking about what you are doing as you are doing it and making sure that you are getting things right as you are doing them.

It also means thinking about not just the main things you need to do in the task but all of the smaller bits too. That might include making sure that:

In written work:

- You don't have any spelling or grammar mistakes when you are writing something
- You double-check any numbers that you use or calculations that you make
- You check facts that you include

In other work:

- You read instructions carefully and don't skip any steps
- You test your work before waiting for someone else to check it

Paying attention to detail also means thinking not just about the tasks that you are doing but about the wider things that are going on too. We often have not only our immediate task to concentrate on, but also have to be aware of all of the other things that might be going on around us. If we are not paying attention, we might easily miss something whether we're learning, or doing our work.

Teaching it

To teach this step:

- The teacher can introduce the idea of what it looks like for learners to work with care and with attention to detail. This lends itself to a class discussion about what this might look like for the learners, and how they might put that into practice.
- Learners could work to put together some tips for working carefully, thinking about what they should do before a task, during a task, and when finishing up a task. The guidance above gives some suggestions of the approach that can be taken.
- Learners can then put these tips into practice in completing an exercise or challenge themselves. This might be a piece of writing, designing something, or following instructions to complete a task. If time allows, trying a little bit of each can be helpful to illustrate how working carefully should be transferred into lots of settings and lots of different pieces of work.

Reinforcing it

This step lends itself to reinforcement in the classroom setting. For instance, before tasks the teacher can take learners through what they need to do to prepare to do good work, how to check their work as they progress, and how to review their work at the end. This can be reinforced through visual reminders.

Learners can regularly reflect on whether they worked carefully and paid attention to detail.

Assessing it

This step is best assessed through sustained observation, to see whether learners can work carefully and with attention to detail over a sustained time. Eventually, they should be able to do this without being reminded to by a teacher.

Aiming High Step 3

Step 3: I work with pride when I am being successful

To achieve Step 3, individuals will show that they recognise and take pride when they are successful.

In the previous step, the focus was on how to work with care and attention. The shift here is to think about success criteria as an important part of being able to recognise when individuals have been successful, and then to take pride in their successes.

Building blocks

The building blocks of this step are learning:

- I recognise when I have been successful
- I take satisfaction in being successful
- I share what I feel when I have done well

Reflection questions

- How do you know when you are successful?
- How can you measure success? Can you give some examples?
- What does it mean to take satisfaction in success?
- Why is that important?
- Can you give examples of when you have done this?

What you need to know

Feeling success

In Step 1, we introduced the idea of knowing what doing well looks like for you. We looked at there being two aspects to this:

- The positive emotional response that you get from doing well which can include feeling happy, excited, or relaxed.
- The other signs that you are doing something well, like positive feedback, or the feeling that you are getting better at something.

This is an important starting point, but we can build on this when we think about what we mean by being *successful* more broadly.

Seeing success

Being successful is about achieving what you set out to do. This means that there are two parts to knowing whether you've been successful:

- Being clear what it looks like to do something successfully
- Being able to see at the end whether you have done that or not

We need both of these parts to know if we are successful. We can think of this as setting *success criteria* for ourselves. What do we need to do to have completed the task successfully?

For example, we might be looking to design a new product. We can only know if we have been successful if we start out by deciding (or being told) what the product needs to be able to do at the end. This might mean that it can store 1 litre of water, be dropped from a height of 2 metres without breaking, and be made out of recyclable materials. We can check against these success criteria once we have finished the product to know if we have been successful.

As another example, we might be writing a report. Our success criteria might be that it gives four different models of environmentally-friendly waste disposal, recommends the best one for us, and is no longer than two pages. This makes it clear whether we have been successful or not.

As a final example, we might be in a competition. Our success criteria might be to reach the final and to improve on our score the last time we entered. We can know then whether we have been successful or not.

In the previous step (*Step 2*) we looked at the ideas of working carefully and paying attention to detail. This is still an essential part of being successful, *but it is not enough*. We also need to keep ensuring that we are working towards the success criteria we have set.

Taking satisfaction in success

It is also important to celebrate and to take satisfaction when we have been successful.

When footballers score a goal, they all celebrate together and share congratulations. When projects are completed, there is often a celebration. When businesses hit their targets, they might pay people bonuses.

These are all examples of taking pride in achievements. Taking pride in achievements is vital because it gives you a reward for the hard work that usually has to go into being successful at something. Because of the effort that goes in, it is essential to balance that out by taking enjoyment from having done something well at the other end.

If we don't spend the time to enjoy and take satisfaction in our achievements, then we feel less *motivated* to try hard to achieve our success criteria in the future. On the other hand, if we know that we will feel good about achieving success, then we will be more willing to put in hard work now to get that feeling later on.

Teaching it

To teach this step:

- The teacher can introduce the idea of *success* and what it means to be *successful*. Learners might already be familiar with the concept of success criteria, and it is worth expanding on these.
- Learners could be given a range of scenarios and be asked to create success criteria for them. Learners might also reflect on times when they knew they had been successful and how they knew?
- The teacher should then lead a conversation about why it is important to take pride and satisfaction from successes, not just because it is nice at the time but because it makes it more likely that learners will feel *motivated* to work hard to achieve success again in the future.

Reinforcing it

This step lends itself very naturally to reinforcement in the classroom. The key concept to introduce if you do not use it already is that of *success criteria*, which can either be set by the teacher or developed with the group of learners.

Once success criteria are achieved, learners should be encouraged to take satisfaction in that success. Initially, this might include praise from the teacher, but the primary focus should be on building their intrinsic motivation.

Assessing it

This step is best assessed through:

- Checking whether learners are able to create sensible success criteria for themselves.
- Using reflective conversations with learners to explore their ability to recognise and take pride in their successes.

Aiming High Step 4

Step 4: I work with a positive approach to new challenges

To achieve Step 4, individuals should show that they can take a positive attitude to new challenges.

In earlier steps, individuals built some of the foundations of this step. They have shown they can recognise and take pride in success, as well as knowing when something is too difficult or dangerous for them to attempt.

Building blocks

The building blocks of this step are:

- I understand why new challenges are a good opportunity
- I look for opportunities in my stretch zone
- I identify the positives of approaching a new challenge

Reflection questions

- Why is it important to be willing to take on new challenges?
- What would happen if we avoided new challenges?
- Can you give any examples of when you have learnt from a new challenge?
- How can you find challenges that work for you?
- What does it mean to work in your stretch zone?

Finding new challenges

In the previous step, we explore the idea of being successful; that is, being able to achieve success criteria. We saw that it was essential to take pride and enjoy that success.

Over time though, we mustn't just stick to safe challenges or only doing things where we think that we are very likely to achieve the success criteria. It might feel that we are very successful initially, but eventually we will take less satisfaction from doing the same things over and over again.

The bigger problem is that if we only do the same challenges or activities over and over again we will stop learning.

Learning through challenges

When we first do an activity or use a new skill, we tend not to be very good at it. We find it difficult because we have to think hard about how to do it, and we will often make mistakes. Over time though, we get better at it; it starts to feel more natural, and we are more successful.

This is because we have learnt how to do the task well, and we will be able to do that task again in the future with success. This expands the range of what we can do and means that we can be confident in lots more situations.

Anything that we have learnt to do in our lives started off being difficult, whether learning to read and write, swim, ride a bicycle, cook, or any number of other skills we have built over time. By working hard at them, and adding those skills to our toolkit, we are much better able to be successful in lots of different situations in the future.

Spotting or creating challenges

Sometimes we will be given challenges to work on, particularly in education where teachers will often think hard about what the next thing to learn is to give the right level of challenge. However, in education it is still good to push ourselves to try difficult tasks. Outside education – in the workplace, or our broader lives – we have to take even more responsibility for finding challenges for ourselves.

In finding or setting ourselves challenges, we need to get the balance right:

- Too easy, and we will just be doing something that we already know how to do. We might be successful, but we won't be learning.
- Too difficult, and we might place ourselves in a situation that is dangerous (see *Step 0*) or where we have no chance of success, no matter how hard we work at something.

Instead, we need to find our *stretch zone*. This is the area where the level of challenge is just right, where we have enough support to help us be successful, but not too much to make it easy. In our stretch zone, we should feel like it what we are doing is difficult and needs us to think and work hard but it should not feel impossible.

The reward of working in our *stretch zone* is lots of learning and therefore being able to get better.

Teaching it

To teach this step:

- The teacher should introduce the idea of why it is essential to take on new challenges through a group discussion with learners.
- Learners could be asked for examples of things that they found to be difficult when they got started but which they are now able to do because they practised.
- The teacher can then introduce the idea of the stretch zone. They could model some examples of where the stretch zone is for them, whether in terms of physical exercise, learning, or a challenge they are doing outside of work.
- Learners should then think about some examples of when they felt that they were working in their stretch zone, reflecting on how it felt and what they achieved as a result.

Reinforcing it

This step lends itself to reinforcement in the classroom. The teacher can introduce opportunities for learners to take on more stretching challenges if they feel that they can quickly achieve the success criteria for tasks that they have been given.

Recognition can also be given to learners who are trying out something new and stretching so that they build new knowledge or skill. This is an essential complement to recognising success.

Assessing it

This step is best assessed through sustained observation and reflection with learners about whether they seek out new challenges or whether they stay in their comfort zone, only doing things that they know they will be successful at.

Aiming High Step 5

Step 5: I set goals for myself

To achieve Step 5, individuals will show that they can set goals for themselves.

Earlier steps focused on building up to this by introducing the notion of what success looks like through success criteria, then the importance of both taking pride in that success but also the importance of seeking out new challenges to support learning. This step combines those elements by introducing the setting of goals.

In the context of the classroom, learners should be able to:

- Set themselves goals that are based on their stretch zones
- Be clear about how they will know if a goal has been achieved

Building blocks

The building blocks of this step are:

- I define and explain what goals are
- I know how to set goals in my stretch zone
- I know how to measure if a goal has been achieved

Reflection questions

- What is a goal?
- How can we set goals in our stretch zone?
- Can you give examples of when you've done this?
- How can you tell if a goal has been achieved?
- How do goals and success criteria fit together?
- Why can numbers help you measure a goal?

What you need to know

Different types of goals

A goal is something that we want to happen, and that we will work towards achieving.

We might set goals in lots of different areas of our lives. For example, we might decide that we want to learn a new language, score more goals for our football team, or pass an examination.

There are different types of goals that we might set ourselves:

- *Short term goals:* These are things that we can achieve quite quickly. These might be things like learning some new vocabulary, mending something, or baking a cake.
- *Mid-term goals:* These are longer goals which may take a few days, a week, or even a month. For example, we might want to improve our fitness or our accuracy at scoring in basketball. Mid-term goals take sustained effort to achieve.

- *Long-term goals:* These are goals that might take a lot longer to achieve. It might be a promotion in work, achieving a particular qualification or something in our personal lives. These are goals that we need to work at for a longer time period and which it might be hard to see progress on day-to-day.

All three of these different types of goals are important, but we need to think about them differently. For mid-term and long-term goals, we also have to think about breaking these into smaller goals to keep us *motivated* to keep trying.

Setting goals in a stretch zone

When we set ourselves goals, it is vital to think about whether they are goals in our *stretch zone*. We explored this in the previous step, but you know if a goal is in your stretch zone if it is:

- Not so easy that you are sure that you will achieve it
- Not so difficult as to make it dangerous or impossible to achieve

Setting goals in your stretch zone gives you the best chance of being successful and learning a lot along the way.

Knowing if a goal is achieved

We have already come across *success criteria*. A goal sets out *what* we are trying to achieve, while the success criteria will be our measures of *whether* we have achieved it or not; the two should work together.

For example, you might set a goal of learning a new language. This could be a great long-term goal, but difficult to know whether you are being successful. So, you could break this goal down into shorter-term goals like being able to learn some important vocabulary, conjugate verbs in the present tense, and have a short conversation.

SMART targets

Even then, if is helpful to start setting clearer *targets*. The best targets are those that are SMART. This means that they are:

- Specific: it is clear exactly what you are trying to do
- Measurable: you can measure whether the target has been met or not
- Achievable: it is in your stretch zone – not too hard or too easy
- Realistic: it is something that makes sense to do
- Timed: you know when it needs to be done by

For example, you could create a target towards learning a language as 'being able to write 50 important words accurately in the language from memory in two weeks' time'.

Putting numbers and deadlines on goals is particularly helpful because it means we can see exactly what success looks like and also see very clearly whether we have been successful.

Teaching it

To teach this step:

- The teacher can introduce goals and why we have them. The teacher can model some goals that they have in their own lives and why they find having goals helpful and motivating.
- The teacher can explain the difference between short-, mid-, and long-term goals and how it is crucial to have a combination of these. Learners could give examples of some of these types of goals for themselves, or a hypothetical example could be broken down together.
- The teacher can then introduce the idea of SMART targets, and why having targets with numbers attached can be helpful.
- Learners can be encouraged to think about setting goals for themselves - perhaps in the context of their learning - and to turn them into SMART targets.

Reinforcing it

This step lends itself well to being reinforced in learning. For example, learners could be encouraged to take responsibility for coming up with their own learning goals and the measures of whether they have been successful. They could also do this in collaboration with a teacher. Learners should review whether they have been successful and to reflect on their progress using these targets over time.

Assessing it

This step can be assessed through an exercise where learners have to create a series of short-, mid- and long-term targets for themselves and turn these into SMART targets. They could alternatively do this by being given a broad goal and having to think about how this can be turned into a SMART target.

Aiming High Step 6

Step 6: I set goals informed by an understanding of what is needed

To achieve Step 6, individuals will be able to think about goals based on broader needs, not just their personal development.

In the previous step, the focus was on individuals setting goals for themselves. By nature, these were primarily focused on individuals' own personal development. The shift here is to think about the needs of their organisations or their teams too.

Building blocks

The building blocks of this step are:

- I identify the needs of myself and others
- I build needs into the development of my own goals
- I build needs into the development of others' goals

Reflection questions

- How can you identify the needs of other people?
- How can you identify the needs of an organisation or community?
- How can you create goals based on the needs of others?
- How can you make a contribution to bigger goals?
- Can you give any examples of when you have done this?

What you need to know

Identifying needs

So far, we have looked at setting goals for ourselves based on what we need.

However, we also need to think about what else is going on when we set goals, not just what is important to us but to others as well. These might include:

- *Other individuals:* Relatives, friends, teachers or learners in education, or colleagues, customers and stakeholders in the working world.
- *Our teams*: Perhaps we are part of a group which has shared goals. In education, that might be a learning group or a class. In the world of work, it might mean teams of colleagues that we're part of, or other partners. In the wider world, that might mean our family or group of friends.
- *Our organisations:* Most of us are part of organisations which have goals , although some might be more clearly expressed than others. In education, that probably means a school, college, or university. In the world of work, that will be the company or organisation. More widely, that might be our town or city, or other groups we are part of like religious groups.

We are all connected to lots of other people in these ways, and so we should think about what our contribution should be to the goals these other groups might have.

For example, how can we support other people? Perhaps we could help a friend who is struggling at something to get better, and that could be our goal. Or we could look at the goals of our team and think about how to make a contribution to that. Or we could look at our organisation's goals and think about whether what we are doing helps.

Building needs into goals

As we think of our part in ever bigger groups of people, we have to be realistic about what we can contribute. We are unlikely to be able to achieve a goal for a whole organisation through our efforts, but we can play a part.

There are several ways we can build others' needs into our goals:

- *Create a goal that is directly about helping someone else*: For example, you could have a goal to help a friend to learn a new language. When they make progress that will be partly your success.
- *Share a goal with someone else:* Some goals might need to be shared – for example, in a sports team, you might have a shared goal with another defender not to let in more than one goal in each match. You both need each other to achieve this goal.
- *Take on part of a bigger goal:* For more significant goals, perhaps of a team, you might need to take part of that goal and focus on that. If each person does this, then the different parts of your efforts might all add up to overall success. For example, if you want to set up a fundraising event, one person might be in charge of finding a good location, another person in charge of getting donations, and another person making sure people turn up.
- *Align your goals with a bigger goal:* In an organisation, sometimes goals are massive. In this case, we might align our goals to make sure that achieving our goals should support the bigger goal and, crucially, that they are not working against this.

As we develop goals for ourselves, we should always be thinking about what the effect of those goals is on others.

Teaching it

To teach this step:

The teacher can remind learners that so far the focus has been on how to set individual goals but that it is essential to also think about other groups. Learners could come up with groups they are part of, and what those groups might be trying to achieve.

The teacher can then introduce the idea of how to think about our contribution to broader goals: Through supporting goals, sharing goals, taking on part of a bigger goal, or aligning our goals. Learners could give examples of each.

Reinforcing it

This is a step that can be reinforced in a classroom setting, through group work exercises or a shared project. Learners could also reflect on the learning goals of the class and how they can align their individual goals with those bigger learning goals.

Learners might even have the opportunity to build this skill step outside of the classroom, and they should be encouraged to reflect on how they are doing this.

Assessing it

This step can be assessed through a worked exercise, where they can be given different scenarios of groups they belong to and asked to consider how they can contribute to the goals of those groups.

Aiming High Step 7

Step 7: I set goals, ordering and prioritising tasks to achieve them

To achieve Step 7, individuals will show that they can start turning goals into action by ordering and prioritising the tasks that are needed.

In the previous steps, the focus was on how to develop goals, first by thinking about what individuals want to achieve, and then thinking about the wider needs of others, whether in groups or organisations. This step looks at how to start to work towards achieving those goals.

Building blocks

The building blocks of this step are:

- I define and explain what tasks are
- I identify tasks that need to be done to achieve a goal
- I put tasks into logical order

Reflection questions

- What do we mean by tasks?
- How do tasks link to goals?
- Can you give examples of how this might work?
- How can we organise the tasks that need to be done?
- What is logical order?

What you need to know

Tasks to be done

So far, we have been thinking of goals as what needs to be achieved. We have looked at targets as how to see whether a goal has been achieved or not.

Tasks are the pieces of work that need to be done. Achieving any goal required lots of individual tasks to be done. Mid- or long-term goals might mean completing tens or even hundreds of tasks to achieve them.

For example, if our goal is to learn a new language, then one of our targets might be to remember 50 pieces of vocabulary accurately. Our task might then be to write out the 50 pieces of vocabulary with their translations, then write them out repeatedly, then cover them and to try to write them again, and then to check whether we have written them accurately. We might repeat these tasks several times until we are accurate.

If we are serious about achieving goals for ourselves, we need to be able to break those goals down into the tasks that we need to complete.

Putting tasks into a logical order

The order of tasks matters. There are several ways to think about how to order tasks:

- *Dependency:* It might be that some tasks can only be completed in a particular order. For example, you can't ice a cake before it has been baked, and you can't bake a cake before all of the ingredients have been mixed together. If something needs to be done before you can do the next task, then this gives you a logical order.
- *Priority:* In some cases, when there are lots of tasks to do and no dependency, then we will want to think about which tasks are most important. For example, we might have twenty ideas about how to get people to come to an event. If we're not sure whether we might have time to do all twenty, then it makes sense to start with the ones we think will have the most significant effect.
- *External dependencies:* It might be that some tasks rely on something or someone else beyond your control to complete them. For example, you might need your oven to be fixed before you can bake a cake. In this case, you could organise tasks to get things ready and then wait until your oven is repaired to moving on to the baking stage. Alternatively, you might need someone to permit you to do something – there will be some tasks that you cannot do until that permission has been received, so you should plan around that.
- *Parallel tasks:* In some cases, it might be possible to work on more than one task at a time. For example, while the cake is baking, we might be making the icing in preparation for the cake coming out of the oven or we might be making a cup of tea to have when the cake is ready. In organisations, individuals are often working on different tasks alongside each other.

We can use these principles to help us to arrange tasks into the order that makes it most efficient to complete them and so to achieve our goals.

We can also think about how long tasks are likely to take, so that we can put them on a timeline and work out how long achieving a goal is expected to take as a result.

Teaching it

To teach this step:

- The teacher can introduce the concept of *tasks* as the means to achieving goals. This is best illustrated by examples, and then by asking learners to create their own ideas of the tasks that might be needed to achieve a particular goal.
- The concept of ordering tasks could be introduced by the teacher creating, with input from the learners, a mind map of all the tasks that would be needed to run some sort of event in school. The mind map can be expanded into areas like publicity to think of lots of ideas of tasks that could be completed.
- The teacher should then guide learners through thinking about how they might organise completing these tasks. This includes thinking about which tasks are dependent on others, where there are priorities, where there are external dependencies, and where it might be possible for tasks to be completed in parallel. Thinking along a timeline can be helpful for this.
- Learners could break down a goal into at least ten tasks. Learners can be encouraged to think about how these tasks are ordered to create a plan, and then present or discuss why they have ordered the tasks in the way they have.

Reinforcing it

Where learners are set projects, extended tasks, or pieces of work, the teacher can encourage them to create a plan. This means taking the goal and identifying all the tasks that need to completed, putting them in order, and putting them on a timeline.

Assessing it

This step is best assessed through an assessed activity. Learners can be set a goal, be asked to break it down into tasks and then to create a timeline of those tasks. Discussion can explore why learners have made the choices they have, and whether these are based on a good understanding of the step.

Aiming High Step 8

Step 8: I set goals and secure the right resources to achieve them

To achieve Step 8, individuals will show that they can set goals, and then be able to secure the right resources to meet them.

In the previous step, individuals focused on how to set goals, ordering and prioritising tasks to achieve them. This step expands on that, by introducing the idea of having the right resources to complete tasks.

Building blocks

The building blocks of this step are:

- I define and explain different resource types
- I identify what resources are needed in order to complete a task
- I know how to secure the resources needed

Reflection questions

- What are resources? Can you give examples?
- Why do we need resources to complete tasks?
- How do resources help us to achieve goals?
- What does it mean to secure resources?
- Is this different for different resources?

What you need to know

Identifying the resources

Resources are those things that we need to use to complete a task.

Lots of things can be described as resources, and we can divide them up into different categories:

- *Human Resources:* These are things that humans bring to complete a task. These include the time and effort of people who can complete tasks, and their knowledge, skills, and experience.
- *Physical Resources:* These are tangible things that we might need to be able to complete tasks. These include machines, technology, buildings, or physical spaces.
- *Financial Resources:* This is the money that we might need to pay for things we might need to complete the tasks.
- *Natural Resources:* These are the materials that we might need to complete the task like water, gas, minerals, and lots of other things.

We are likely to need a combination of different resources to complete a task.

Securing the resources

To turn a plan into reality, we need to know not just the resources we need, but also how to secure them. Securing them might not mean owning the resource; we might hire or borrow the resource instead for the time we need it to complete the task.

How we do this depends on the type of resources:

Resources	How we might secure them
Human resources	- It might be that you can provide the effort required if you have the right expertise and enough time. - If not, you might need to persuade other people to help you out – sometimes you pay people for their time, other times you might be able to convince them to help you without paying.
Physical resources	- If you need special equipment for a short time, then you might be able to hire this. However, if you use up the resource through use, then you will have to purchase it. - In terms of space, you might be able to hire that space, or you might be able to borrow it.
Natural resources	- Natural resources are the raw materials that you need to produce something. We will usually need to purchase these, although we might be able to recycle something already existing, or to have them donated if we need.
Financial resources	- Financial resources are the money you need. How much finance you need will depend on the other resources that you need to secure. - You might be able to fund this work yourself, you might need to borrow for someone else, or if you might be able to secure the budget from your organisation if you can convince them it is a good idea.

As you can see, there are several ways to secure the resources you need. It is also worth remembering that if you can't obtain particular resources, there might be other ways of achieving your goals without them, or by changing some of the tasks you decide to carry out.

Teaching it

To teach this step:

- The teacher can introduce the step as an essential part of being able to achieve goals: goals are broken up into tasks, which then use resources to complete.
- The teacher can facilitate a discussion about the different types of resources that might be needed for different kinds of tasks, gathering ideas together in a mind map.
- The teacher could then model how a goal can be broken down into tasks, and then identifying the resources that would be needed to complete them.
- Learners can work on a team challenge to take a goal and then to identify the tasks (reinforcing *Step 7*) and resources they need. They should share why they have identified those resources as being essential. They could be challenged to think about what they might do as an alternative if some of the resources were unavailable. Could they adapt the tasks or resources?
- This can be extended by giving learners a challenging project – for example, to organise an event. Learners could be given scope to plan the event having first identified their goal and any targets they might have (see *Step 5* and *Step 6*). This will ground their thinking about resources they could access, and how they would secure them, in reality.

Reinforcing it

This step can be reinforced in the classroom by encouraging learners to set their own goals and make plans to achieve them. This might be linked to learning goals, completing projects, or broader activities. For older learners, this might be related to qualifications or college and university applications.

Assessing it

This step can be assessed through an extended project or challenge where learners are responsible for creating a plan to achieve a goal. If an extended project is not possible, then a shorter planning activity might be sufficient.

Aiming High Step 9

Step 9: I set goals and plan to involve others in the best way

To achieve Step 9, individuals will have to identify where they need to involve other people in their plans and how to engage them with the effort.

In earlier steps, individuals explored how to set goals and start to develop plans by thinking about the required tasks and resources. Although the previous step touched on the importance of human resources, involving others in plans is worth additional focus.

Building blocks

The building blocks of this step are:

- I recognise people are different to other types of resources
- I identify how I can involve others in my plans
- I know how to engage people in my plans

Reflection questions

- When do we need to involve other people to achieve our plans?
- Why are people different to other types of resources?
- How can you convince people to support you in achieving your plans?

What you need to know

Why you might need to involve other people

Sometimes, we cannot complete our goals by ourselves. This is particularly true for bigger goals, or long-term goals.

Other people can play a critical role in bringing plans into action. They might offer support in many different forms:

- Advising on your goals or plans
- Making connections or introductions to other people who can help
- Helping you to secure the resources that you need, including financial resources
- Completing some of the tasks
- Sharing the goal with you if it is something you want to achieve together
- Setting your goal to start with if they in a position of authority

Who to involve in your plans

Involving the right people to support you to achieve your goals is essential. You will want to think about how they might be able to help you by thinking about:

- Do they have particular skills, expert knowledge, or experience of what you are trying to do so? If so, they might be good for advice or to help.
- Do they have strong networks of people they know who might be able to help you or provide you with resources, even if they can't do so directly? If so, they might be good for connections.
- Do they control particular resources that you might need, like a space you need or a physical asset like a machine or technology? In which case, they can help you to secure that resource.
- Do they also have a strong interest in achieving the same goal – for example, if you are on a team together? In this case, you might be able to work together to share the goal.
- Do you need them to give permission for you to work towards your goal, perhaps because they are in a senior position? In this case, you will need to get them to agree to what you want to do.

How to engage other people

When you engage people to support your plans in any of the ways above, you will need to *convince* them. Convincing them means persuading them so that they make the decision that they want to help you out.

There are several parts to persuading people to support you:

- *Showing them why the goal that you are working towards is worthwhile*: What will be different if you achieve the goal? Why does it matter to you personally? How have you already shown that you are committed to achieving the goal?
- *Explaining why helping you will be good for them*: What will their reward for helping you? This might be financial if you are paying them for their help, or it might be that your achieving your goal helps them to complete one of their goals, or it might just be that they can take satisfaction out of seeing the goal completed.
- *Giving them confidence that you can do it:* If people are going to help you, they want to know that you are likely to be successful. How can you show that you are likely to be successful? What have you done in the past that was similar?
- *Showing how their support will make the difference:* Why do you need them to help you? What would be the problem if they did not help you?
- *Being open to their advice:* Show that you are prepared to change or improve your plans if they have good advice.

There are also some traps to avoid:

- Just telling people they should help you, or presuming that they should
- Trying to make people feel guilty about not helping you or threatening them to make them help
- Assuming that people will know any of the answers to the questions above without your talking about it

If you use these ideas, then you are much more likely to be able to get the support you need to achieve your goals.

Teaching it

To teach this step:

- The teacher can introduce the idea that, for most of our goals, we need other people to help us. The teacher can model this with some examples from their own lives about how they have to engage other people to achieve lots of their goals and tasks.
- The teacher could ask learners to reflect on some of the different ways that people could help them to achieve their goals, and mind map some ideas. These should tally with the broad areas outlined above.
- The teacher can then ask learners to think about what sort of people they would need to help them in those different ways, and how they might be able to find them.
- Learners could put this into practice by thinking about a goal they might have, and who they would need to help them and in what different ways.
- Finally, the focus switches to how to persuade people to help. Learners could try out some of the ideas by scripting what they might say or trying it out in role-play conversation. The teacher could also introduce some of the things to avoid, so learners can see what the effect would be.

Reinforcing it

This is another element that can be reinforced in classrooms where learners take responsibility for their goals and create plans to achieve them. It might also be possible for them to think about how they persuade people to support or help them, and to try out this persuasive talk in the classroom.

Assessing it

This step is best assessed through an extended project, where learners have to put their ideas into practice and persuade people to help them to achieve their goals. Where this is not possible, a shorter simulation could be used, including the use of scripting or role-play to act out persuasive conversations.

Aiming High Step 10

Step 10: I create plans that are informed by my skill set and that of others

To achieve Step 10, individuals will be able identify their own skill set and those of others, and reflect that in their plans.

In earlier steps, the focus was on setting goals, and gradually building those out into plans by identifying the tasks, resources and other people required to achieve them. The focus is now on the creation of more detailed plans.

Building blocks

The building blocks of this step are:

- I identify my own skill set
- I identify others' skill sets
- I build skills into plans I create

Reflection questions

- What do we mean by skills?
- What types of skills are there?
- How can you identify your skills? How can you identify those of others?
- Why is it important to think about skills when making plans?
- How can you use the knowledge you have of your skills and those of others?

What you need to know

Types of skills

A *skill* is the ability to *do* something. As you've seen, there are a huge variety of skills from being able to balance, to playing chess, to making or building something. We use so many skills every hour that we hardly notice them. Indeed, when we have mastered a skill, it can often seem so easy that we forget that we are doing something that other people can't do.

We can think about three broad types of skills:

- *Basic or foundational skills:* These are the skills that are the foundation for everything else and include numeracy (the ability to work with numbers), literacy (the ability to read and write), and basic digital skills (like being able to access the internet and find information).
- *Essential skills:* These are the skills we focus on in the Skills Builder Framework – those skills which we need to do almost anything, and which support the application of technical knowledge and skills. We define these as listening, speaking, creativity, problem solving, staying positive, aiming high, leadership, and teamwork. However, the steps show that there are lots of smaller skills that make up these bigger themes.
- *Technical skills:* Those skills which are specific to a particular subject specialism, sector, or role. These are hugely diverse as a group, where some are skills held by quite a lot of people, like driving, and others that are highly specialist like writing computer code.

Identifying skills

We can identify skills in a number of ways:

- Sometimes our *interactions* with people help us to build up a sense of their essential skills and how well they can do things like listen, speak, solve problems, or work with other people.
- We might also *observe* how people carry out tasks, and we can use this as a way of seeing what skills they can put into use, and with what level of mastery. This can be done in a real-life situation, or through a simulation.
- *Interviews* are another way to explore the skills that people have. This is the method used most often by companies when they are recruiting. They often ask people for examples where they have used different skills to work out whether they have them or not.
- *Qualifications or certificates* are a final way of identifying skills and are particularly important for some technical skills where real expertise is involved, or where there is danger if mistakes are made.

None of these methods is entirely failsafe. People may be lucky or unlucky when you are observing them, our intuitions about people are often wrong or biased, some people are good at interviews while others are not, older certificates or qualifications might not reflect someone's current skill level. Using a combination of approaches, though, can be most helpful in getting a sense of what someone else can do.

Building skills into plans

A goal is something that you want to achieve, and a plan is how you will get there. Since putting a plan into action is all about *doing*, the ability to do is crucial.

There are two ways of thinking about skills:

- *The first is when you are setting your plans and making your goals.* Back in *Step 5*, we explored the idea of working in your stretch zone. This is only possible if you know the level at which you are working in your skills, and so an understanding of your skills will inform how you set your goals. In this case, your plans can be informed by your skills and those of others involved.
- *The second is when your goal is already set, and you need to find people to help.* In this case, you need to identify where there are gaps in the skills that you need to deliver a plan successfully. It is essential to be honest and thorough about these gaps. You can then try to find the right people to help fill those gaps.

Teaching it

To teach this step:

- The teacher should ask learners for their understanding of what a skill is and work towards a shared understanding, using the definition given. Learners could share lots of examples of skills, with the teacher sharing a few to get them started – the point is that there is are an overwhelming number out there.
- The teacher can then introduce the simple split between basic, essential, and technical skills, and ask learners for examples of each to check understanding.
- Learners could be asked to reflect on the technical skills that they feel they have and how they know that they have them.
- The teacher can then lead a class discussion about how you might identify those skills in other people, highlighting the four main ways outlined above. Learners might be asked if they have any experiences of their skills being assessed, or assessing others, using these methods.
- Finally, the teacher can lead a conversation about how to either build plans around those skills, or to identify skills gaps if a plan is already in place.

Reinforcing it

This step can be reinforced in the classroom by raising learners' awareness of the skills that they are building or using day-to-day. Learners could also be encouraged to audit the skills that they feel they have built – particularly in the context of looking towards university or college applications for older learners.

This step can also be used if learners are undertaking any sort of work experience or sustained project where they have to create and enact a plan towards a real goal.

Assessing it

This step is best assessed through a sustained project, where learners have to put their ideas into practice. If that is not possible, learners could be encouraged to audit their skills, and then think about the skills that would be needed elsewhere if they were to achieve different hypothetical goals as part of a team.

Aiming High Step 11

Step 11: I create plans that include clear targets to make progress tangible

To achieve Step 11, individuals will show that they can develop plans that include clear targets in them, to support making progress as tangible as possible.

In the previous step, the focus was on how to create plans informed by your skillset and that of others. This step builds on this, by thinking about how to make plans focused, and to be able to track progress through those plans.

Building blocks

The building blocks of this step are:

- I identify what elements are important in creating a plan
- I define and explain how goals and targets differ
- I know how to turn goals into tangible assets

Reflection questions

- What are the steps to creating a plan?
- What is the difference between a goal and a target?
- Why is it important to take care when setting targets?
- Have you created plans that include targets?

What you need to know

Creating plans

Creating plans has been a major focus of Aiming High throughout the steps. Before plans can be created, of course, the most vital thing is to know what the purpose or goal of the plan is.

We can then work back from that goal to think about what needs to happen, how to order and prioritise those tasks, securing the right resources, involving others, and drawing on the skills we need to complete our plan.

This step builds on this further by asking how we can make progress tangible as we implement our plans.

Setting targets

You are already familiar with goals, and targets are the complement to goal setting. Targets become the tangible measure of whether a goal has been achieved.

For instance, our goal might be to increase the number of young people participating in competitive sport. We might turn this into a target of having a 10% increase in participation over one year.

As a reminder, targets should always be SMART:

This means that they are:

- Specific: it is clear precisely what you are trying to do
- Measurable: you can measure whether the target has been met or not
- Achievable: it is not too hard or too easy
- Realistic: it is something that makes sense to do
- Timed: you know when it needs to be done by

Targets matter

It is important to think carefully about the targets that you set. They will inevitably become a key focus of your efforts, and so you want to make sure that they are really representative of achieving the goal.

As you develop your targets, there are some key questions to think about:

- Why is this target important?
- Could I achieve the goal without hitting this target? If so, is it really the right target?
- How does the target achieve the SMART principles?

Teaching it

To teach this step:

- The teacher should start by explaining how targets are an important part of being able to see if we have achieved a goal.
- The teacher should introduce learners to SMART targets and why each of the components is important.
- Learners could then be asked to create their own targets for different scenarios, checking that they have fulfilled each of the SMART elements in turn. Peer assessment could be a useful tool at this point.
- Finally, the teacher can lead a discussion of why it is so important to get targets right – this could include sharing some examples of government or other targets, and how they ended up distorting practice to fulfil the target.

Reinforcing it

This step can be reinforced whenever learners are being asked to set targets for themselves or for some aspects of their work. It can also be reinforced whenever learners are exploring relevant topics in business, politics, economics, or other subject areas.

Assessing it

This step is best assessed by setting learners an exercise giving them a scenario and asking them to develop SMART targets that support that help to make that goal tangible and measurable.

Aiming High Step 12

Step 12: I create plans that are informed by external views, including constructive criticism

To achieve Step 12, individuals will show that they actively seek external views in developing their plans, including constructive criticism.

In the previous steps, the focus has been on building plans based on an understanding of the goals, resources, and skills available. This step develops this further by also looking at how to engage with external views and seek constructive criticism to improve these plans.

Building blocks

The building blocks of this step are:

- I understand and recognise the role of constructive criticism
- I identify appropriate people and how to ask for constructive criticism
- I identify how to build external views into plans I create

Reflection questions

- Why is it important to include external views as we develop our plans?
- What is constructive criticism, and how can it be helpful?
- How can we ask for constructive criticism?
- When should we time asking for external views?
- Have you had any experience of doing this, and what was the result?

What you need to know

The value of external views

The best plans are informed by a wide range of external views. This is a common theme between many of the other skills, including Listening, Speaking, and Creativity.

Engaging with a range of external views can help us to:

- Learn new information
- See a new perspective on a problem
- Challenge our preconceptions or misconceptions
- Force us to articulate our ideas
- Generate new ideas
- Solve problems together

For this reason, all organisations that create effective plans consult widely with team members, clients, customers, and other stakeholders to ensure that their plans are informed and challenged as widely as possible.

Constructive criticism

Constructive criticism is one part of gathering external views. It is about asking others to identify what might be wrong in your existing plans and to suggest ways of making improvements or addressing some of those shortcomings.

It is quite different to criticism because it is focused on making improvements more than just telling you what is wrong. Constructive criticism is normally defined by:

- A positive, helpful tone
- Identification of what is working well, as well as what can be improved
- Considered, reasoned opinions
- Explanation of points
- A willingness to discuss the critique more widely

In some cases, you will have an open, trusting relationship with someone where giving and receiving constructive criticism is a normal part of how you work together. This is invaluable for your development and that of your plans.

However, in other cases you will need to be proactive in encouraging others to feel they can share what they really think. You should not believe that generally encouraging comments are necessarily a true reflection of what the other person is thinking – they might just be being polite.

Asking for constructive criticism

To encourage others to give constructive criticism, you need to first be explicit about the fact that you welcome it. For example:

- "This thinking is at an early stage, and I would really value your input to make it better."
- "This plan is just a starting point, so I'd love to hear your thoughts."

You can then ask questions to encourage others to give constructive criticism:

- What do you like about the plan at the moment?
- What do you have concerns about?
- What do you think I should also think about?
- Do you think there are any mistaken assumptions I've made?

This questioning will help the other individual to feel like they have permission to be honest and open with you in their feedback – and this sort of feedback will definitely be the most helpful.

When are external views most valuable

External views can play an essential role at all different stages of putting together and implementing a plan. That includes when goals are being devised, analysis carried out, and action plans being written.

The crucial thing is to get external input early so that it can be built into your thinking rather than needing to change plans later on – or receiving feedback when it is too late to do anything with it.

If you can engage people early, then they can become your most engaged partners, because they will share a sense of ownership with you about the plan and the outcomes. That also means that they are much more likely to support you along the way to realise those plans.

Teaching it

To teach this step:

- The teacher should start by asking learners to think about what they might get out of engaging with external views when they are developing their plans. This should include some of the ideas that were shared earlier, and potentially others too.
- Learners can be asked to define constructive criticism, and what makes it different to just criticism. The teacher can lead a discussion of why this sort of feedback can be helpful, but also why it is not always easy to come by.
- The teacher can introduce some of the approaches for asking for constructive criticism from others, modelling how they might ask. Learners can practice this in pairs, with an emphasis on giving permission for the other person to provide feedback.
- Finally, learners can reflect on the stages in the planning process when external feedback can be valuable, and how they might go about gaining it.

Reinforcing it

This step can be encouraged across learning, as it is a good habit for learners to seek out constructive criticism across many aspects of their work and personal development. This could be extended to reviewing one another's work as peers and being able to give helpful, constructive feedback to one another.

Assessing it

This step is best assessed by observing whether learners can give and receive constructive criticism and actively seek external views when developing their ideas and plans.

Leadership

Supporting, encouraging, and developing others to achieve a shared goal

Why it matters

Leadership and teamwork are two critical parts of interpersonal skills. Both are about how we relate to others and collaborate to shared goals – the difference is our role relative to others.

This is a skill which is at risk of being seen as innate; we talk too easily about 'natural leaders'. However, there is good evidence that teachable, learnable skills underpin being an effective leader.

Building leadership skills will enable learners to play an active role and make a good contribution in their school or college, or in their wider lives. Leadership skills are particularly valued when they leave school and join the working world or become entrepreneurs. It is possible to put some of those building blocks in place early.

How Leadership is built

This skill is relevant not only for individuals in leadership positions, but also for learners working with peers in teams.

At the earliest stages, the focus is on basic empathy – understanding their own feelings, being able to share them, and recognising the feelings of others.

After that, the focus turns to managing – dividing up tasks, managing time and sharing resources, managing group discussions, and dealing with disagreements.

Beyond that, individuals build their awareness of their own strengths and weaknesses, and those of their teams. This allows them to allocate tasks effectively. They then build techniques to mentor, coach and motivate others. At the highest steps, individuals will be able to reflect on their own leadership style and understand its effect on others.

Ultimately, they should be able to build on their strengths, mitigate their weaknesses, and adapt their leadership style to the situation.

Skills Builder Framework for Leadership

Supporting, encouraging, and developing others to achieve a shared goal

Step 0	I know how I am feeling about something
Step 1	I know how to explain my feelings about something to my team
Step 2	I know how to recognise others' feelings about something
Step 3	I manage dividing up tasks between others in a fair way
Step 4	I manage time and share resources to support completing tasks
Step 5	I manage group discussions to reach shared decisions
Step 6	I manage disagreements to reach shared solutions
Step 7	I recognise my own strengths and weaknesses as a leader
Step 8	I recognise the strengths and weaknesses of others in my team
Step 9	I recognise the strengths and weaknesses of others in my team, and use this to allocate roles accordingly
Step 10	I support others through mentorship
Step 11	I support others through coaching
Step 12	I support others through motivating them
Step 13	I reflect on my own leadership style and its effect on others
Step 14	I reflect on my own leadership style, and build on my strengths and mitigate my weaknesses
Step 15	I reflect on my own leadership style, and adapt my approach according to the situation

Leadership Step 0

Step 0: I know how I am feeling about something

To achieve Step 0, individuals will need to be able to identify their feelings about something, whether positive or negative.

This is the first step for Leadership and focuses on building empathy as an essential foundation for being able to lead others.

Building blocks

The building blocks of this step are:

- I know what different emotions might look and feel like
- I recognise positive emotions and what might cause them
- I recognise negative emotions and what might cause them

Reflection questions

- What are different emotions?
- When do you feel different emotions?
- Can you give examples of what has caused different emotions for you?

What you need to know

Different emotions

An emotion is a strong feeling that is caused by something that is happening. There are broadly two different types of emotions:

- Positive emotions: These emotions make us feel good, and that we want to continue to feel like this. We might describe ourselves as being happy, excited, or calm.
- Negative emotions: These emotions make us feel bad, and we want to stop feeling like this. We might describe ourselves as feeling sad, angry, or scared.

Lots of different things cause our emotions, and they are lots of them:

Positive emotions	Negative emotions
Happy: • Joy • Grateful • Optimistic Excited: Amused • Energetic • Inspired Calm: • Kind • Loving • Relaxed	Sad: • Disappointed • Tired • Fed up Angry: • Irritated • Angry • Upset Scared: • Nervous • Anxious • Frightened

Positive emotional responses

An *emotional response* is how we feel about something that has happened. We often have an emotional response before we have time to think about what has happened fully – people sometimes call this our 'gut reaction' to what has happened.

If you think something is a good thing, you will typically have a positive emotional response.

Positive emotions	What might cause you to feel like this
Happy: • Joy • Grateful • Optimistic	Getting good news or getting positive feedback where someone tells you have done something well.
Excited: • Amused • Energetic • Inspired	When you are enjoying something, or you think that something good is going to happen soon.
Calm: • Kind • Loving • Relaxed	Knowing that everything is alright and that you don't need to worry about it.

Negative emotional responses

If something is a bad thing, you will typically have a negative emotional response:

Negative emotions	What might cause you to feel like this
Sad: • Disappointed • Tired • Fed up	This is usually caused by bad news, something going wrong or getting some negative feedback from someone.

Angry: • Irritated • Angry • Upset	This is typically caused by feeling that something has been unfair, or someone has been rude or aggressive to you.
Scared: • Nervous • Anxious • Frightened	This is generally caused by uncertainty or the feeling that something terrible is going to happen in the future.

Teaching it

To teach this step:

- The teacher can introduce a discussion about emotions, and what some of the different emotions are that a learner might feel.
- Learners can contribute their ideas of what some of the different emotions are that they might feel at different times, and the teacher can help to organise those ideas into the broad groups suggested:
    - Positive emotions: happy; excited; calm
    - Negative emotions: sad; angry; scared
- The teacher can then facilitate a discussion about when learners have felt different emotions and how they knew that is what they were feeling.

Reinforcing it

This step can be effectively reinforced through learning. It might be helpful to have a visual reminder of the different emotions up in the classroom, and learners could be encouraged to stop and reflect on how they are feeling at different times.

The key at this stage is to help learners to recognise and be able to name the emotions that they are feeling in response to different things.

Assessing it

This step is best assessed through discussion with learners and asking them to share how they feel at different points or in reaction to different ideas.

Leadership Step 1

Step 1: I know how to explain my feelings about something to my team

To achieve Step 1, individuals will be able to communicate how they are feeling about something to their teams.

In the previous step, the focus was on individuals being able to recognise their feelings about something. This step builds on this by thinking about how to share those feelings with others.

Building blocks

The building blocks of this step are:

- I recognise why it is helpful to explain how I am feeling
- I know there are good ways to express how I am feeling
- I know there are bad ways to express how I am feeling

Reflection questions

- Why is it helpful to be able to explain your feelings to others in your teams?
- What should you be careful about doing when you talk about your feelings?
- Can you give any examples of when you have done this? What was the result?

What you need to know

Why it is helpful to explain how you feel about something

When we are working with other people, it can be useful to share how we feel about things.

If we are feeling negative emotions:

- *People can support us:* If we are feeling negative emotions, other people might help us understand a situation better or help us feel better about it.
- *People can understand our view:* We might be feeling differently about something to other people, so it's useful to explain this. This difference might be because we see problems that other people don't, or what someone has said has affected us in a way other people have not seen. This is essential information to share.
- *People might share their views:* If we share our opinions well, it encourages other people to share theirs too. It might be that actually everyone shares feels the same view, but no one has said it yet.

If we are feeling positive emotions:

- *People might feel encouraged:* If you share positive emotions about something with people, they tend to feel more positive about it too. This encouragement is critical to make people want to do something.
- *People can see the positive side of something:* It might be that other people have negative emotions about something – if you share how you feel it can help them to see the other side of the situation.

Expressing your feelings badly

We have to be careful, though, because it is easy to share how you're feeling poorly – which can be much more damaging than not sharing your feelings at all.

- Sometimes people share how they are feeling about something through their *body language* without explaining how they are feeling or why. If you feel negatively about something, other people in your team can probably tell, but if you do not explain how you are feeling and why, they cannot do anything to help and might feel that you are not trying to make something better.
- Sometimes when people are *angry,* they cannot stop themselves from shouting, pointing, or behaving aggressively. This is a poor way of sharing how you feel because it will upset other people or make them angry too.
- Sometimes when people are *sad*, they don't want to talk to the group because they feel too upset. However, not talking means that others don't understand your concerns and might think that you are just not interested.
- Sometimes when people are *scared,* they become nervous and want to leave the situation. Leaving the situation can sometimes be the right answer if you are in danger. At other times, it is better to talk about why you feel like that so the problem or situation can be resolved.

How to express your feelings in a good way

It is possible to express how you are feeling, whether positive or negative, in an effective way if you are careful. There are a few things you should do:

- *Think before you speak:* the most important thing to remember is that you have an emotional feeling about something quicker than your head can think about it. Get into the habit of stopping yourself, thinking first about why you feel the way you do before reacting.
- *Try not to make it personal if it is negative:* don't say "she made me feel…" or "he makes me angry…" Instead, try not to blame other people. For example, you could say "I felt angry because…". This will stop an argument.
- *Try to explain why you feel that way:* sometimes it can be challenging to tell why we feel the way we do about something, but if you can explain it, it will make it a lot easier for other people to understand how they can help.
- *Ask other people how they are feeling too:* t can be helpful to know how other people are feeling in case it changes your mind or makes you think about something differently.

Teaching it

To teach this step:

- The teacher can introduce the skill step by asking learners to reflect on why it can be valuable to express feelings to others they are working with. These ideas can be gathered and discussed.
- The teacher can then facilitate a discussion of how this can be poorly done and what the impact would be. Learners could reflect on times when they feel they have shared their feelings poorly.
- The teacher can then ask learners to come up with a series of tips for how to express emotions well. These can be used as helpful visual reminders.
- Finally, learners could use role-play to practise how they would share their feelings effectively in various hypothetical scenarios.

Reinforcing it

This step can be reinforced in the classroom quite easily. When learners are in groups, it can be good to encourage them to express how they are feeling about things that their groups are discussing or working on – and to talk about how to share their feelings effectively. This might also be a helpful approach to resolving conflicts outside of learning.

Assessing it

This step is best assessed through observation of group tasks and reflection when incidents have occurred. You will be looking to see that learners can effectively share their feelings without causing further harm or upset, and where possible to resolve differences.

Leadership Step 2

Step 2: I know how to recognise others' feelings about something

To achieve Step 2, individuals will show that they can recognise the feelings of others.

In earlier steps, the focus was on individuals understanding their feelings and being able to explain them to others. This step is recognising the emotions of others and how to react well to those.

Building blocks

The building blocks of this step are:

- I know how to recognise how people might be feeling
- I link how people might be feeling to what has happened
- I explore others' feeling to understand why they feel that way

Reflection questions

- How can you tell how other people are feeling without them speaking?
- How can you explore how other people are feeling through questioning?
- How should you react to others' feelings?

What you need to know

How to recognise others' feelings

It is not always easy to tell what emotion someone is feeling, and some people might choose to try to hide how they are feeling for different reasons. However, we can also pick up some clues about how people are feeling:

Positive emotions	How you might be able to tell
Happy: • Joy • Grateful • Optimistic	Happy people tend to smile, and to look at you directly. They might also laugh and seem comfortable.
Excited: • Amused • Energetic • Inspired	People who are excited tend to be very active and look like they have lots of energy, like they want to get on and do something.
Calm: • Kind • Loving • Relaxed	Calm people are likely to have a more neutral facial expression, although they might smile a bit. They seem to be content to stay where they are, rather than having lots of energy to use.

We might also pick up clues for negative emotions that people might be feeling. For example:

Negative emotions	How you might be able to tell
Sad: • Disappointed • Tired • Fed up	People who are feeling sad are unlikely to be smiling and might have downturned mouths. They are unlikely to laugh and might cry or look like they could cry.
Angry: • Irritated • Angry • Upset	Angry people tend to have a lot of energy. They might shout or talk loudly and might look red-faced. They might frown or clench their teeth together.
Scared: • Nervous • Anxious • Frightened	Scared people might not look directly at you but look around. They might seem twitchy and are unlikely to laugh or smile.

Over time, you might well be able to get better at recognising emotions in other people by looking for some of these signs.

How to explore how other people are feeling

Although we might be able to get a sense of how other people are feeling through their facial expressions and body language, we should not just presume that we understand:

- We might have *misread* how they are feeling – we might easily confuse sadness and nervousness.
- We could also have misunderstood *what* they are thinking. We might think they are reacting to what we're thinking about, but they are upset or excited about something entirely different in their own lives.
- We might not know *why* they are feeling that way. It is easy for us to assume that we understand why they have a particular reaction, but it is just a guess.

For all these reasons, we should try to learn more about why people feel the way that they do about something. To do this, we can use:

- *A safe space*: making sure people feel that they can share how they are feeling about something without getting into trouble.
- *Open questions:* these are questions that do not presume to know the answer. For example, you might ask someone "What do you think about that?" or "How do you feel about that?"
- *Ask follow up questions:* to check your understanding, you can use follow up questions but, again, try not to presume you know the answer. For example: "What is it that disappoints you about that?"

How to react to people's feelings

Sometimes you might not understand why someone feels the way they do or feel that it does not make sense. That is why it is important not to end up arguing with people about how they feel or how they should feel.

Instead, the focus should be about *acknowledging* how someone is feeling ("I understand that you feel…" or "I hear that you feel…"). You can then try to understand why and see if anything can be done to make them feel better if they are feeling negative about something.

Teaching it

To teach this step:

- If the teacher feels confident, they could act out different emotions and ask learners to try to guess what emotion they are feeling. This can lead into a discussion about how we recognise the feelings of others.
- Learners could capture their ideas on how you spot different emotions, either in a written form or in drawings.
- The teacher should then discuss why we shouldn't just rely on what we see to presume we understand others' emotions. Instead, we should check what we think and try to understand why someone feels that way.
- Learners can practice these ideas through role-play, thinking particularly about the way they would ask questions.

Reinforcing it

This step can be reinforced in the classroom setting when learners are working collaboratively, and new ideas are introduced, or disagreements worked through. In some settings, this can also be a helpful way to encourage learners to resolve misunderstandings or to work together more effectively.

Assessing it

This step is best assessed through observation of an activity where learners have to explore the feelings of others about something. The assessor is looking for whether the learners can think about the emotions someone else might be feeling and then explore this further through questioning. A reflective discussion after the exercise can help check learners' understanding.

Leadership Step 3

Step 3: I manage dividing up tasks between others in a fair way

To achieve Step 3, individuals will be able to divide up tasks between others in a justifiable way.

In the earlier steps of Leadership, the focus was on individuals being able to identify and express their own emotions and then those of others. The focus now shifts to thinking about task management.

Building blocks

The building blocks of this step are:

- I know how to divide up tasks
- I know how to share tasks out in a fair way
- I spot if there are problems

Reflection questions

- What do we mean by tasks?
- How can you share tasks between people in a fair way?
- How can you tell if there are problems with how you have divided up tasks?
- Do you have any examples of having done this?

What you need to know

Dividing up tasks

When we want to do something as a team, it often does not make sense for everyone to be trying to do the same thing at the same time.

Instead, we might want to divide up the job into smaller tasks that different people can do. In the end, all of these various tasks should add up to the job being completed.

When we divide up tasks, we want to think about some questions:

- Is the task something that one person can do, or does it depend on something else happening?
- Does the task need some special skills so that not everyone will be able to do it?
- How long will the task take to complete?
- How difficult is the task – will it use a lot of thinking effort, or lots of physical effort?
- How enjoyable is the task?

How to share out tasks in a fair way

When we share tasks out, we will be limited by:

- Only being able to give tasks using specialist skills to those who have them
- Some tasks being limited in who they can be given to, if they are dependent on other tasks being completed too.

Otherwise, we can try to be as fair as possible. Ideas of what is fair will be different from person to person, but we should try to make sure that everyone has tasks which:

- Use a similar amount of physical or mental effort (unless someone prefers these sorts of tasks when we might give them more of them).
- Take a similar amount of time (unless team members differ in how much time they have).
- Are about as enjoyable or unenjoyable as each other.

How to spot if there are problems

In the previous step, we looked at how you might be able to understand how other people feel about things. It might be that when you shared tasks out, you did not have enough information about how long the different tasks would take or know enough about what people enjoyed or felt able to do.

If you can tell that people are unhappy, then you should use some of the ideas in *Step 2* to have a conversation about what is wrong and then think again about how to share the tasks.

You might also spot a problem if some tasks are taking too long, or someone is struggling to complete a task. In this case, you might be able to help them out, or ask someone else to take on that task or some other tasks to share things out evenly again.

The best way to avoid problems, though, is to talk to your team about how you have divided up tasks, and how you decided how to share them between people before you start. This way, people can talk about any concerns before you get started.

Teaching it

To teach this step:

- The teacher should introduce the idea of how we work with people to get things done and how we have to think in terms of tasks. Learners could think of examples of tasks that might need to be completed as part of a bigger job – for instance, in setting up an event like a cake sale or a simulated challenge like building a newspaper tower.
- The teacher can introduce how to think about sharing out the tasks among team members. For example, thinking about how long the different tasks would take, the skills they would need, and how difficult or enjoyable they are. This could be applied to either a hypothetical event or, better, to the simulated challenge.
- In the simulated problem, learners could then put their ideas into action, and use reflection to explore whether they had managed to divide up tasks in a fair way, and how they dealt with any mistakes as they came up.

Reinforcing it

This step can be reinforced by encouraging learners to divide up tasks between them when there are opportunities for them to work together. The teacher can help to raise awareness of what they should be thinking about when making these decisions and encouraging them to reflect on how effective their approach was at the end.

Assessing it

This step is best assessed through a structured activity, where learners are given a job and have to think about the tasks and how they might be divided up fairly between the team they have been allocated. A reflection discussion at the end will help to show whether they applied sensible thinking to how to divide up tasks fairly.

Leadership Step 4

Step 4: I manage time and share resources to support completing tasks

To achieve Step 4, individuals will show that they can manage the completion of tasks within time constraints, and make sure team members have the resources they need to complete the tasks.

In the previous step, the focus was on how to divide up tasks between others fairly. This step builds on this by thinking about other things that need to be managed to complete a job.

Building blocks

The building blocks of this step are:

- I manage the team's time effectively
- I ensure my team has the right resources
- I know how to support my team to complete tasks

Reflection questions

- Why is it important for a leader to be able to manage time and resources?
- What sort of resources might you have to manage?
- How can you support your team?
- What could you do if things don't go to plan?
- Do you have any examples of having managed a task like this?

What you need to know

Managing the time of your team

A critical part of managing is to be aware of time. Lots of tasks will have *deadlines* attached to them which is the time that a task has to be completed by. If a deadline is missed, it might mean that:

- The task is no longer worth doing - for example, a newspaper that misses its publishing deadline won't be in the shops the next day
- Other tasks that rely on this task being finished can't start
- There are delays that cause inconvenience to others

It is critical from the beginning to be clear about how much time you have, and then telling the team this very clearly. You should also explain why this deadline has been set, so that they take it seriously.

You can then work out how long the different tasks will take, and by allocating them between team members how long everything will take. You should always allow extra time because things often take longer than we expect.

Once you have shared the tasks out among your team, you need to think about how you will know if you're on track. Some jobs might all be done in an hour or a day, others will run over weeks or months. In either case, you cannot afford to wait until the deadline to work out if you are on time or not.

Instead, you should think about asking your team to think about when they will finish each of their different tasks. This way, you can check at that time whether they are finished, which helps you to understand that everything is going correctly. It is also helpful for them because it is motivating to see progress made and will be calming for them to know if they are on track to finish on time.

Giving your team the right resources

Resources are those things that people need to complete the tasks that you have given them. They might include:

- Tools like stationery, screwdrivers, saws
- Technology like computers, printers, tablets, phones
- Materials like paper, wood, metal, plastic, screws
- Money to buy resources they need

It is your job as the leader to make sure that people have what they need to complete their tasks or can acquire those resources.

At times, it might be that team members need to share resources to complete their tasks. If this is the case, then you need to think carefully to ensure that those tasks are not planned to happen at the same time.

How to support your team

Before the tasks begin, you can support your team by:

- Being clear about what needs to happen and inviting questions or alternative ideas to make how you divide up tasks better. Remember, in the end you have to make the decision.
- Reminding the team about what the timeline is and when different things need to be ready.
- Telling your team that you are prepared to help them if they need it.

Once tasks are underway, there are a few key things that you should do as a leader to ensure that the tasks are a success:

- *Check how everyone is getting on:* if someone is struggling, then help them out or think about whether you have shared out tasks in the right way (see *Step 3*)
- *Remind people of the time:* check that tasks are completing at the time they were meant to be. If they are not, then you should decide whether it is okay for them to run a bit late, or whether you need to share tasks out differently or give them extra help.
- *Be positive about progress:* people feel encouraged to keep working, but don't ignore problems, just try to fix them quickly.

Teaching it

To teach this step:

- The teacher should introduce the idea of how we lead a team to complete a set of tasks, starting by how we allocate tasks between different individuals. This is a recap of *Step 4* but provides essential context for this next step.
- This step can be taught effectively by walking learners through a simulation or a real-life task – for example, by creating a production line for greetings cards. Each team will have one allocated leader, but will have to discuss the decisions together, so all learners have the experience of decision-making.

- Using this simulation, learners can create a plan of how to allocate different tasks and how to plan out how to reach a deadline. They also have to decide how to assign a limited number of resources between their teammates.
- Once underway, the leader should follow the guidelines discussed to support their teammates and ensure that the task is completed successfully.
- The teacher can introduce most of the ideas in structuring the exercise as runs, and it would also be valuable to lead a reflection at the end of the session so that learners can firm up their understanding of what this looks like in practice.

Reinforcing it

This step can be reinforced when learners have the opportunity to work together in teams on a project or extended task.

Assessing it

This step is best assessed through observation of an individual through a simulated task, as laid out above, or on a real-life project. The teacher can look for evidence that they were able to think about the tasks that needed to be completed, the time available, and how resources should be allocated. During the task, they can look for evidence that the leader is working to support the others in his team.

Leadership Step 5

Step 5: I manage group discussions to reach shared decisions

To achieve Step 5, individuals will have to show that they can manage group discussions towards shared decisions.

In earlier steps, the focus was on how leaders manage tasks by sharing them thoughtfully and fairly, and then managing time and resources so that team members can complete those tasks. This step expands on that by engaging team members in that decision-making process.

Building blocks

The building blocks of this step are:

- I identify the different roles that exist in a meeting
- I chair meetings so everyone has a chance to contribute their ideas
- I support the team to reach a decision

Reflection questions

- What do you need to do to plan a good meeting?
- How do you make sure everyone has a chance to contribute their ideas?
- How do you get to decisions?
- Have you had experience of bad meetings? What went wrong?

What you need to know

How to organise a meeting

In some jobs, there are endless meetings – in others, they are only occasional. A meeting is when two or more people come together for a discussion for one or more of these reasons:

- To share information
- To create new ideas
- To debate different views and perspectives
- To get to know someone and build a relationship
- To make decisions

To run a meeting effectively, there are some things that you need to have decided in advance:

- *Who is organising the meeting?* This is the person who will ensure that the right people are invited, that the *agenda* is decided, information is shared in advance, and there is an appropriate location.
- *Who is chairing the meeting?* There is usually a leader for a meeting, who makes sure that the session runs smoothly, keeps to time, covers the agenda, and makes decisions.
- *What is being covered?* The agenda of the meeting is the document which says what is being discussed in the meeting. These different things are typically called *Items,* and they often have a time allocation for them

- *Who needs to be invited?* For meetings to work well, there needs to be careful thought about who is invited: if you ask people who are not required they will have wasted their time; if you miss people out you might have to repeat the meeting so that they get the information. Also, remember that the more people there are in the meeting, the more difficult it is to manage.
- *How much time is needed?* This will depend on how many things need to be covered and how many people are involved. Meetings can vary in length from a 10-minute catch-up to a whole-day or multi-day event.
- *Where will be the meeting be held?* The location will depend on how many people are involved and how formal or informal the meeting is. It could be a quick catch-up over coffee, a large meeting around a table, or even need a hall for a very large meeting.
- *What information do attendees need in advance?* Think about what you need attendees to think about before the meeting to make the best use of the time. Lots of formal meetings have pre-reading for attendees so that the time can be used on conversation, rather than just sharing information.

Different roles in a meeting

There will be different roles during a meeting itself. If it is a small meeting, then it is likely that one person will take on more than one of the roles:

- *Chair:* this is the person who leads or facilitates the meeting. Their role is to make sure that the *Agenda* is covered, that the meeting keeps to time, that a range of people speak, and that decisions are made. The Chair is often the leader, or the more senior person at the meeting.
- *Notetaker:* for formal meetings, usually there will be someone responsible for writing down a summary of what happened and the decisions. These notes are called *Minutes* and are shared with the attendees after the meeting. They mean that everyone has a record of what was agreed, and what they need to do next – these are called *Actions.*
- *Timekeeper:* meetings will often have a timekeeper to help ensure that the Agenda is being covered at a reasonable speed, although the Chair will often take this role.
- *Presenters:* in some meetings, information will be shared, and this will be given by people called presenters. These people will typically have prepared in advance what they want to say and will share this information.

How to chair a meeting

Chairing a meeting is an important role. One of the most critical parts is giving everyone a chance to contribute their ideas or reflections. There are several things to think about to do this well:

- *Be clear on the question you want to answer:* this should be the focus of the discussion. This will help to keep people on point.
- *Make sure people have the information they need:* if there are presenters, you should make sure they have covered everything that the other attendees need to know to contribute to the discussion.
- *Tell everyone how long you have:* if you only have time for short points from people then tell them that, and then they should talk for less time – and it is more comfortable to stop them when they speak for too long.
- *Make sure people stick to the question you want them to think about:* you can politely say that you will come back to other points later on, or outside that meeting.
- *Check who has spoken:* some people will want to talk more than others and so it is important to encourage quieter people to contribute if they wish.
- *Remember who has particular expertise:* if people are experts or have particularly helpful experience on the question, then encourage them to talk.
- *Keep everyone to time:* conversations can continue indefinitely if they are not stopped.

- *Don't let people talk over each other*: it is your job as Chair to make sure that only one person speaks at a time. Politely tell them you will come to them next.
- *Summarise the discussion*: remind everyone of what has been discussed and share the decision.
- *Clarify decisions*: if the decision is not clear, you can either share what you think the choice is, ask further questions to try to understand what everyone thinks, or vote to make a choice.

Throughout, the way you chair is the most important thing – you need to be polite, calm, and clearly in control of what is going on.

Teaching it

To teach this step:

- The teacher should ensure that learners have a shared understanding of what a meeting is, and that meetings come in all sorts of shapes or sizes. Images can help to illustrate that – from the UN General Assembly to two people catching up for coffee.
- The best way to teach this step is to simulate a meeting of the whole class in the first instance, modelling how to set an agenda, and all the other preparatory steps.
- The teacher could chair at this stage, encouraging all learners to participate and keeping the points focused. Another learner could be given the role of note-taker, and another as timekeeper.
- Throughout the meeting, the teacher can model how they are following good practice in how they run the meeting. These guidelines can then be shared with learners.
- It would then be good for learners to have the opportunity to run their own meetings in small groups. They can all be given a meeting purpose, and then come up with their own agendas, chair the meetings, and share the Minutes at the end.

Reinforcing it

This step can be well reinforced if learners have an extended project, although it can also be reinforced through shorter tasks. Reminding learners of the role of a chair and what makes a productive meeting, and then carrying out a reflection afterwards will help them to build their confidence in running sessions in this way.

Assessing it

This step is best assessed through observing a meeting and how the leader organises and then chairs a meeting. The teacher should look for evidence of effective chairing using some of the guidelines above.

Leadership Step 6

Step 6: I manage disagreements to reach shared solutions

To achieve Step 6, individuals will show that they can manage disagreements towards achieving shared solutions.

In the previous step, the focus was on how to set up and manage a group discussion in the format of a meeting. This step focuses on when there are disagreements, how these can be positive opportunities, and how to work towards a shared solution.

Building blocks

The building blocks of this step are:

- I recognise that disagreements can be helpful
- I know how disagreements can be unhelpful
- I know how to turn disagreements into shared solutions

Reflection questions

- When have you experienced disagreements that end up being helpful?
- When have you seen disagreements that are unhelpful?
- What do you think works to turn disagreements into shared solutions?
- Do you have any examples of having done this, or seen others do it?

What you need to know

When disagreements are helpful

It is easy to fall into the trap of imagining that all disagreements are unhelpful. We might believe that it is much better if everyone immediately agrees what the right thing is to do and gets onto it. Sometimes this is the case, particularly for routine or straightforward decisions.

However, when trying to decide on something more complicated, it can be damaging to all just agree with one another. This risk is called *groupthink*.

Groupthink occurs because people tend to want to agree with each other. It is much more pleasant than arguing, and the more it seems that everyone agrees with each other, the more difficult it will be for any individual to disagree with the rest of the group. It might also be that group members believe the decision has already been made. In this case, there is little to gain by questioning or disagreeing with what is proposed.

There are lots of examples of when group think has led to bad decisions. These bad decisions occur because there are often good reasons for people to disagree. They might have:

- *information or insights* that others in the group don't have
- a *different perspective* that others in haven't seen – for example, seeing an effect that others haven't imagined
- *better ideas* of how a problem could be solved
- insight into *problems* that haven't been considered

If shared well, these disagreements are healthy and helpful, and a good leader will encourage their team to contribute to discussions and actively encourage different views and perspectives. This giving permission for people to disagree is essential – the leader should be clear that they are not fixed on the answer before the conversation has taken place.

When disagreements are unhelpful

While disagreements are often helpful when built into conversation well, they can be harmful if the timing or way they are delivered is wrong. Sometimes that differences become negative include when:

- *Offered in the wrong way:* It is possible to disagree without being unpleasant. People disagreeing can always show that they understand another person's perspective, can always be polite, and can always speak calmly and pleasantly.
- *Delivered at the wrong time:* Disagreements are much more difficult to manage if they are shared after a discussion, when tasks are underway. This doesn't mean that they should never be shared – for example, some new information might come to life, or an unexpected danger might be spotted. However, it is much more difficult to adapt if disagreements arise late.
- *An unwillingness to change:* Most differences come about because of different information or views and can generally be resolved. Sometimes though, people hold on to their opinions and refuse to listen to others or think differently. In these cases, disagreements can become hard to resolve and so are much less helpful.

How to reach shared solutions

An essential part of a leader's role is to resolve disagreements to achieve reasonable, shared solutions. There are several steps to doing this effectively:

- *Give everyone to the opportunity to share their views*: be clear that a decision has not yet been made, so people feel it is worth sharing what they think.
- *Actively encourage a range of views*: make sure that you are not just hearing from the same people that you always hear from and be clear that everyone has something to contribute. Ask if anyone disagrees or sees things differently.
- *Build a shared understanding*: ask questions to check what people think and why. Don't let people just make assertions without backing up the reasons *why* they believe that. This might mean sharing data, past experiences, or other facts.
- *Frame the choices*: sometimes, you will need to *choose* between two or more different options. Other times there will be a *compromise* where you do a bit of two or more options, or sometimes you can *combine* ideas to reach a better answer.
- *Reach consensus:* in the end, you want everyone to agree so that you have a shared plan. You can help to achieve this by asking whether people are happy with the proposed approach. If you do not all agree, then you can use voting to help make the decision.
- *Be clear about what has been decided and why:* it might be that in the end, not everyone is totally pleased. You can bring them along most effectively by talking them through the different views and why the decision has been made. This transparency will help to get people behind the approach, even if they don't agree entirely.

Teaching it

To teach this step:

- The teacher should first model why it can be that disagreements can be positive, giving some examples of silly decisions and the adverse effects they could have if no one had disagreed with them.
- Learners could expand their ideas of ways that disagreements can be helpful. The teacher can capture and record these different ideas.
- The conversation can then expand to talk about when differences can be unhelpful. This might be drawn from learners' experiences.
- Good and bad disagreements could be modelled by giving learners an exercise where they have different perspectives on a question that has been proposed – for example, selling the school or college's playing fields. They could be allocated different roles and bring diverse perspectives to the discussion. In this scenario, the leader has a vital role in encouraging different views and trying to reach a consensus.
- Learners can reflect on the lessons they have learned and potentially repeat the exercise with a different question – for example, whether the school week should be shortened to four days.

Reinforcing it

This step lends itself well to being reinforced in the classroom. For example, when there are interesting or controversial topics, learners could be asked to take a view as a group, and this will give them a chance to air different perspectives and then to try to reconcile them. The teacher could provide learners with differing pieces of information to encourage discussion.

Assessing it

This step is best assessed through observing an activity like that outlined above. The teacher should look for evidence that the leader sees the value of disagreements and actively encourages different contributions. This can be supplemented by a reflection conversation or written reflection, where the learner thinks about how they used some of the approaches outlined above.

Leadership Step 7

Step 7: I recognise my own strengths and weaknesses as a leader

To achieve Step 7, individuals will show that they are aware of their strengths and weaknesses as a leader.

In earlier steps, the focus has been on how to manage groups to achieve tasks: thinking about how tasks are shared out, resources and time managed, and how to manage discussions and disagreements. The focus of the next steps is thinking about leadership more broadly, starting with thinking about their strengths and weaknesses as a leader.

Building blocks

The building blocks of this step are:

- I know the elements of being an effective leader
- I identify my own strengths as a leader
- I identify my own weaknesses as a leader

Reflection questions

- What do we mean by strengths and weaknesses?
- What are good leaders able to do?
- How can we identify what strengths and weaknesses are?
- What can we do about our strengths and weaknesses?

What you need to know

What good leaders do

The most important thing to remember is that there is no perfect leader, there are leaders who are better or worse in different situations. In the Skills Builder Framework, Leadership is defined as *supporting, encouraging, and developing others to achieve a shared goal.*

We think about there being four different elements to being an effective leader:

- *Knowledge and understanding:* To be effective, leaders usually have to expertise and experience in an area that is more than most of their followers. A leader might be better at something so can support and develop others.
- *Relationships:* A vital part of being an effective leader is having the trust of the team who they are leading. These relationships are built up over time – you might be able to build trust quickly, but you can lose it even quicker.
- *Character strengths:* Leaders will also need different character strengths. Character is about the choices that we make. Do you want leaders who are thoughtful, decisive, confident, humble, or lots of other things? We will explore this more in a minute.
- *Skills*: There are lots of practical elements to leadership too – what does a leader need to be able to do? These are the things we have focused on in the Skills Builder Framework.

Leadership beyond character traits

For a long time, a lot of academic focus on Leadership was about trying to find those *character strengths* that explained why some people were much better leaders than others. These *traits* included:

- Endurance
- Decisiveness
- Responsibility-taking
- Compassion
- And many hundreds more

Many of the traits identified appeared to be contradictions. For example, the need to be decisive and to reach consensus.

The thinking now is much more focused on the *situations* in which different traits are more or less useful. For example, a leader like Winston Churchill was built for wartime conflict but was less effective during peacetime.

Lots of character strengths have a negative side if they are too extreme. For example, endurance might lead to bloody-mindedness or the desire to complete something at any cost. Or decisiveness might lead to arrogance or an inability to listen.

For this reason, it is not that helpful to think about a list of traits as being the absolute goal in becoming an effective leader.

How can we identify our strengths and weaknesses?

All of this means that thinking about your strengths and weaknesses is difficult, but there are some important questions that can help to guide you:

- When do you feel *most* confident as a leader?
- When do you feel *least* confident as a leader?
- In what situations do you feel you have shown your best leadership?
- When have you found being the leader more difficult?
- How do you think you could improve further as a leader?
- What do you think are the things that you do well that you want to do more?

It is also useful to ask other people what they see as your strengths and weaknesses. Sometimes other people have a much clearer view than you because they are not in your head. You might ask people who you have led, and those who are experienced leaders who can give you a different perspective.

How to use these insights

We can use these insights in a few different ways:

- We can see the *skills* that we want to get better at, which can support us as leaders. This is what we focus on in the Skills Builder Framework – the practical tools that you can use.
- We can think about the *relationships* that we need to develop and how we go about acting in ways that build trust.
- We can think about how to put ourselves in *situations* which play to our character strengths as leaders. If we have characteristics that we want to address – for example, we feel that sometimes we are arrogant, or indecisive – then we try to practice getting better at these.
- We can build *knowledge and experience* in an area which will help us if we want to be a leader in that area.

The key thing is that everyone, however much or little they have been a leader in the past, has areas of strength and areas of weakness. We can all get better.

Teaching it

To teach this step:

- The teacher can open the discussion by asking learners to reflect on what they think about when they think of great leaders. They might talk about historical or political figures, or more familiar examples.
- The teacher can then lead a discussion of what makes those leaders effective – what are their strengths and weaknesses? It is worth challenging learners to think about how some leaders' strengths have a negative flip side and exploring that.
- The teacher can also introduce the different elements to being an effective leader, emphasising the idea that we can all get better at leadership.
- Learners could be asked to complete a self-reflection based on some of the questions above and then discuss their ideas. These could then be built into a set of actions they could take to improve their leadership skills.

Reinforcing it

This skill is less likely to be regularly built in the classroom setting. However, the big opportunity is that whenever learners do have the chance to take a leadership role – whether in the classroom, co-curricular activities, or their wider lives – they are encouraged to reflect on how it went, and what they can learn from it to become better leaders.

Assessing it

This step is best assessed by encouraging learners to complete a self-reflection and action plan and using this as a way of exploring whether learners can think about their strengths and weaknesses as leaders. This can be extended through conversation or discussion.

Leadership Step 8

Step 8: I recognise the strengths and weaknesses of others in my team

To achieve Step 8, individuals will show that they can identify the strengths and weaknesses of others in their team.

In the previous step, individuals showed they could reflect on their own strengths and weaknesses as a leader. In this step, a similar approach is taken, but extended to thinking about others in the broader team.

Building blocks

The building blocks of this step are:

- I identify areas of strength for others in my team
- I identify areas of weakness for others in my team
- I recognise the different types of skills people have

Reflection questions

- What are some of the areas that you might think about when it comes to strengths and weaknesses?
- What sort of skills might you need to look for?
- How can you identify strengths and weaknesses in others?
- Do you have examples of where you have done this?

What you need to know

Areas of strength or weakness for your team

In the previous step, we talked about the importance of thinking about your leadership strengths and weaknesses in a broad and balanced way. It is exactly the same attitude that you need to take to think about the strengths and weaknesses of your team.

No one is great at everything, and no one is terrible at everything. People are often great in some situations, and not in others. A balanced approach to thinking about the strengths and weaknesses of your team members might include these four areas:

- *Knowledge and understanding:* The expertise and experiences that individuals have, which might consist of formal qualifications, or years of doing something similar.
- *Relationships:* The people that they know, and how positive and trusting those relationships are.
- *Character strengths:* The traits that people have and the choices they make – perhaps including being honest, reliable, careful, enthusiastic, for example.
- *Skills*: These are the things that individuals can do.

Which of these areas you need will depend a lot on the task – this is explored more in *Step 9* when we think about how to use this understanding of strengths and weaknesses to help allocate roles in a team.

Different types of skills

Skills are things that you can do, and we all have lots of them. We can think about three types of skills:

Basic or Foundational Skills: Being able to read and write (literacy skills), work with numbers (numeracy skills) and use some technology (digital skills).

Essential Skills: The essential skills that almost everyone needs to some degree to do almost anything – these are the focus of the Skills Builder Framework.

Technical Skills: Skills that are job or role-specific – like plumbing, nursing, or accounting qualifications and a lot more.

With all skills you might have them to different levels. That is why the Skills Builder Framework, for example, is split up into steps that get progressively more difficult, and which introduce all the different parts of the skills in turn.

How to recognise skills and other attributes

There are different ways of recognising the strengths and weaknesses that people have, and this is also explored in *Aiming High Step 10*.

- Sometimes our *interactions* with people help us to build up a sense of their skills and how well they can do things like listen, speak, solve problems, or work with other people. We can also get a sense of how they behave, make choices, their knowledge and expertise, and how they can build relationships.
- We might also *observe* how people carry out tasks, and we can use this as a way of seeing the strengths they can put into use, and where they appear weaker. This can be done in a real-life situation, or through a simulation.
- We might *ask other people* who have worked with them in different settings to get a fuller picture of their strengths and weaknesses.
- *Discussions* are another way to explore strengths and weaknesses. This is the method used most often by companies when they are recruiting. They often ask people for examples or reflections to help build up a picture of an individual.
- *Qualifications or certificates* are a final way of identifying skills and knowledge and are particularly crucial for some technical skills where real expertise is involved, or where there is danger if mistakes are made.

Remember, there is no perfect way of understanding someone's strengths and weaknesses because they are not always the same, and different situations will draw on them differently.

Teaching it

To teach this step:

- The teacher should ask learners to reflect on how they would think about their individual strengths and weaknesses. This will be a problematic exercise without any structuring because we have strengths and weaknesses in so many different areas of our lives.
- The teacher can talk through some of the different areas we might consider when getting a view of an individual's strengths and weaknesses, and why some areas might be more important at different times.

- Learners can think about some of the different ways of finding out individuals' strengths and weaknesses and contribute to a class discussion.
- This could be applied through an activity when learners reflect on their own strengths and weaknesses in different areas or carry out those reflections based on a choice of character, perhaps from television.

Reinforcing it

This skill step can be reinforced in the classroom by emphasising the critical message that everyone has strengths that they bring to different situations, and everyone has areas of weakness where they can improve. It can be helpful to encourage learners to articulate improvements they are making, and to recognise when they or others are building skills, knowledge, relationships, or character strengths.

This could be extended when learning about individuals in history, geography, literature, or world events as learners could use this approach to analyse those individuals.

Assessing it

This step is best assessed through a simulated exercise where learners are asked to appraise the strengths and weaknesses of a character based on the information they are given or what they can research. They should be encouraged to think about each of the four domains when making their appraisal.

Leadership Step 9

Step 9: I recognise the strengths and weaknesses of others in my team, and use this to allocate roles accordingly

To achieve Step 9, individuals will be able to use their knowledge of the strengths and weaknesses of others in the team to allocate roles effectively.

In the previous step, individuals showed that they were able to appraise the strengths and weaknesses of members of their team. This step builds on this by looking at how to use these insights to allocate roles effectively.

Building blocks

The building blocks of this step are:

- I define what roles are with examples
- I identify the requirements in different roles
- I know how to allocate roles by matching others' strengths with role requirements

Reflection questions

- What do we mean by roles?
- How can we understand what we need from people carrying out particular roles?
- How do we match strengths and role requirements?
- What can we do if there are still gaps?
- Have you had the experience of having to allocate roles in this way?

What you need to know

Understanding roles

A role describes what someone will do in a particular situation. When we think about jobs and tasks, a role describes what that person will do.

When individuals are employed, they have to be given a clear job description which explains what they should do, and what their responsibilities.

A role might be a whole job, or it might be a smaller part of it. For example, when working with a team, we might be asked to take on various different roles, or to take on different roles at different times. This does not mean that it is our entire role forever.

A leader has to decide how to allocate different roles so that the tasks get done. Making the decision about who is best-placed to take on these different roles is an important one.

Identifying the needs in a role

When companies or organisations look to recruit people to join them, they will usually put together a pack of information that includes:

- *What job the person will do:* This includes the title of their job, what they will be expected to do day-to-day, and what or who they will be responsible for.
- *The skills that will be needed:* The job pack will generally explain what skills the employer is looking for in the job, and at what level. This will include basic skills, essential skills, and technical skills (see *Step 8*).
- *The knowledge or qualifications that will be needed:* The job pack will say if particular qualifications or certificates are needed, or if the applicant needs to know about any sector or technical area.
- *The required experience:* Lots of job packs will say that they expect a certain level of experience in a particular industry or type of role. They often put this as a number of years.
- *The behaviours needed:* Lots of job packs will also talk about the character of the individuals they are looking for – for example, reliable, committed, enthusiastic, honest, and more.

Lots of employers put a lot of time and effort into thinking about new roles, and this is why they are a good model.

If we are just allocating smaller roles to complete projects or tasks, a leader is unlikely to put all that time into thinking about exactly what they need, but they should think about the main things those different roles need.

Allocating roles

Once you have a clear view of the strengths and weaknesses of your team in the broad areas that we have discussed, and the needs you have for a role, you can match up who is best for the different roles. You want as many of the needs for the role to be filled as possible by the strengths of the team member.

If you can't fill every need, then you should think about whether a need is either of the following:

- *essential*: the role *cannot* be completed without it
- *desirable*: it would *help* if the individual had this, but it is not essential

You can then prioritise making sure you fulfil all of the *essential* elements. If you can do this, you should think about some of the earlier ideas about sharing out tasks and make sure that they are fair (see *Leadership Step 3*)

At the end of this exercise, you might find that there are things you need from your team that you haven't been able to match perfectly. This is where mentorship and coaching are critical, and these are explored in the next two steps.

Teaching it

To teach this step:

- The teacher should start by revising the key areas that individuals might have as strengths or weaknesses from *Step 8*: knowledge; relationships; character; and skills.
- Learners could be shown (or find) some example job packs to explore how employers share what they need applicants to know, how they behave, and what they can do.

- Learners can then apply this to creating a role description for a task that they imagine or are given. For example, for someone who was going to be a prefect in the school or who would support them with their learning.
- They could then be given some artificial profiles of individuals and think how to allocate them to different roles based on an assessment of the needs to the role and the strengths and weaknesses of the individuals.

Reinforcing it

This step can be reinforced if learners are given an extended collaborative project where there will be lots of opportunities for them to think about the different roles that need to be completed and allocated.

This exercise can also be used by reflecting on individuals that learners come across in their wider studies – for example, in geography, history or literature.

Assessing it

This step is best assessed through a structured activity where learners have to make an assessment of characters' strengths and weaknesses based on profiles they are given, and then allocate roles accordingly. A reflective discussion can help uncover learners' thinking through this process.

Leadership Step 10

Step 10: I support others through mentorship

To achieve Step 10, individuals will show that they can use mentorship to help support and develop others.

In previous steps, the focus was on individuals understanding the strengths and weaknesses of themselves as leaders and of other team members. They then use this insight to allocate roles accordingly. This step and those that follow look at how to support team members to build those strengths further and to address areas of weakness.

Building blocks

The building blocks of this step are:

- I define and explain what mentorship is
- I identify what makes mentoring work for the mentee
- I support my mentee to identify goals

Reflection questions

What does mentorship mean?

- Have you ever had a mentor or been a mentor?
- What do you think makes mentoring work well?
- When does mentoring not work well?

What you need to know

What mentorship means

Mentorship is where one person provides advice or guidance to another, normally based on their higher level of skill, knowledge, experience, or networks.

It is a way of an individual providing support to another and using their resources to support them. There is usually a clear split between the roles of the mentor and the mentee (the person who is being mentored), with the mentor typically being more senior.

Mentorship can happen in the context of education, in employment, in entrepreneurship, and in the wider world. As a result, an individual might have more than one mentor, spanning different areas of their lives. An individual might also have a mentor and be a mentor to someone else at the same time.

How mentoring varies

Mentoring comes in lots of different forms:

- It might be an *informal arrangement* between two people who have got to know one another outside of any organisation.
- It might be *brokered* – that is, that another organisation has helped to set up and support the mentoring relationship. This is often the case when young people are being mentored, for example.
- It might be a *formal programme*, organised by an organisation for its employees, or by a school, college, or university for its learners.
- It might be *structural* – for example, when a line manager in a business becomes a *de facto* mentor for those they manage.

Mentoring can also differ by:

- *How it is delivered:* It could be in person, over the telephone, or virtual. There are good examples of each of these different types of mentorship.
- *How regular it is:* How frequently mentoring happens varies a great deal. It might be a daily event or it might be monthly, or even less often than that.
- *How long the relationship lasts:* Some mentoring relationships are only ever planned to last for a fixed period, perhaps a couple of months or a year. Others run indefinitely for as long as they are useful.

The type of mentoring that works best depends on the relationship between the mentor and mentee and their goals.

What makes mentoring work

When mentoring works well, it can be a powerful tool which has benefits both to the mentee and to the mentor too. Some important things for mentoring to work effectively are:

- The mentor and mentee get on with each other, and can have a positive relationship
- The expectations of both are clear and understood by each other – what they think the purpose and focus should be, how long the relationship will last, and agreed norms of how they will communicate
- Both respect each other's time and the expertise and efforts of the other

Teaching it

To teach this step:

- The teacher can introduce the idea of mentorship and the value that it can bring, and how many different ways it can be found.
- Learners could be asked to reflect on people who have been mentors in their lives. These might be through formal mentoring schemes, informal support from older learners or family members, or outside of school. It might be helpful to clarify the difference between mentoring and coaching here (see *Step 11*)
- Learners could reflect on those experiences and think about when they have worked well or not and turn this into a set of guidance that they can share, and perhaps turn into a poster or other visual reminder.

Reinforcing it

This step can be reinforced most easily when learners have the opportunity to mentor others. For example, some schools have a programme that allows older learners to mentor to support younger learners, which can be an invaluable experience for both.

Assessing it

This step is best assessed through observing learners taking on a mentoring role and reflecting on what they felt that they did well in it, and what they could do better.

Leadership Step 11

Step 11: I support others through coaching

To achieve Step 11, individuals will show that they can use coaching as a means to support other people.

In the previous step, the focus was on using mentoring as a way to develop people. Coaching builds on this by supporting someone to reach an answer for themselves without being directly told what to do.

Building blocks

The building blocks of this step are:

- I define what coaching is and explain how it differs from mentoring
- I understand what a coach does
- I identify how coaching can be used effectively to improve performance

Reflection questions

- What is coaching?
- How does coaching differ from mentoring?
- What does a coach do?
- What are the benefits of using a coaching approach?
- Have you had any experience of coaching or being coached?

What you need to know

What is coaching

Coaching is about supporting another individual to achieve their potential. Sometimes this is about the coach providing a soundboard, asking questions, and helping the individual being coached to work out the answer for themselves.

Individuals might be supported by coaches to help them to achieve professional or personal goals, and often find them invaluable.

How coaching differs from mentoring

In the previous step, we explored the idea of mentoring. This is normally where a more experienced, skilful, or knowledgeable individual will give guidance to a more junior person.

Coaching is quite different. The coach is not expected to provide the answer – indeed, they might not even *know* the correct answer themselves. Instead, their role is to act as a 'sounding board' to support the individual to explore ideas for themselves and work through a problem to get to a solution.

This means that they do not necessarily have to be an expert in the field, although that can be helpful in supporting someone to reach a technical solution. Instead, their expertise lies in facilitating the other person to structure their thinking.

It should be noted that coaching in the context here is quite different to sports coaching, which is much more directive and draws on the expertise of the sports coach.

How coaching can be used effectively

Coaching can be a useful and effective tool, but there need to be certain things in place before it can achieve that potential:

- A shared understanding of the goal that is to be achieved
- An appreciation of the role of the coach, and how it differs to that of a mentor
- A positive, respectful working relationship where the incentives of the coach and the individual being coached are aligned

An effective coach has to be a great listener (see *Listening*). That is because the most critical tool that a coach has is good questioning. The coach can use a careful sequence of open questions to open up and explore a topic, and then encourage the individual towards taking action.

- An effective coach uses listening tools along the way like:
- Asking questions to clarify what a speaker has said
- Demonstrating active listening through eye contact and engaged body language
- Summarising or rephrasing what they have heard

Ultimately, to be a good coach, you take to take the other individual on a journey from uncertainly exploring their idea, through evaluating their thoughts, through to a commitment to action.

The power of coaching

Coaching is such a powerful tool for leaders because the leader cannot be expected to know the answer to every possible question. Equally, there is good evidence that individuals who develop their own ideas have a much greater sense of ownership of the solutions and ideas that they have generated. This means they are more motivated to implement those ideas and tend to need less oversight and direct management.

Teaching it

To teach this step:

- The teacher should start by asking learners to differentiate between mentoring and coaching, and when they think each is more or less appropriate. It is worth explicitly addressing that sports coaching is a bit different to coaching as we're discussing it here.
- Learners can identify what coaches need to be able to do and what needs to be in place for a coaching relationship to be an effective one.
- The teacher should highlight that much of coaching draws on advanced Listening skills like active listening, asking open questions, and summarising and rephrasing.
- Learners should have the chance to coach one another to give them the opportunity to put this step into practice. If there is time, it works well to have a reflection after as short stint of coaching (say, 10 minutes) and then reverse roles so that all learners have the chance to coach and to be coached.

Reinforcing it

Peer coaching can be an effective mechanism for helping one another to think through ideas and plans, and so can be incorporated into learning where possible.

Assessing it

This step is best assessed through observing a learner coaching another. The teacher should be looking for evidence that they are able to set clear goals at the start of the coaching, and then use active listening, open questions, and summarising as a way to support the coaching conversation. The teacher's observation can be supplemented by a reflective conversation with the learner after the coaching session.

Leadership Step 12

Step 12: I support others through motivating them

To achieve Step 12, individuals will show that can motivate others in different situations.

In the two previous steps, the focus was on support others through mentoring and coaching respectively. This step builds on this by looking at how to boost motivation in a range of settings, which is a vital part of leadership.

Building blocks

The building blocks of this step are:

- I define what motivation is and what factors can influence motivation
- I know how understanding my team can boost motivation
- I know the critical things a leader can do to maintain motivation in their team

Reflection questions

- What is motivation?
- When do you feel more or less motivated?
- What are the critical things that a leader can do to maintain motivation in their teams?
- What do you think are the most important things to prioritise?
- Have you had any experience of motivating others as a leader?

What you need to know

What is motivation

Motivation is the drive that someone feels to commit energy and effort to completing tasks in the expectation of some future benefit.

If humans were rational, then motivation would simply be a function of the reward that would be expected from completing a task, and the probability of being successful based on the level of effort put in.

In reality, though, there is more complex psychology involved in how humans are motivated and how to keep them motivated when going through difficult situations. As a result, an effective leader will think hard about how to keep their team motivated, even through difficult times.

There are four things that underpin being able to motivate your team:

- Understand your team, know them, and what excites them
- Provide the resources, tools, and training for success
- Recognise success and support through challenges
- Ensure a sense of shared endeavour

Understanding your team

There are a few basics that a leader can put in place as the foundations of ensuring a motivated and committed team:

- *Getting to know their team:* It is powerful to get to know your team as individuals, and to understand their individual strengths as well as their wider interests.
- *Spending time to support them:* Making time available to support them is a good sign that you consider them worth your time, and that you value them.
- *Finding out what excites them about their role:* It may not be obvious what it is that excites people day-to-day, but if you find this out you can help to ensure that they have plenty of opportunities to do what does.

Provide the resources, tools and training for success

Individuals want to be successful. A large part of the role of the leader is to help to support and facilitate that success. That means:

- *Finding out what team members need from you:* Many leaders make the mistake of thinking leadership is about getting people to do whatever you want. In reality, successful leaders think more about how to support and help their teams.
- *Providing the resources they need:* It is demoralising and demotivating if individuals don't have the resources they need to get the job done. As their leader, you are best-placed to help secure these resources.
- *Seeking the right training and development opportunities:* Individuals want to feel that they can do more tomorrow than they can today, so helping them to find the best development opportunities and chances to try something new are vital.

Recognise success and support through challenges

Individuals not only want to succeed but want that success to be seen. The leader can boost motivation here by providing this recognition by:

- *Praising individuals for hard work and achievements:* Everyone likes to feel that they are recognised for good work and to feel that their efforts are appreciated. The leader has a key role in providing this praise and support.
- *Recognising individuals in front of their peers:* It can also be meaningful and motivating for the work of individuals to be recognised more widely, including in front of their peers.
- *Providing appropriate rewards:* Traditionally, having the right rewards was thought of as being the most important thing to motivate people. Nowadays, rewards are seen as being more of a minimum requirement (or *hygiene factor*) – so long as the reward is good enough, then it is not that motivating beyond that level.

Ensure a sense of shared endeavour

Finally, it is vital that there is a sense of shared endeavour. This means:

- *Involving the team in decision making:* In other steps, the idea of involving people in decision-making, problem solving, and creative thinking has been highlighted as a route to get people more invested in achieving the solution. If you can involve your team in the decision-making process, they will feel greater ownership of the solution, and so will be more motivated to achieve it.
- *Working through problems together:* Where problems emerge, it is unhelpful for individuals to

feel that they cannot talk to a leader about it, but equally unhelpful if they feel they can just hand over the problem for someone else to fix it for them. Working together through problems helps to maintain that motivating sense of ownership and shared endeavour.
- *Demonstrating trust:* Finally, demonstrating trust is motivating as it helps people to know that they have real responsibility and that their leader believes that they can complete the tasks well.

Teaching it

To teach this step:

- The teacher should start by asking learners what they think motivation means, and to reach a shared group definition. The teacher should explain that, as humans, we are far from completely rational, and there is a strong element of psychology in how we are motivated and maintain motivation.
- The teacher can ask learners to generate ideas of what makes them feel motivated in their own lives. The teacher can mind map these ideas.
- The teacher can then introduce the four main categories above: understanding your team; providing the resources, tools, and training for success; recognising success and supporting through challenges; giving a sense of shared endeavour. Learners can reflect on what each of those means and what are some practical things a leader might do in each of those categories.
- Learners could consolidate their learning by either putting those principles into practice through a project or create a presentation or written reflection on those principles.

Reinforcing it

This skill step can be reinforced whenever there is an opportunity for learners to work in groups and for one of them to take on a leadership role. The teacher can also model how they apply some of these approaches to motivate their class or when leading other activities.

Assessing it

Ideally, this step would be assessed through observation of an extended project where a learner has a leadership position, to see whether they are able to really apply these motivational principles. If that is not possible, then learners could create a written piece of work or presentation to outline the principles and how they could be applied.

Teamwork

Working cooperatively with others towards achieving a shared goal

Why it matters

Teamwork is the other side of interpersonal skills, alongside leadership.

All learners have the capacity to make a contribution when working with others, but it won't come as naturally to every learner as to others. We should also avoid making the mistake of assuming that those learners who are the loudest or seem to have the most friends are the most effective at teamwork.

This skill is important for support different types of project-based learning and encouraging peers to work together. This is true in the classroom but is absolutely vital in employment or entrepreneurship where working with others is vital to get things done.

How Teamwork is built

This skill applies to working within both formal and informal teams, and also with peers, teachers, community members, and others.

Initially, this is about learners fulfilling expectations around being positive, behaving appropriately, being timely and reliable, and taking responsibility. This extends to understanding and respecting diversity of others' cultures, beliefs, and backgrounds.

The next steps focus on making a contribution to a team through group decision making, recognising the value of others' ideas, and encouraging others to contribute too.

Beyond that, individuals improve their teams through managing conflict and building relationships beyond their immediate team. At the top steps, individuals focus on how they influence their team through suggesting improvements and learning lessons from setbacks.

Ultimately, individuals support the team by evaluating others' strengths and weaknesses and bringing in external expertise and relationships.

Skills Builder Framework for Teamwork

Working cooperatively with others towards achieving a shared goal

Step 0	I work with others in a positive way
Step 1	I work well with others by dressing and behaving appropriately
Step 2	I work well with others by being on time and reliable
Step 3	I work well with others by taking responsibility for completing my tasks
Step 4	I work well with others by supporting them if I can do so
Step 5	I work well with others by understanding and respecting diversity of others' cultures, beliefs, and backgrounds
Step 6	I contribute to group decision making
Step 7	I contribute to group decision making, whilst recognising the value of others' ideas
Step 8	I contribute to group decision making, encouraging others to contribute
Step 9	I improve the team by not creating unhelpful conflicts
Step 10	I improve the team by resolving unhelpful conflicts
Step 11	I improve the team by building relationships beyond my immediate team
Step 12	I influence the team by reflecting on progress and suggesting improvements
Step 13	I influence the team by evaluating successes and failures and sharing lessons
Step 14	I support the team by evaluating others' strengths and weaknesses, and supporting them accordingly
Step 15	I support the team by bringing in external expertise and relationships

Teamwork Step 0

Step 0: I work with others in a positive way

To achieve Step 0, individuals will show that they can work positively with others.

This is the first step in the skill of Teamwork and provides the foundation of being able to work cooperatively with others towards achieving a shared goal.

Building blocks

The building blocks of this step are:

- I understand why working with others can be helpful
- I know what working positively looks like
- I recognise when it is difficult to work positively

Reflection questions

- What does behaving positively look like to you?
- When do you find it easier or more challenging to work with others in a positive way?
- Can you give examples?

What you need to know

Working positively

Working positively is all about working with other people in a way that helps everyone to achieve what they want to:

- *Sharing things* like tools or materials
- *Encouraging other people* by saying positive things about what they are doing
- *Being pleasant,* by being polite, kind, and thoughtful about others
- *Showing you want to the work to go well* by being enthusiastic

When it is difficult to work positively

Sometimes it is easier to work positively than at other times:

- If we are in a positive emotional state to start with, then we find it easier to work positively. This includes the feelings of calm, excitement, or happiness.
- If we are in a negative emotional state to start with, then we normally find it much more difficult to work positively. This includes if we are feeling sad, angry, or scared.

If we are feeling negative emotions, we might end up showing the opposite behaviours of what we should:

- We might refuse to share our tools or materials
- We might be discouraging to other people, criticising or being unfair about what they are doing
- We might be unpleasant, being rude to other people, or thoughtless in what we say
- We might moan about our work, or be pessimistic about how it is going

Why we need to keep trying

None of us will be able to work positively all the time – sometimes we our negative emotions get the better of us. The most important thing with working positively is to keep trying at it, and know that is what we are aiming for, even though sometimes we find it easier than at other times.

We explore more about how to recognise and manage negative emotions in *Staying Positive Step 0*.

Teaching it

To teach this step:

- The teacher should introduce the step by asking the learners what they think it means to work positively, and to ask for examples. Depending on the age of the learners, that might be phrased as "taking turns" or "being friends with everyone in the class".
- Learners can discuss these, and then create a set of posters or guidance about how they should work positively with each other. The language of how this is shared will depend on the age of the leaners.
- The teacher should ask learners to think about when they struggle to work positively and what causes that. This can open into a conversation about how negative emotions affect working and how learners can manage them effectively.

Reinforcing it

This step can be reinforced in the classroom by reminding learners regularly about what working positively looks like. Visual reminders could help reinforce this.

Assessing it

This step is best assessed through observation of learners working with others. A teacher can look for evidence that they are able to work in the positive ways outlined above, and then to make a judgement about the consistency with which they work positively.

Teamwork Step 1

Step 1: I work well with others by behaving appropriately

To achieve Step 1, individuals will show they understand what appropriate behaviour looks like in different settings and act in that way.

In the previous step, individuals showed that they could work positively with other people. This step builds on this by focusing on what appropriate behaviour looks like in different places.

Building blocks

The building blocks of this step are:

- I define what behaviour is with examples
- I know how behaviour might vary
- I identify the appropriate behaviour for different situations

Reflection questions

- What do you think appropriate behaviour means?
- Is appropriate behaviour the same in every setting?
- How can we know what appropriate behaviour looks like in different places?
- Can you give some examples of what behaviour is appropriate in different settings?

What you need to know

What behaviour means

Behaviour is how we act or what we do in different situations, particularly towards other people. When we talk about appropriate behaviour, it means that we are acting correctly for the situation.

Behaviour includes things like:

- *How we talk to other people*: being polite, friendly and helpful
- *What we talk about*: the topics that we cover
- *How we dress*: whether there is a uniform or dress code
- *The attitude we have towards what we are doing*: including being on time and working hard
- *The values we demonstrate*: honesty, kindness, courageousness, and many others

Behaviour which is never appropriate

There is some behaviour which is never appropriate:

- Bullying someone
- Harassing or annoying someone
- Causing other people upset or distress

- Offending someone
- Breaking the law or persuading someone else to
- Putting ourselves or others in danger

How appropriate behaviour varies

Beyond those behaviours which are never appropriate, there are some behaviours which might be fine in some settings which are not acceptable in others. As some examples:

- *We might dress differently* in work or attending school or college to how we might dress with our friends or when taking part in sports activities. Some workplaces have uniforms you are expected to wear, and others might have a broader range of acceptable clothes.
- *What we talk about* might vary in different settings. With friends or family, you might be able to talk about anything and express your opinions freely and heartily. In school or a workplace, you have to be more careful to avoid upsetting or offending people. There might also be humour that you could share with friends you know well that you wouldn't share with other people.
- *How we talk to people* is likely to be different too. With friends, we are probably relaxed in our language but might use slang or other words. In work or school, we might think more carefully about being polite.

Working out what is appropriate in new settings can take a little bit of time, and it is always worth starting carefully and relaxing a little bit more if you see that is acceptable later on.

In the end, the acceptable behaviours are all down to the values of where you are, and what is considered 'normal' there.

Teaching it

To teach this step:

- The teacher can ask learners to think about what the word behaviour means to them. Younger learners are likely to immediately link this to being "well-behaved" which is undoubtedly part of it, but not the whole picture, so do encourage them to think about what this looks like.
- Next learners should explore the idea of what behaviours are never acceptable.
- They are likely to start by thinking about the school rules – this is a helpful example, but the teacher could challenge them on whether these same rules would apply in their homes?
- This can open the conversation up to how different behaviours may be appropriate in different places. Learners can identify how they behave differently in different settings.

Reinforcing it

This step lends itself well to being reinforced in the classroom, as a set of norms of behaviour. The teacher can also make the contrast between appropriate behaviour at break time and during learning time to help learners recognise the differences.

Assessing it

This step is best assessed through sustained observation of behaviour, particularly if learners are able to identify and follow norms of behaviour in different settings.

Teamwork Step 2

Step 2: I work with others well by being on time and reliable

To achieve Step 2, individuals will show that they can be on time and reliable.

In earlier steps, the focus was on how to work positively with other people and recognise appropriate behaviour in different settings. These are crucial foundations for effective teamwork, as is this next step of being on time and reliable.

Building blocks

The building blocks of this step are:

- I understand why being on time matters
- I can define reliability and why it matters
- I identify how to get better at being reliable

Reflection questions

- What does it mean to be reliable?
- Why does it matter to be on time?
- What is the effect if someone is not reliable, or not on time?
- Have you had an experience of that?

What you need to know

Why being on time matters

The importance of being on time varies a lot in different cultures and different parts of the world.

In some parts of the world, being late is seen as being rude, as it is seen as suggesting that you do not respect the time of the person you are keeping waiting. In other places, the idea of timings is much more relaxed.

In the context of work or education, timings tend to be more important. This is because getting tasks done relies on things happening in the right order and at the right points. If you work in a factory, the production line might be held back if you are not in post at the right time. In a hospital, the previous shift cannot leave until the new one has arrived to take over. In education, classes have to start and end at the right time.

The other side to being on time is being on time with getting work done. Pieces of work often need to be finished by a particular time - called a *deadline* - because this work is required in order to allow something else to happen. If you don't meet those deadlines, then it stops the whole process of other things that were due to happen afterwards.

Why reliability matters

Reliability is about being consistently good at something so other people can trust in you. That might mean completing work to a good standard and trying hard every day. It also means that if you promise to do something that you get it done.

Being reliable also means that you can be relied on to follow the expected behaviours where you are (see Step 1) and that you can always work positively with others (Step 0). It also means being on time, as we've just seen.

If you are reliable, you will find that:

- You get greater freedom to manage your work because people trust that you can get it done
- You might get more opportunities or new challenges because you have proven that you are likely to be able to get them done
- In the workplace, this can lead to opportunities for promotion, which come with chances for different work and potentially more pay

Unfortunately, the reverse is the case you if you are unreliable:

- You will be more carefully monitored in our work, because you are not expected to be able to get it done otherwise
- You might find that you have opportunities taken away because the feeling is that you need to get better at the basics first
- In the workplace, there will be little opportunity for progression and being consistently unreliable is considered possible grounds for losing your job

How to get better at being reliable

There are a few things that you can do to become more reliable:

- Make the *commitment* that you think it is important to be reliable and that you are going to focus on improving.
- *Get advice* from your teacher or manager about what they believe you should do to become more reliable in your work. Take their help and ask them to support you.
- Think about *what stops you being reliable at the moment*. Perhaps it is that you are easily distracted, that you need to improve your skills, or that you find it hard to follow instructions. This then gives you something to work on.
- Make sure you are clear on the *expectations* that people have of you and your work and write them down. This includes what the tasks are, when they need to be done by, and any other instructions. If you are unclear, then ask more questions (See *Listening Step 2* for more on this)
- *Work hard to try to meet those expectations*. Sometimes that might mean putting in more work than you might expect or finding ways of working that stop you being distracted. You might also need to do some additional learning to improve your skills.
- Finally, *keep getting feedback* – this helps to show that you are dedicated to getting better, and people should want to support you.

In the end, we can all become reliable, and we all benefit from that too.

Teaching it

To teach this step:

- The teacher can ask learners to consider why being on time matters. They can explore why being late to school or to lessons has a negative effect, and learners could extend to thinking about why this matters in their wider lives. The teacher can also ask learners to reflect on the impact of missing deadlines or not getting work done on time.
- This can then be extended into a discussion about what it means to be reliable and why this matters. Learners can think about whether they think they are reliable in different aspects of their lives.
- A discussion can be structured around how learners could become more reliable. This could culminate with learners capturing some tips on how to boost their reliability or create actions for themselves to get better.

Reinforcing it

This step lends itself well to reinforcement in the classroom. The teacher can use the language of being on time and reliability as a way to support learners to develop positive attitudes towards these. Learners should also see that there are steps that they can take to get better too.

Assessing it

This step is best assessed through sustained observation of learners, and whether they are on time and reliable over a sustained period.

Teamwork Step 3

Step 3: I work well with others by taking responsibility for completing my tasks

To achieve Step 3, individuals will show that they can take responsibility for completing their tasks.

The earlier steps have been about building the foundations of being able to work effectively with others by working positively, behaving appropriately, and being on time and reliable. This step builds of this by focusing on taking responsibility.

Building blocks

The building blocks of this step are:

- I can define what responsibility means
- I identify ways to take responsibility
- I understand when taking responsibility works well

Reflection questions

- What does it mean to take responsibility?
- What are the positive effects of taking responsibility?
- What are some of the risks of taking responsibility?
- How can you get the balance right?
- Do you have any experience of taking responsibility?

What you need to know

Taking responsibility

Taking responsibility is taking charge of something and working to ensure that it is a success. It means that you get the praise if it goes well, but it also means that you have to take the blame if it goes badly.

In this context, it means that when given a task, you work hard to make sure that it happens and don't make excuses or blame other people if things go wrong. Instead, you try to fix any problems yourself or find someone else to help, rather than giving up.

There are lots of positive sides to taking responsibility for something:

- It gives you a greater sense of ownership over your work and what you are trying to do which makes it more enjoyable.
- If you are taking responsibility, you are likely to be given more control and freedom in what you are doing.
- Showing that you take responsibility helps to build trust with others.
- Taking responsibility also helps you to learn better, because you have to work harder to overcome setbacks and problems – you cannot just give up.

There are also potential negatives to taking responsibility:

- You are being asked to take responsibility, but don't have enough control to affect whether the tasks are a success or not, this can be very difficult.
- You do not have the training or skills to be able to complete the tasks.
- Something goes wrong – even though it is beyond your control, you might still be blamed for what has happened.

When taking responsibility works well

To get the balance right, there are certain things you should try to push for when taking responsibility:

- A clear view of what you are - and are not - responsible for
- Ensure you have enough control to be able to achieve what needs to be done
- Believe there is a good chance of success
- Know you have the skills and training you need to complete the tasks

In these cases, it is a good thing to take responsibility, for all of the positive reasons that we have already talked about.

Showing that you can take responsibility is a key part of being able to work with others and make a contribution to a shared goal.

Teaching it

To teach this step:

- The teacher can introduce the concept of 'taking responsibility for a task' and ask learners what they think it means. The teacher can model this by talking about things that they have to take responsibility for.
- Learners can give examples of when they have had to take responsibility for getting a task completed, and how they felt about it.
- The teacher can then lead a discussion about why it can be useful to take responsibility, but what you need to be clear about first.
- This can be illustrated by giving the learners a challenge to work on in a team, where each individual has to take responsibility for their tasks for the whole job to be completed. For example, creating a picture where each of them creates a piece and then they are all put together at the end, or a presentation where each of them needs to write and say part of it in turn.

Reinforcing it

The concept of taking responsibility for completing tasks is a good one to build and reinforce in class. When learners receive tasks for themselves, they should be told how they are being given responsibility for completing them (whether they are individual or group tasks) and the teacher can reinforce clear expectations.

Assessing it

This step is best assessed through observation over a sustained period to see whether learners are able to demonstrate taking responsibility for completing tasks over the long-term.

Teamwork Step 4

Step 4: I work well with others by supporting them if I can do so

To achieve Step 4, individuals will show that they are willing to support others, but with an awareness of when they can.

Earlier steps have focused on the building blocks of working with others, looking at working positively, behaving appropriately, being on-time and reliable, and then taking responsibility for completing tasks. This step builds on this further by thinking about supporting others too.

Building blocks

The building blocks of this step are:

- I understand what it means to support others
- I explain why supporting others is important and helpful
- I know how to identify if I can support others

Reflection questions

- What does it mean to support other people?
- Why is it important to try to support other people?
- When should you not try to support someone else?
- Do you have experiences of having supported others, or been supported yourself?

What you need to know

What it means to support others

Supporting others is about helping them to complete a task. This might happen in one of a few ways:

- *Sharing tasks* that benefit from there being two or more people involved – for example, when painting a room, lifting things, or digging a hole.
- *Providing advice* or showing how to do something if you have higher expertise and they ask for it
- *Taking on tasks* if you have time available while someone else still has lots to do
- *Providing encouragement* if someone seems unsure or is lacking in confidence

Why it is important to support others:

There are lots of reasons why it is good to support others and why it is such an essential part of the skill of Teamwork:

- Your team are more likely to be able to get tasks finished on time and to a good standard.
- By showing that you will support others when they need it, you are more likely to be offered support when you need it.
- All of us benefit from encouragement at times, to help us feel that we are doing a good job and to keep us feeling *motivated* about continuing to work hard.
- Supporting others is an excellent way to use our skills, and to help others to build their skills too. Lots of skills we learn, we are shown by someone else.

How to know if you can support with something

Although it usually is helpful and welcome to support someone else, there are a few things you should think about:

- Do you have the expertise to help out the other person?
- Would it be dangerous for you to try to get involved?
- Do they want support? It is always good to check before you get involved.
- What is the best way to support with a task? Some tasks can be easily divided between people, but others need one person to complete them.

If someone does not want your support, then it is critical not to get upset about it because it is probably for a good reason. Instead, you can ask others in your team if there is anything else that you can be doing to help any of them.

Teaching it

To teach this step:

- The teacher can introduce the idea of supporting other people to complete their tasks, and why this is an integral part of Teamwork.
- This can broaden into a discussion with learners about when others have supported them and how it helped. The teacher might also contribute and model some examples themselves. It is crucial to illustrate the range of ways that support might be presented and how different types of support are appropriate in different settings, depending on the task and the skills involved.
- Learners can then be given a piece of work to work on as a team, but with tasks designed and allocated so some learners have a much quicker easier task than others. The challenge is then to see whether learners are able and willing to support one another to get everything done.

Reinforcing it

This step can be reinforced whenever there is group work, reminding learners that they should think not just about completing their own tasks, but also about how they can support others in their teams too. Good examples can be shared and rewarded.

Assessing it

This step can be assessed through long-term observation of how learners interact with one another and whether they show that they can support one another in an appropriately. It can also be assessed through a structured group activity which relies on learners supporting one another to complete the task.

Teamwork Step 5

Step 5: I work well with others by understanding and respecting diversity of others' cultures, beliefs, and backgrounds

To achieve Step 5, individuals will show that they can work with others with diverse backgrounds, and with different cultures and beliefs.

In previous steps, the focus has been on how to work well with others, thinking about positive working, appropriate behaviour, reliability, taking responsibility and supporting others. This step focuses on understanding and respecting diversity and inclusivity.

Building blocks

The building blocks of this step are:

- I define and explain what diversity means
- I define and explain what equality means
- I define and explain what inclusivity means

Reflection questions

- What does diversity mean?
- What does it mean to be inclusive?
- What does it mean to discriminate?
- How do you create an environment where everyone is respected and able to make a full contribution?

What you need to know

What is diversity

To be effective in a team, it is essential to recognise that everyone is different and so your team members will all be different from one another - and you. This difference is called *diversity*.

Diversity is a strength for a team, because:

- People will bring different perspectives and experiences
- The world is diverse, so it is good to have that reflected in your team
- You can make better decisions if you do not all think about the world in the same way

Diversity might come from lots of different things including: gender; race; religion; socio-economic background; age; experience; disability; and other things too. Appreciating diversity means appreciating the value of these differences.

What is equality

Equality is the vital idea that everyone is of equal value in the world and deserves the same opportunities to make the most of their skills and talents.

In many ways, equality has still not been achieved for many groups, or individuals with particular characteristics, as mentioned above. This is an area where we all have an essential part to play in working towards equality for all.

What is inclusivity

For your diverse team to achieve its potential, it needs to be an *inclusive* team. That means that everyone needs to be included and to feel included.

This starts by ensuring that no one is *discriminated* against. Discrimination is the unfair treatment of different people based on something about them. This is both wrong, and illegal in UK law: you must not treat anyone differently based on their age, disability, race, religion, gender, or sexual orientation, among other things.

There is a lot more though to make sure that everyone is included:

- What can you learn from the range of experiences that other team members might have, or the perspectives they might take?
- How can you make sure that activities or tasks are considered so that everyone can take part fully?
- Do you ensure that everyone has equal opportunities to take part?

Being inclusive does not mean that everyone is necessarily treated precisely the same, because some people will have different needs to others. Instead, being inclusive is about making sure that everyone has equal opportunities to contribute and participate. This is an essential part of working well in a team.

Teaching it

To teach this step:

- This topic is covered most effectively as a group discussion where the teacher can support discussion and contribution of ideas following the three key concepts above.
- Depending on the age of the learners, some of the language might have to be simplified to make it accessible. However, the core concepts are accessible and can be brought to life with examples.
- It is important to be aware and sensitive of the learners in the group and how to make sure they all feel comfortable and confident to engage with the lesson.

Reinforcing it

These are important values that should be reinforced through school life. This step helps to bring an additional angle that diversity makes the team more robust, while inclusivity is critical for working effectively as a team and to making the most of everyone's strengths.

Assessing it

This step can be assessed in a combination of ways:

- Firstly, ensuring that learners understand and are comfortable with the key vocabulary and concepts.
- Secondly, asking learners to reflect on why the different concepts are important and what they look like practically.
- Thirdly, observing that learners can put those principles into practice, and don't behave in ways that are counter to that.

Teamwork Step 6

Step 6: I contribute to group decision making

To achieve Step 6, individuals will show that they can contribute to group decision making.

The previous steps were focused on the essential parts of being able to work well with others. The focus now shifts to how to make a contribution as part of a group, starting with how to contribute to group decision making.

Building blocks

The building blocks of this step are:

- I define and explain what group decision making is
- I recognise the benefits of contributing to group decision making
- I know how to contribute positively to group discussions

Reflection questions

- What is meant by group decision making?
- How can you make good contributions to group decision making?
- What are things to avoid?

What you need to know

Group decision making

Group decision making is when a decision is discussed and decided upon by a group. It might be that ultimately the leader has to make a final decision, but there is a process that gives everyone the chance to feed in their expertise, ideas, and opinions.

There are some benefits to group decision making:

- The group benefits from the broadest possible range of views and perspectives
- Group members understand where decisions have come from
- Group members are generally more *invested* in making the ideas work because they feel more of a sense of *ownership* over what has been decided

There are also some limitations:

- It can take much longer than an individual just making a quick decision
- It can open up debates and disagreements which cannot be resolved

As a result, group decision making is not always the best thing to do; it depends on the complexity of the problem, the time available, and how positively the team can discuss difficult issues.

How to make good contributions

Effective group decision making depends on the contributions of the members of the group. There are some essential things to think about when making contributions, to make sure that they are helpful:

- Always think before you share something – so you believe what you are saying
- Make contributions positively – avoid becoming aggressive or too forceful when making your points
- If you disagree with someone else, then you should say so politely and keep the focus on what they were saying, not about them personally
- Be ready to change your mind if other people share other perspectives or ideas

Some people feel much more confident in contributing to group decision making. This is particularly the case if they know the others in the group well, are in a more senior position, or if they have more experience.

You should always feel that you have something to contribute, even if it is just to say which perspective you agree with based on what you have heard. You don't always have to present a new idea - it is still helpful for the team to understand what everyone is thinking.

Teaching it

To teach this step:

- The teacher should introduce that this step focuses on how learners contribute to their teams, starting with group decision making.
- The teacher could model where they have contributed to group decision making – perhaps in a staff meeting or in life beyond school. Learners could be encouraged to offer their experiences too.
- The teacher can ask learners when they think group decision making works well, and when it doesn't, perhaps turning this into some shared guidelines, based on the ideas above.
- It then works well to simulate group decision making. This could also link to some of the content in *Leadership Step 5,* which looks at how to run a meeting. Depending on the learners, this could be done as a whole class or split into smaller groups. Learners could be given a question or problem and have to come to a solution as a group. The focus is for each learner to contribute something to that process.
- In reflection, learners could think about what tips they would capture for how to make useful contributions, and make sure these are recorded for future use.

Reinforcing it

This step lends itself well to the classroom where there is the opportunity for learners to work together on problems or questions. Before such activities, learners could be reminded of the goal to make a helpful contribution to group discussion and some ideas of how best to do that.

Assessing it

This step is best assessed through an observed activity, similar to that outlined above. The teacher would be looking for evidence that learners can make positive contributions to group discussion. This could also be assessed over a more extended period if there are regular opportunities for group work that gives the opportunity for this skill to be used.

Teamwork Step 7

Step 7: I contribute to group decision making, whilst recognising the value of others' ideas

To achieve Step 7, individuals will show that they can contribute to group decision making, whilst recognising the value of others' ideas.

The previous step changed the focus of Teamwork to how to contribute to group decision making. This step builds on this, thinking not just about how to add your ideas, but how to think about others' contributions too.

Building blocks

The building blocks of this step are:

- I understand that sharing my ideas is just one part of group decision making
- I identify why group decision making can go wrong and take steps to avoid this
- I recognise the value of others' ideas

Reflection questions

- Why is it not enough just to focus on sharing your own ideas?
- If everyone did this, what would be the effect on group decision making?
- Why do different people have different ideas?
- How can you ensure that you think about others' ideas and recognise the value in them?
- Do you have any experiences of this going badly or well?

What you need to know

Sharing your ideas is just the start

In the previous step, the focus was on how to contribute to a group decision-making process. To have achieved that step, you would have to show that you could contribute helpful ideas to the discussion.

However, that is only part of being an effective part of group decision making. If everyone just focused on what they were saying, then they would be missing out on the other critical part of communication – listening effectively.

Listening is vital to make sure that we are making helpful additional contributions, rather than restating points that have already been made.

However, even listening is not effective if you are not ready to expand or change your perspective based on what you have heard.

When group decision making goes wrong

One of the causes of group decision making not working, is people being unable or unwilling to contribute their ideas. This is why the previous step was about having the confidence and skill to be able to make contributions.

However, one of the other leading causes is when everyone focuses on what they are saying and the points *they* want to make but fail to listen to other people. This can particularly happen when there is a lack of trust in the team, so everyone feels like they need to defend their interests and perspective.

Instead, a team can only make effective decisions when they move away from being competitors with each other to being real collaborators. In this case, the success of the group is more important than who came up with the ideas, or who gets to take the most credit.

This means being able to recognise the value of other people's ideas.

Recognising the value of others' ideas

One of the great opportunities of group decision making is the chance to learn from a range of different views. It is quite possible that everyone in a group discussing a particular challenge or opportunity might start with a different *perspective*. These different perspectives might come from:

- Seeing the world differently and holding different values about what is important – this might lead to different *priorities*
- Having diverse *expertise*, *knowledge,* and *skills*
- *Being affected by the decision in different ways* – a choice is often useful for some people but might have adverse effects for other people
- Having had *different ideas* – good ideas can come to anyone

If we only think about our thoughts, then we miss the chance to learn from other people, and to make the best possible decision for our team.

How to open your mind to other ideas

There are several things that we can do to be more open to valuing other people's ideas:

- Make the *decision* that you are going to listen and try to learn (this is a critical approach that is discussed a lot more in *Listening*).
- Present your ideas as a *perspective* rather than presenting too adamantly, which makes it harder to change your mind later. You could use language like "My thinking on this was…" or "My perspective coming into this was…" or "It seems to me that…" – all of this language makes clear that you are open to changing your mind.
- *Always explain your perspective* – this will encourage others to explain theirs too and will help you to see the thinking behind their ideas.
- *Actively try to understand* why someone has a different view to you. What is it that is giving them a different view? This is sometimes called *cognitive empathy* – trying to understand where someone else is coming from.
- *Check that you are not biased against someone else's perspective* because of your biases or other forms of discrimination. (See *Step 5* for more on diversity and inclusion)
- *Ask questions* to expand your understanding and to make sure you have had a chance to think about what someone else's idea is, and why they have come to that idea (see *Listening Step 7* for more on this)
- *See changing your mind as a strength* if you can explain why you have changed your mind. People will respect you for it if you have shown that you can take on different perspectives and make an intelligent appraisal of different views.

Teaching it

To teach this step:

- The teacher should introduce the topic by asking learners why is it important to value other people's ideas? This can be linked to wider ideas about the diversity of experience, the importance of equality, and ensuring that no one is discriminated against.
- Learners should then be given a task to help model to them how to make sure that they are truly listening to one another and to demonstrate the value of different experiences. You could set whatever question you like, but it should be one that can cause debate. For example, which subject should no longer be taught? Or what should we do to improve our school community?
- Before they start, learners should think about how they will make sure they really listen to and value the ideas of others. Some of the guidance above should be shared with them. They should be told that at the end of the exercise, they will have had to make a decision as a group and then explain how they came to it. Each individual learner should be given 1 minute to make their case, and then there will be 10 minutes for discussion.
- At the end of the session, reflection can help to ensure that all learners have listened to the ideas of others, been open to them, and possibly even changed their thinking as a result.

Reinforcing it

This step can be reinforced in learning whenever there is a debate or discussion in class. Learners should be reminded not just to think about contributing their own ideas but also to ensure that they are learning from others and potentially changing their point of view as a result. Visual reminders of some of the guidance above might help this process too.

Assessing it

This step is best assessed through a structured group activity, as outlined above. Learners have to complete an exercise that requires them to share their views, but also demonstrate that they can widen and change their perspective in response to the ideas of others.

Teamwork Step 8

Step 8: I contribute to group decision making, encouraging others to contribute

To achieve Step 8, individuals will show that they can contribute to group decision making, while actively encouraging other people to participate too.

In the previous two steps, the focus was on how to contribute to group decision making – firstly, by having the confidence to make contributions yourself, and then by valuing others' ideas and views and being open to changing your mind as a result. This step builds on this by actively encouraging others to contribute too.

Building blocks

The building blocks of this step are:

- I recognise why everyone in a group should contribute
- I understand why sometimes people don't want to contribute
- I encourage others to contribute effectively

Reflection questions

- Why might you need to encourage others to contribute their ideas?
- What might you miss out on if you don't?
- How can you do this effectively?

What you need to know

Encouraging others to contribute ideas

From previous steps, we have already seen that for a team to make the best possible decisions it needs to benefit from the fullest possible set of views, experiences, and information.

At times, it is not necessary to have group decision making – perhaps the problem or challenge is a simple one, or there is not the time to have a full group decision. If the decision is made, though, to have a group approach, then it is vital that everyone in the group has the opportunity to contribute. If they do *not*:

- The group does not benefit from the collective experience, knowledge, perspectives, and ideas of all its members
- Individuals who have not had the chance to contribute might feel excluded from the decision – this might lead to feelings of not being valued and lead to disengagement with the tasks
- It increases the risk of bias in the group and goes against the ideas of equality and inclusivity.
- Too much power in the group ends up residing in a smaller number of individuals who do contribute.
- The group may end up suffering from *groupthink* where the group moves too quickly to consensus and stops challenging itself (see *Leadership Step 6*)

These damaging effects are reinforced over time if some individuals do not contribute to group decision making and end up feeling that their views are never sought and therefore are not valued. Similarly, the need for consensus can end up overwhelming the need for good decisions, and diverse opinions are no longer welcome.

Why people don't contribute

Individuals might not contribute to collective decision making for several reasons:

- They do not feel that they have the expertise, knowledge, or skills to contribute.
- They do not have the confidence to participate – perhaps because they are shy at speaking, or they have had an adverse reaction to their contributions in the past.
- They do not think that their contribution will be welcome – perhaps because they are not senior enough in the group.
- They disagree with the majority of the group and fear being on the 'losing side' of an argument.
- They have additional needs that have not been taken into consideration for them to participate in decision making fully.

How to encourage others to contribute effectively

The key to encouraging everyone is to make group discussions a *safe space*. That does not mean that people cannot disagree – instead, it means that everyone's contributions are:

- *Encouraged:* People are actively encouraged to participate. For example, if someone has not spoken, any team member could say "We haven't yet heard from X – what do you think?" or "I think X might have an interesting perspective on this?" If you know that someone has particular expertise, skill, or knowledge in the area, you can include that in your invitation for them to speak.
- *Appreciated:* People should be thanked for their contributions, especially if they are not in line with everyone else's view. This is particularly important because some people might find contributing to a group stressful.
- *Included:* People's opinions should all be included in the discussion. There is no point in thanking someone and then not thinking about their ideas, or ignoring all together what they have said.
- *Supported:* People might have additional needs to take part fully in a group discussion – for example, if they have specific disabilities. In these cases, it is vital to provide support so that they can be fully included.

Reaching a final decision

At the end of all the contributions, it is the role of the leader to secure a final decision. At this point, you can be helpful by suggesting:

- *Combining ideas:* Where people have different views, it might be possible to combine ideas to get to a better solution (See *Creativity Step 5*).
- *Compromises:* You might be able to suggest a middle path that gets some of the benefits of two or more ideas if it is not possible to do both.
- *Ways of reaching a decision:* If the group is getting stuck, or starting to go round in circles, you could suggest some ways of reaching a decision. For example, through voting, or seeking additional information or data (if time allows) that might help resolve two different views.

In the end, working hard to make sure that everyone contributes to collective decision making will make the team stronger, and able to make better decisions.

Teaching it

To teach this step:

- The teacher should lead learners in a reflection of what is meant by group decision making and why it is valuable.
- Learners can then reflect on when they feel comfortable contributing to group decision making and when they feel uncomfortable. The teacher could get this started by sharing some examples from their own life.
- Learners should then develop some ideas of how they might be able to encourage other people to contribute. The guidance above might also be helpful for this and provide a useful visual reminder for the next task.
- To consolidate learning on this step, learners should take part in a group activity. This can be based around making a decision where some learners are given tips to hold back on contributing their ideas unless encouraged to. The decision might be something like: "How long should the school be shut over the summer holiday?" The focus is on ensuring that those learners who have been briefed to be reticent are encouraged to participate by their peers.
- This activity can be repeated with a different challenge so that the reticent learners are switched over. This will mean that all have the chance to encourage participation from their peers.

Reinforcing it

This step can be effectively modelled in the classroom by the teacher who can make a point of encouraging the participation of everyone in the class. The four steps of how to model ways of encouraging participation might also be available as a set of visual cues.

Assessing it

This step is best assessed through the observation of group activities and looking for examples of when learners have actively encouraged participation from their peers.

Teamwork Step 9

Step 9: I improve the team by not creating unhelpful conflicts

To achieve Step 9, individuals will show that they can avoid unhelpful conflicts.

This step marks a shift away from contributing to the team, to thinking more actively about how to make the team as effective as possible. This starts by not creating unhelpful conflicts.

Building blocks

The building blocks of this step are:

- I define what unhelpful conflicts are and what effect they can have
- I recognise the common causes of unhelpful conflicts
- I know strategies to help avoid conflicts starting

Reflection questions

- What is an unhelpful conflict?
- How is conflict different to disagreement?
- How can unhelpful conflicts be avoided?
- Do you have any examples of having managed this?

What you need to know

Unhelpful conflicts

Disagreement is often an important part of a team coming to a better decision about what they should do and the actions that they should take. (See *Teamwork Step 8*)

This is very different, though, to *conflict*. A conflict is an extended agreement which grows into a more significant clash. The results can be destructive if, over time, individuals descend into a negative cycle of conflict as they:

- Lose trust in one another
- No longer see themselves as having compatible goals – if one wins, the other must be losing
- Stop cooperating with one another
- Start actively seeking to undermine one another

The result is that effective teamwork can't flourish: our definition of teamwork, if you recall, is working cooperatively with others towards a shared goal.

What causes conflicts

Conflicts can start from several different places and can often be quite minor before they escalate and become very destructive. Some common causes of conflict include:

- Different views for a range of reasons including diverse perspectives, experiences, knowledge, or skills.
- Feelings that people have been rude or disrespectful
- Shortages of resources
- A sense of unfairness about the allocation of tasks and the level of effort required
- Differences in how different team members are recognised or rewarded
- Limited opportunities

How we can avoid causing conflicts

We can all help to avoid conflicts starting in the first place:

- We can apply the principles of encouraging and valuing a diverse range of perspectives when working in a group (See *Steps 6, 7 and 8*).
- We can stay focused on the task, rather than the other individuals.
- We can be polite to everyone, even people we do not naturally get on with - perhaps because we have very different styles or views.
- We can talk to the leader if we feel that there are elements that are unfair, or we are concerned about resources not being allocated.
- We can share any concerns with the other individual or individuals early on before they have grown and turned into conflicts that are much more difficult to resolve later on.
- We can seek out additional opportunities for ourselves, rather than waiting for them to be given to us.
- We can find someone else to help arbitrate disagreements if we cannot fix them ourselves. This means someone who is not involved in the controversy can help us work out a compromise or solution.

The critical thing is that conflicts are much easier to resolve early on. Most conflicts started from a small beginning that led to a loss of trust and then escalated over time.

We should always keep an eye out for potential conflicts and try to avoid getting into any. If they start, we should try to fix them as quickly as possible.

Teaching it

To teach this step:

- The teacher should emphasise the difference between *disagreements*, which are a healthy and regular part of working in a team, and *conflicts* which can be unhelpful and destructive.
- Learners can reflect on occasions when disagreements turned into conflicts and what the effect of those were. This may need some thoughtful and sensitive facilitation from the teacher.
- The teacher can then illustrate some examples of times when conflicts have emerged. These might be drawn from current affairs, geography, history, or literature. In each case, the emphasis should be on how small differences spiralled into conflict. Learners can be encouraged to identify these patterns for themselves.
- The focus can then move to thinking about how to avoid or diffuse conflicts before they develop. Learners can give their ideas and suggestions, and compare these to some of the tips above.
- Finally, role-play can give learners the opportunity to practice some of the techniques to avoid ending up in conflict with others.

Reinforcing it

This step lends itself to reinforcement in the classroom context when disputes or disagreements might emerge among learners. It might be good to turn some of the guidelines as things to remind learners of before group working, or to use them as visual reminders in the classroom.

Assessing it

This step is best assessed through observation of group learning, but also of a learner's interactions with their peers over a sustained period.

Teamwork Step 10

Step 10: I improve the team by resolving unhelpful conflicts

To achieve Step 10, individuals will show that they can resolve unhelpful conflicts.

In the previous step, the focus was on how to avoid creating conflicts with others. This step builds on this by exploring how to resolve disputes that have started whether of the individual's own making or not.

Building blocks

The building blocks of this step are:

- I prepare to resolve my own conflicts
- I use conversation to resolve my conflicts with others
- I know how to help resolve the conflicts of others

Reflection questions

- What do we mean by an unhelpful conflict?
- How can we avoid these conflicts developing in the first place?
- How can you resolve your own conflicts with others?
- How can you help others to resolve their conflicts?
- Do you have any examples of having done this?

What you need to know

Why you need to resolve conflicts

As we saw in *Step 9*, conflicts can emerge from all sorts of differences, misunderstandings, feelings of being excluded, or a sense of unfairness or injustice. These conflicts can escalate quickly through a downward spiral:

- Losing trust in one another
- No longer seeing yourselves as having compatible goals – if one wins, the other must be losing
- No longer cooperating with one another
- Actively seeking to undermine one another

The way to resolve a conflict is to stop this downward cycle, and the earlier that it can be stopped the better.

Things to do in preparation

There are some basic things that you can do to resolve your own conflicts:

- *Do not ignore the conflict*: it can easily get worse by being ignored.
- *Stop and try to think objectively about the situation*: that means trying to stop your emotional responses drowning out the opportunity to think logically. Some ways of doing this were discussed in *Staying Positive Step 4*.
- *Try to see things from the other person's perspective:* think about what it is that might have caused the conflict to start with.
- *Do not think about blame:* the focus should not be about who was right or wrong, but on trying to find a solution.

Using conversation to resolve conflict

You will need to talk to the other person, speaking openly about the conflict, where it has come from, what the impact is on you both and on your wider team, and how you might be able to resolve it. This might be a challenging conversation, so it is essential to go into it prepared:

- Make sure you are feeling calm – do not start the conversation if you are not feeling in a good emotional place
- Expect that at some point in the discussion you might expect to feel negative emotions and be prepared with some strategies for reduce this stress
- Pay attention to the feelings that the other person is sharing, and make sure that you are respectful about what they are sharing – it is not easy for them either
- You can share the emotions you are feeling too but try to avoid blame
- In the end, you are likely to both feel wronged, so trying to work out who to blame is not worth it, and will not resolve the conflict
- Try to agree on a way forward and to work together well in the future

Rebuilding trust

The good news is that if you can resolve a conflict, then it can improve your relationship with someone else and build confidence. This means that you can get back onto a positive upward cycle again:

- Building trust
- Seeing yourselves as having the same goals – if one of you wins, you both do
- Actively supporting one another
- Sharing successes

Resolving the conflicts of others

As part of a team, it might be that at times you need to help resolve conflicts between other members of your team. In this situation, you need to set up a context where it is possible to have a good conversation.

This means:

- Encouraging team members to talk if they seem to be in conflict.
- Set up a time and place so team members can talk without outside interruptions. If you are helping to facilitate this, make sure that each individual has time to speak and say what they feel they need to.

- If you are facilitating, you can use active listening methods like summarising to help the conversation to be productive and to encourage the participants to engage (see *Listening Step 8* for more on this).
- Look for areas of agreement where individuals agree on elements of the situation, even if they have different perspectives. Do not take sides and try to encourage both sides to recognise how they better support the other in the future.
- In the end, you want to reach a resolution where the challenges have been aired and learnt from.

Teaching it

To teach this step:

- The teacher should start by recapping what is meant by unhelpful conflict, how the spiral of negative conflict can emerge, and why this can be so damaging in a team.
- Learners could reflect on times when they have ended up in this sort of conflict and whether they were able to resolve it.
- The teacher should model some of the ways of helping to address and resolve conflict through discussion. This might be about walking through how they get into the right mindset and then talk through the issues without focusing on blame.
- Learners could practice how to have these conversations through role-play.
- This can then be extended to learners practising how to facilitate a conversation to resolve a conflict between two of their peers based on a created scenario.
- At the end of the session, learners should reflect and capture some of the lessons that they have learned that they can use in the future.

Reinforcing it

This step lends itself effectively to being reinforced in the classroom setting, where conflicts often emerge. Learners can be encouraged to take an active approach to resolving conflicts, or to use a peer to support those conversations.

Assessing it

This step is best assessed through observing a structured activity using role-play where the learners are given different information and perspectives on a problem that has led to a conflict and have to resolve this between them. A similar activity could assess whether learners can facilitate a conversation between their peers to resolve a dispute.

Teamwork Step 11

Step 11: I improve my team by building relationships beyond my immediate team

To achieve Step 11, individuals will show that they can build productive relationships beyond their immediate team.

In earlier steps, the focus was on how to improve the team by avoiding or resolving unhelpful conflicts. This step is about being able to widen the range of external relationships that the team can benefit from.

Building blocks

The building blocks of this step are:

- I recognise why relationships beyond the team are important
- I understand what external relationships might be based around
- I know how new relationships can be started, maintained, and developed

Reflection questions

- Why is it helpful to have relationships beyond your immediate team?
- What might be valuable about these relationships? What could they do?
- How can you start new relationships?
- How can you build them?
- How can you maintain those relationships over time?
- Have you had any experiences of building relationships like these?

What you need to know

Relationships beyond the team

In organisations it can become too easy just to focus on how we work with those who are around us and to become focused internally. It is vital to have good working relationships with others in the team, for all the reasons that we have explored in the steps up to here.

However, it can also become limiting to only take this *internal* perspective. All teams and organisations exist in a much wider sector of people who are potential partners, customers, clients, suppliers, or competitors. At more advanced steps of Teamwork, it is essential to start to engage with this wider array of *external* stakeholders.

The focus of external relationships

Broadly, external relationships might be based around:

(a) Sharing information and learning

- Sharing information and learning as peers
- Mentoring or coaching someone outside of the organisation (see *Leadership Steps 10 & 11*)
- Being mentored or coached by someone outside of the organisation

(b) Supplier and customer relationships

- Supplying a good or service to the other party
- Receiving a good or service from the other party

(c) Partnership working

- Working together as partners on a joint project or endeavour
- Engaging stakeholders who have an in interest in a project – for instance, local community members who are affected by a project

You are less likely to have good relationships with your competitors (indeed, in some areas of commerce such relationships could be illegal) but you might end up developing one of the other ways of working above.

How new relationships can be started

New relationships can be started in a range of different ways. This might include:

- *Networking:* There is a range of networking events where it is possible to build new professional relationships. Sometimes, these events are explicitly designed for meeting new professional contacts who you might end up working with, like speed networking events. Other times, the event is nominally about a launch, celebration, or a conference – although you might learn something interesting at these events, many participants will see these chiefly as networking opportunities.
- *Introductions:* Sometimes, an existing partner or stakeholder will make an introduction to a new contact. This might be in-person or by email. This can be helpful as it builds trust and credibility from the outset.
- *Research:* Another approach is to research the field that you are looking at. You might be able to find individuals who are offering to act as mentors, or who are professional coaches, for example. In other places, you might identify individuals who have similar professional interests to you.
- *Cold approaches:* Finally, a cold approach might be necessary if you have no way to meet the person for real or have no possibility of an introduction through a mutual contact. In this case, a short introductory email or call, explaining who you are, and why you would be interested in talking to them is the best start.

How to develop relationships

Once a relationship has started, it needs to be deepened and reinforced if it is to be helpful. Some of the key steps to achieving this are:

- *Getting to know one another:* Most relationships benefit from meeting in person, getting to know one another informally over a coffee or similar. This includes discussing both what they are working on, and a bit about them as a person too. This is essential to answer the question of whether you like each other enough to have the possibility of working together.
- *Understanding one another's goals and priorities:* It is important to understand what each of you might be hoping to get out of working together. At this stage, it is vital to do a lot of listening so that you can understand their position.
- *Exploring avenues for shared interests and areas of learning or working together:* As you explore a professional relationship, it would be helpful to hone down the number of possible priorities that you might be able to work on together. This should not be a forced exercise – if there is no overlap that is fine, but it is probably not worth pursuing the relationship further.
- *Starting with small projects, so that there are tangible rewards to working together:* By this stage, you should have a sense of whether you could work together and the focus, but the real test is whether you can undertake a short project together successfully. This should be something low-stakes so you can work out whether the arrangement works for you both.
- *Building trust and understanding over time towards bigger projects:* If the small project is a success, this can build confidence that more ambitious things will be possible over time.

How to maintain relationships

Not every professional relationship is meant to last forever. Sometimes, the relationship is about getting something done, and so when that has been achieved, that is a natural end.

However, many professional relationships can develop over time, from being transactional to a much greater alignment and deeper partnership. To reach this deeper level of partnership, there are certain fundamentals:

- Mutual respect between the partners
- Trust that the other partner is reliable and will do anything that they promised
- Shared goals where there are aligned interests, and both are benefiting
- Commitment to continuing to work together

Most external relationships are not bound together by obligation in the way that team relationships sometimes are. This means that it is particularly important to maintain consistency and transparency in external relationships if they are to be maintained.

Teaching it

To teach this step:

- The teacher should start by reminding learners that although most of the focus in Teamwork so far has been on how to build relationships within the team, there are lots of ways that other relationships can be important too.
- Learners could reflect on when external relationships are helpful and how they could help. They could share examples they have had, and what they got out of them.
- The teacher can then talk learners through the stages of starting and then developing a new professional relationship. At each stage, learners can work in groups to develop ideas about what they should do at that stage to ensure success.
- Again, discussing examples and experiences is likely to be invaluable here for bringing the concepts in this step to life.
- Finally, learners could think about where they might be able to get value from an external relationship, obviously carefully guided by the teacher as to what might be appropriate.

Reinforcing it

This step can be reinforced if there are mentoring or coaching opportunities available to learners, or where they might need to seek external advice or help – for example, on college or university applications, social action projects, or parts of their studies.

Assessing it

This step is best assessed through observing and reflecting with learners on how they have developed a professional relationship, and the steps that they went through to start that partnership, to develop it, and then to sustain it over time. If observation isn't possible, then a written reflection might be enough.

Teamwork Step 12

Step 12: I influence the team by reflecting on progress and suggesting improvements

To achieve Step 12, individuals will show that they can reflect on the team's progress and suggest improvements as a result.

In the previous steps, the focus was on how to work well with others, how to contribute to team decision-making, and then how to improve the team through managing unhelpful conflicts and building external professional relationships. This step focuses on how to influence the team to make it more effective.

Building blocks

The building blocks of this step are:

- I use evaluative questions to reflect on a team's progress
- I make suggestions for improving team performance
- I know how to work with the leader to positively influence my team

Reflection questions

- What are some of the things to consider when evaluating whether your team is making good progress?
- What is worth considering when thinking about team morale and motivation?
- How can you reflect on operational and impact effectiveness?
- Why is it important to spot unintended effects?
- How can you ensure your suggestions are taken well?
- How can you work with different types of leader?

What you need to know

How to reflect on a team's progress

There are a few different dimensions that you could consider when reflecting on the progress of a team:

- Team motivation and morale
- Operational effectiveness
- Impact effectiveness
- Unanticipated effects

1. Team morale and motivation

Morale and motivation are explored further in *Leadership Step 12*. In essence, motivation is the drive, commitment, and energy that a team has to achieve particular goals. This can fluctuate at different times depending on the likelihood of success and the rewards that will be achieved (not just financial) if the task is completed successfully.

However, there is also a deeper psychological element where individual motivation will also fluctuate according to whether the team members feel:

- Known as individuals, that they are safe in the team, and that they are working on a goal that excites them
- They have the resources, tools and training for success
- Their successes are recognised, and they are supported through challenges
- They have a sense of shared endeavour

These are all areas where, as a team member, you can help to ensure the continued motivation of other members of your team.

2. Operational effectiveness

Sometimes there are operational challenges as you implement a plan. Perhaps you were unable to secure the resources that you need, or tasks were completed incorrectly, or external factors have undermined your efforts.

It is important to recognise these challenges so that you can adapt your plans accordingly, securing additional resources, moving timelines and milestones, or changing some of the tasks you had planned. Reviewing progress regularly against milestones will help you to spot operational challenges early and make changes.

As a team member, you have particular insight into the areas that you are working on directly and how you might go about improving operations. You might also be able to reach out to others to support them directly or find ways around problems.

3. Impact effectiveness

At other times, you might experience a challenge around the impact of what you are doing. Perhaps you are delivering the operational plan, but it is not leading to the outcomes that you were expecting.

As a team member, you can support taking learning from the situation. What was it in the original model that was wrong? What were the logical assumptions that did not hold up? Are there hypotheses that were disproved unexpectedly?

This is likely to be an area which needs a wider team conversation, as it will involve revisiting some of our assumptions, improving them with what we see in reality, and then adjusting our strategic plan accordingly to get back on track for our impact goals.

4. Unanticipated effects

It's important as a team member to keep scanning for unanticipated secondary effects. This might include talking to those individuals you are working with or looking at the broader social and environmental effects of the work that you're doing.

Once you have identified a secondary effect, you can analyse why that has happened, and what actions you might need to take as a team to take to mitigate that effect – or whether it means that you need to go back to the drawing board on the whole approach.

How to suggest improvements effectively

If you can't enact an improvement yourself, you will have to think carefully about how to deliver the suggestion or the *constructive criticism*, including:

- A positive, helpful tone
- Identification of what is working well, as well as what can be improved
- Considered, reasoned opinions
- Explanation of points
- A willingness to discuss the critique more widely

There is a lot more on how to influence people in *Speaking Steps 12-15*.

Working with the leader

If your team has a clear leader, then the dynamic between you and the leader will be critical if you are going to suggest improvements in a way that will encourage them to be taken on and used.

You can find out more about different leadership styles in *Leadership Steps 13-15*. Essentially, the style of leadership will affect the openness of the leader to take on board your reflections and make improvements as a result.

If your leader takes a democratic approach to decision-making, encourages change, and believes in coaching and developing the team, then you are in luck. They are likely to delegate considerable authority, or at least be open to taking on board the ideas of the team, and you are likely to get a positive reception. In a democratic structure, you are likely to need to bring the whole team along with you, so open conversation and debate is likely to be important.

On the other hand, if your leader takes an autocratic approach, prefers stability and consistency to change, or takes a transactional approach to their team, then you will find it a lot tougher to get the change to be incorporated. In this case, you probably have a couple of options:

- Try to enact the ideas without the leader – this might be possible, depending on the size of the team
- Get the leader to see the improvement as their suggestion by coaching them towards the idea, although this can be difficult to pull of.
- Help the leader to see how this improvement will help them to achieve their goals – this is called *alignment* and is most likely to be successful

Teaching it

To teach this step:

- The teacher should start by introducing the idea that all members of a team have the opportunity and the responsibility to make the team more effective, and to help the team achieve its goals.
- The teacher can introduce the four main areas where team members can have a positive influence and ask learners to work in groups to explain what is meant by each of these: team morale and motivation, operational effectiveness, impact effectiveness, and unintended effects.
- Learners should then discuss what could be difficult about just telling people to do things differently, and how a team member can think about carefully influencing others (this is covered more in *Speaking Steps 12-15*)
- Finally, the teacher should introduce the challenge of how to work with different leaders. They should remind learners that leaders might be quite different in their styles (see *Leadership Steps 13-15*), and they will have to adapt their approach to influencing the team accordingly.

Reinforcing it

This step can be reinforced whenever learners are working in a group. The teacher can pause the group and ask learners to think about how their group is working across the four dimensions shared above. Learners can reflect and then make changes.

At a more advanced stage, the teacher can ask them to reflect on this at the end of a task, which will be a better indication of whether they were able to both recognise where improvements could be made, and then actually make them.

Assessing it

This step is best assessed through an observation of an extended project or challenge, then coupled with a reflection. It should be clear to the teacher during the observation that the learner is proactive in identifying issues and is then trying to influence their team to address them.

This observation can be complemented by a reflection which is either discussed, presented, or written.

Glossary

Aiming High: In the Skills Builder Framework, aiming high is defined as 'the ability to set clear, tangible goals and devise a robust route to achieving them'.

Building block: A building block is a key learning or competence which supports achieving a skill step. They can be used to provide additional scaffolding for learning – for example, for learners with special educational needs.

Basic skills: Basic skills, also known as foundational skills, comprise literacy, numeracy and basic digital skills. They are important for underpinning learning and essential skills but are not included in the Skills Builder Framework which only focuses on essential skills.

Creativity: In the Skills Builder Framework, creativity is defined as 'the use of imagination and the generation of new ideas'.

Essential skills: Those highly transferable skills which are used by almost everyone to do almost any job and which support application of technical skills and knowledge. In the Skills Builder Framework, these eight skills are: Listening; Speaking; Problem Solving; Creativity; Staying Positive; Aiming High; Leadership; and Teamwork.

Leadership: In the Skills Builder Framework, leadership is defined as 'supporting, encouraging, and developing others to achieve a shared goal'.

Listening: In the Skills Builder Framework, listening is defined as 'the receiving, retaining and processing of information or ideas'.

Problem solving: In the Skills Builder Framework, problem solving is defined as 'the ability to find a solution to a situation or challenge'.

Skills: We define a skill as the ability to enact a repeatable process. These can be further broken down in basic or foundational skills, essential skills, and technical skills. Essential skills are the focus of the Skills Builder Framework and approach.

Skills Builder Approach: The approach combines the Framework which breaks down what essential skills are and the Principles which define best practice for how to go about teaching them.

Skills Builder Framework: The Framework helps to break down the essential skills into a sequence of steps which are assessable and teachable. The steps go from Step 0 as an absolute beginner through to Step 15 which is mastery.

Skills Builder Partnership: The Partnership is the global group of more than 800 organisations who are actively adopting and championing the *Skills Builder approach*.

Skills Builder Principles: These six principles capture best practice around how to build essential skills in educational settings. They include: keeping the language simple; working across all ages; measuring skills effectively; directly teaching the skills; practising those skills in lots of settings; and linking the skills to the wider world.

Skills Step: This is an incremental progression within an essential skill. In the Skills Builder Framework there are sixteen progression steps which go from an absolute beginner (Step 0) through to mastery (Step 15).

Speaking: In the Skills Builder Framework, speaking is defined as 'the oral transmission of information or ideas'.

Staying Positive: In the Skills Builder Framework, staying positive is defined as 'the ability to use tactics and strategies to overcome setbacks and achieve goals'.

Teamwork: In the Skills Builder Framework, teamwork is defined as 'working cooperatively with others towards achieving a shared goal'.

Technical skills: Those skills which are specific to a sector or role, sometimes drawing off a particular body of knowledge. These skills are not easily transferred beyond the sector or role to which they relate.

Thanks & acknowledgements

This Handbook is the culmination of twelve years of wrestling with the question of what it would look like for every child and young person to build the essential skills to thrive in the rest of their lives.

Over that time, I am extremely grateful for the insights and ideas that have come from so many different places. Sometimes that has been through conversation, but often through educators putting these ideas into practice and our learning together.

That collaborative aspect has been so fundamental that in 2020 we changed the name of the organisation from Enabling Enterprise, as it had been, to Skills Builder Partnership. Our mission is to ensure that one day, everyone builds the essential skills to succeed and collective impact is the only way that something so ambitious could ever be achieved.

There are now 800 partners actively championing the Skills Builder approach – educational institutions, businesses, and impact organisations. Ultimately though, that ability to work and learn together is driven by individuals and I'm grateful to everyone who has helped make Skills Builder a reality. That includes the tens of thousands of teachers in ten countries who have boosted the essential skills of their learners.

Our team at Skills Builder Partnership is pretty special. Each team member brings energy, commitment, and a focus on having the greatest possible impact. That might be on the frontline, working directly with partners, or behind the scenes creating and managing our systems, fundraising, and advocacy efforts. I feel fortunate every day to work with such a brilliant group.

As a not-for-profit organisation, our non-executive directors play a critical role in helping to support and challenge our thinking and directing our energies and priorities. I'm grateful to Richard Bronze, Alex Shapland Howes and Sam Butters for being such sterling board members.

We also benefit from the connections, insights and expertise of our Strategic Advisory Group who generously give their time to further our mission. Thanks go to: Brett Wigdortz, Professor Lynda Gratton, Sir Peter Estlin, Sir Ian Davis, Dame Julia Cleverdon, Professor Bill Lucas, Professor Tristram Hooley, Honor Wilson-Fletcher, Peter Cheese, John Yarham, Daniel Sandford Smith, Nicola Inge, Sir John Holman, Professor Anne Bamford, and Jo Owen.

Finally, I'm ever grateful to my parents, brothers, and wider family for their enduring love and support. I couldn't be prouder of my two sons, Joshua and Alex and their burgeoning essential skills. My wife, Charlotte, helped me set up Enabling Enterprise originally back in 2009, and has been its staunchest champion ever since. Thank you.

About the author

Tom Ravenscroft

Founder & CEO, Skills Builder Partnership

Tom founded the Skills Builder Partnership in 2009, whilst a secondary school teacher in London. The Skills Builder Partnership brings together a global group of more than 800 partners around a common language and approach to building essential skills like teamwork, communication, and self-management. The Partnership, which includes educators, employers and impact organisations, delivered 1.46 million opportunities for individuals to build those skills in 2020-21.

The approach that Tom pioneered has now been widely adopted in the UK, and is being replicated in ten further countries – including the Czech Republic, Kenya, Ghana, Uganda, Egypt, Pakistan, and India. The Partnership has won the UK Social Enterprise Award for Impact.

Tom was the UK Entrepreneurship Teacher of the Year. He has served as a non-executive director of Teach First and has also been recognised as one of the UK's leading social entrepreneurs by being elected an Ashoka Fellow in 2017. He holds a BA in Economics & Management from the University of Oxford.

Printed in Great Britain
by Amazon